CW01033144

TAKEN BY SPEED

TAKEN BY SPEED

Fallen Heroes of Motor Sport and Their Legacies

Connie Ann Kirk

ROWMAN & LITTLEFIELD
Lanham • Boulder • New York • London

Published by Rowman & Littlefield
A wholly owned subsidary of The Rowman & Littlefield Publishing Group,
Inc.
4501 Forbes Boulevard, Suite 200, Lanham, Maryland 20706
www.rowman.com

Unit A, Whitacre Mews, 26-34 Stannary Street, London SE11 4AB

British Library Cataloguing in Publication Information Available

Library of Congress Cataloging-in-Publication Data

Name: Kirk, Connie Ann, author.
Title: Taken by speed : fallen heroes of motor sport and their legacies / Connie Ann Kirk.
Description: Lanham, Maryland : Rowman & Littlefield, 2017. | Includes bibliographical refer-
    ences and index.
Identifiers: LCCN 2017021431 (print) | LCCN 2017047003 (ebook) | ISBN 9781442277625 (elec-
    tronic) | ISBN 9781442277618 (hardcover : alk. paper)
Subjects: LCSH: Automobile racing drivers—Biography. | Automobile racing—History.
Classification: LCC GV1032.A1 (ebook) | LCC GV1032.A1 K58 2017 (print) | DDC 796.72092
    [B]—dc23
LC record available at https://lccn.loc.gov/2017021431

Because I could not stop for Death –
He kindly stopped for me –
The Carriage held but just Ourselves –
And Immortality.

—Emily Dickinson, c. 1862

CONTENTS

PREFACE

People who know of my previous works in literature always ask me what got me interested in, of all things, motor sport. The subjects seem so different, after all. How does a writer who studies the likes of the nineteenth-century American poet Emily Dickinson go, in the span of only a few years, from researching and writing about Dickinson's life of composing fierce poetry in her upstairs bedroom in Amherst, Massachusetts, to studying the roar, color, and speed of a Formula One international racing circuit? A "Renaissance woman," one racer on the historic circuit once jokingly called me.

I suppose the diversity jumps out to observers, but art and science, literature and technology have been dual interests of mine since I was a girl. I used to take long walks, thinking about the future. Which way should I go? One day I wanted to become an astronaut; the next day I wanted to write the Great American Novel. Though writing eventually won out, I never gave up my interest in science and technology, even to the point of acquiring a two-year degree in chemical engineering technology along the long and circuitous journey toward my PhD. Many people are surprised to learn that I also worked in a Fortune 300 company's research and development lab for a few years.

Add to this oddity the fact that I am not a lifelong fan of motor racing, either, as are many of the people I work and speak with now. I remember going to the 1978 United States Grand Prix (USGP) in Watkins Glen, New York, and wanting to see the famous Mario Andretti race there. All I remember about it now is how intense and exciting the whole scene was and my subsequent confusion at the end of the race. I did not understand then how Andretti could lose the race but still be world champion. (He did not even finish the race, as it turned out—his Lotus 79 retired with engine trouble after twenty-seven laps.) Andretti had secured enough points before the USGP—in fact, at the Italian Grand Prix immediately before it on the schedule—that he could compete in that race already a champion. I remember that it took what seemed like forever to get out of the parking lot at Watkins Glen International and make the way down Route 414. People alongside the road waved and provided entertainment to the stalled line of spectators' cars. These two memories were about the extent of my following of the sport back then.

Drive three decades further down the road, on through an advanced degree in English and a dozen or so books on literary topics, including several biographies of writers. In 2011, I attended the U.S. Vintage Grand Prix in Watkins Glen. I'd seen it advertised for years but had never gone myself. "Vintage" racing is a branch of motor sport in which collectors of retired race cars buy them and, instead of keeping them in their garages, take them out to a racetrack and race them against other like-minded collectors. This is also called "historic" racing. "Historic cars?" The words struck me as odd. How could a Formula One race car from thirty years ago, a time I could still remember, be regarded as "historic" now? (Disregarding the aging process appears to be just one of my many character flaws.)

Too reserved to go to the paddock as I was told I was welcome to do and not even knowing what a racing paddock was in the first place, I sat in the grandstands and watched practice after practice, qualifying after qualifying, race after race. Around early morning fog and rain delays and through the September sunshine, the action on track rarely stopped all day, every day, for three days straight. Among cars of many colors, years, shapes, and sizes, this amateur event did have a few 1970s-era Formula One cars in competition. The sights and sounds brought back memories from 1978 that had been long buried. The excitement revved up in me again—this time I was ready for it. Even relatively later in my life's experience, the racing "bug," as they say in motor sport, bit me that day. I couldn't get enough and went back early each morning and stayed until the very end of the last session each day for the whole three-day event. By the end of the weekend, the racing bug had not only bitten but moved in for a long stay.

Between writing projects as I was at the time, I had wanted to write something different—something away from literature perhaps but also, in particular, something closer to home so that I need not seek out research fellowships and travel grants to distant libraries quite so often. But motor racing? That would have to pass the snicker test before I would invest the necessary time and energy to learn an entirely new subject. I read a little bit and visited the International Motor Racing Research Center in the village of Watkins Glen. To my surprise, my curiosity was welcomed; the people there did not flinch at my naive questions. I talked with amateur racers who participated in the historic/vintage event. They came from a variety of occupations and professions, and that surprised me. The more I found out, the more I wanted to know. The subject and the unending questions it brought would not leave my thoughts. Before long, I knew I had found a new subject for writing, and I knew I may as well plunge in, commit, and go forward with trying to learn as much as I could.

Perhaps due in part to my literature background, this book arose out of the intense drama I found while researching and learning about the sport. As much as participants and spectators alike may not talk about it, the danger of the sport remains part of its allure. Racers and race teams compete against one another, but everyone is competing against the physical properties of nature that make us, as human beings, slower than the horse or the gazelle, that keep us limited by the laws of physics from moving faster on this earth without some sort of assistance. Speed was the desire; speed was the goal; and the faster one could go, the more speed was desired. Pushing the "limit"—that edge of adhesion, the moment before a driver and car lose control and cannot stay on the road—the border between control and chaos, I have discovered, may not be so different from pushing the envelope of what is possible with language and the mind in excellent poetry like Dickinson's. Odd as it may sound at first, I have found that passion and challenge fuel both the driven poet and the gifted racer.

This book is about a few of the many racers who did not survive their pursuit of perfection through speed. It is not my aim to dwell on the morbid aspect of the sport or of these racers' tragic ends, in particular. My goal instead is to reflect on these people and their adventures in life by retelling their stories to a wider audience and to hopefully shed a little light along the way on a few of the legacies they have left behind. Going in, general readers who may not be motor racing fans may think these people are foolish. I can certainly understand that way of thinking and see that point of view. What appeals to me, however, and draws me back to the sport each time is the passion its participants have for what they do.

Who among us, I ask, is not interested in people who are chasing their dreams flat-out?

ACKNOWLEDGMENTS

Many thanks go to several individuals and organizations for their warm welcome of this student of motor racing and motor sport history into their world. They have been generous in their willingness to share what they know and think about this exciting sport. I would likely not have pursued this area of interest and study were it not for their open and ready adoption of me into the motor sport "family." Any good that this book may bring to readers I share credit for with them; any blame for problems, of course, belongs entirely with me.

Deep respect and appreciation go to the legendary icons of the sport who were willing to share their thoughts, opinions, and memories with me directly for this modest project—Mario Andretti, Derek Bell, Sir Stirling Moss, Bobby Rahal, Brian Redman, and Sir Jackie Stewart. I am especially pleased that their participation in this book indicates a desire on their parts to share motor sport history with an audience beyond the track and the sport's own enthusiasts. Thanks, too, to the following folks who helped facilitate conversations or various communications with one or more of the racing stars mentioned above: Helen Bramley, Patrick Crew, John R. T. Monson, Lady Susie Moss, Patty Reid, and Mandy Shepherd.

Other individuals from the motor sport community have shared their valuable time at the racetrack, chatted in person at related events elsewhere, or engaged in conversations remotely via Skype, telephone, or e-mail. Still others have helped along the way by going above and beyond their role as media or other contacts at racetracks or through tangential support of this work. Whether in conversations sustained over time or fairly quick discussions, all have helped and are appreciated. These generous people include, but are not limited to, J. C. Argetsinger, Michael Argetsinger (RIP), Josh Ashby, Chris Banker, Samy C. G. Beau-Marquet, Steve and Marilyn Bieler, Randy Cook (RIP), Tom and Jenn Fitzgerald and the Fitzgerald family, Glenda Gephart, Marc and Cindy Giroux, Bill Green, Kevin Hughey, Rick Hughey, Larry and Karen Kessler, Betsy Mayer, Bud Moeller, John R. T. Monson, Lady Susie Moss, Michael Printup, Rick Roso, Maxa Whitford, and Kip Zeiter.

Several organizations have helped this writer gain firsthand knowledge and experience at the racetrack or at related events by granting me professional media credentials. These special passes offer behind-the-scenes access and up-close views of the action about which long-time fans can only dream; credentials are a privilege that, especially as a relative newcomer to the sport, I do not take for granted. These organizations include, but are not limited to, the International Motor Racing Research Center and Watkins Glen International, both in Watkins Glen, New York; the website Examiner.com, Boulder, Colorado; Lime Rock Park, Lakeville, Connecticut; Circuit of the Americas, Austin, Texas; Indianapolis Motor Speedway, Indianapolis, Indiana; the Federation Internationale de l'Automobile, Paris, France; the professional motor racing series of Formula One, IndyCar, NASCAR, and IMSA; the Sportscar Vintage Racing Association, based in Southlake, Texas; and the Goodwood Circuit at the Goodwood Estate in Chichester, West Sussex, England.

As part of holding the above-mentioned credentials, it is also a privilege to have access to currently racing professional drivers at their busy places of work as well as at press conferences and other media events. To all the drivers in the various racing series who have answered my questions, I thank you for sharing your time and insights.

Friends and colleagues offer support for my writing efforts, no matter the subject. These folks include, but are not limited to, Margaret H. Freeman, Marie Hannan-Mandel, Nancy Pridgen, Emily Seelbinder, Byron Shaw, and Marcy Tanter. Thank you for your interest, help, and kindness!

Of course, a bouquet of thanks goes to editors Christen Karniski and Kellie Hagan and the staff at Rowman & Littlefield for accepting this project for publication and helping shepherd it into being. Special thanks go to Jenny Ambrose and Josh Ashby at the International Motor Racing Research Center for their tireless help in locating and providing the many archival photographs that appear in this book as well as some of the source material used.

Finally, where would any of us be in our work if not for the love, support, and unending patience of our families? My family of men is exceptional in its support of a writer—and all that entails—as a wife, mother, and daughter. Ken, Ben, John (fellow racing fan and track buddy!), and my dear father, who was taken from us so suddenly during the writing of this book—I love you all.

INTRODUCTION

The Cruel Beauty of Motor Sport

"To race is to live. But those who died while racing knew, perhaps, how to live more than all the others." —Juan Manuel Fangio, Argentinian racing legend[1]

Motor sport has intrigued human beings ever since they created the first motorized vehicles that could get them around more quickly and efficiently than their bodies alone could do—motorcycles, automobiles, trucks, boats, airplanes, snowmobiles, even lawn mowers are all housed under the umbrella of recreational competitions around the world known today collectively as "motor sport." Arguably, the most popular and best known of these is motor racing in cars.

Motor racing with automobiles probably began the first time two drivers pulled up next to one another in two vehicles. No one knows when or where that exactly happened. The birth of the automobile as we know it now is traditionally said to be January 29, 1886, the date Carl Benz of Germany filed a patent application for the first "vehicle powered by a gas engine," Patent #37435.[2] It didn't take long for the testing of automobiles to take the form of exhibitions and competitions. Both auto manufacturers and the press benefited from the spectacles caused by such events. These moving machines were a novelty to almost everyone at the time, and people came out to watch them. The press sold newspapers by hyping the contests before they happened and by covering the day of the race and its aftermath, just as they and other forms of media still do today.

By 1894, the press was so involved in the new endeavor that it actually sponsored the competitions. The first such recorded contest took place when people lined up to watch the *"La Petit Journal* Competition for Horseless Carriages" run from Paris to Rouen. People turned out again for the Paris-Bordeaux-Paris competition in 1895. The same year in the United States, spectators gathered to watch the vehicles running the first recorded American auto competition, the *Chicago Times-Herald* race, from Chicago to Evanston, Illinois. The average speed in that fifty-four-mile race was just 7.3 mph! The second race in the United States, on May 30, 1896, interestingly, was sponsored by *Cosmopolitan* magazine and went fifty-two miles from New York's City Hall to Irvingston-on-Hudson and back.[3]

By late 1896, it became obvious to organizers that a closed track where tickets could be sold for access rather than racing on open public roads would be a source of revenue. In the United States, the first "closed-circuit" race was held as part of the Rhode Island State Fair at Narragansett Park in Cranston, from September 7 to 11, 1896. The "horseless carriages," as they were called, competed on the horse racing track at the fairgrounds. According to the August 1, 1896, issue of *Scientific American*, "Official Rules and Conditions" for that race stipulated that "only vehicles propelled by other than animal power [were] allowed to compete"; vehicles must be able to go at least 15 mph; there was a $100 entry fee covering five heats, with a first-prize purse of $1,500; and the winner of the most heats won the overall competition. Importantly, there was this statement concerning risk even back then: "All legal responsibility is thrown upon the contestants, the association declining to assume any whatsoever."[4] The popularity of automobile racing in a ticket-charging venue was off and running when fifty thousand spectators showed up to watch this event. Another American early track first used for horse racing is the Milwaukee Mile, which dates its auto racing history from 1903 and is also the location of the Wisconsin State Fair. The close connection between automobile and horse racing did not end when the horseless carriages left the stables and stalls of their four-legged forebears—horse racing terms like "paddock," "livery," "stable," and "pole position" remain integral parts of motor racing's vocabulary to this day.[5]

Unlike with many sports that a child can grow up playing in the backyard or on a neighborhood ball field or playground for little money, motor racing was a grand spectacle from the start, involving cutting-edge technology, high finance, and the press touting it all to the public. The first inventors and car companies were eager to sell this new mode of transportation to consumers who, for centuries, had relied on the horse for their livelihoods and to get around. It is hard to think of it now, but there was a time when the whole concept of the automobile needed to be sold to the hearts and minds of the general public. In *Story of the Automobile*, published in 1917, for instance, H. L. Barber attempts in chapter 5, titled "Benefits Conferred by the Automobile," to rebut arguments presented by some "medics" of the day that the automobile will be bad for human health. "Some of them think it does not give people enough exercise," Barber writes, "and that at the rate its use is increasing it will not be long before man loses his ability to use his legs!"[6] The medics of the early twentieth century may have been on to something that walkers and bicyclists of the early twenty-first century might agree with wholeheartedly; however, these objections were quickly swept aside by most people at the time in the name of progress.

As interest in the automobile and racing evolved, purpose-built tracks (facilities constructed for the sole or primary reason of racing or testing cars) were eventually constructed where manufacturers could test their new machines and organizers could continue to charge admission to spectators. Long-standing purpose-built tracks around the world now have their own histories, legacies, and lores. Many claim to be the "first" or the "longest continuously running" racetrack. It is important to look at the wording of the claims carefully. Brooklands in the United Kingdom, for instance, dates itself from 1907 and claims it is "the world's first purpose-built motor racing circuit." The Milwaukee Mile bills itself as "the oldest operating motor speedway in the world," with its first auto race happening on its dirt horse racing track in 1903. The Indianapolis Motor Speedway (IMS) in the American Midwest, first built for testing automobiles in America's heartland, dates its opening from the balloon, motorcycle, and auto races run there in the summer of 1909; the first Indy 500 took place there in 1911.[7]

Racetracks, both ovals and circuits (irregular tracks that involve both right and left turns), were established, and enthusiasts ran car competitions on them. The races also still ran occasionally on public roads closed for the day for that purpose. With its better roads than most countries had at the time, thanks in part to Napoleon Bonaparte's initiative at the turn of the nineteenth century, France was particularly keen on running city-to-city races in the early days of the sport. The country essentially banned road racing in 1900 after an accident in a race from Paris to Roubaix injured dozens of spectators, but by then motor racing had gotten under the skin of the French, and the strict bans did not stick. Automobile manufacturing took off in France among those who were eager to put France's lackluster performance in the First Industrial Revolution behind them. Small artisan companies in metalworking and the like were primed to embrace the new opportunity. As a result, at the turn of the century, France had six hundred automobile manufacturers compared to one hundred such companies in other countries of western Europe and the United States combined.[8]

As with most expensive new inventions today, the wealthy and well connected were the first to own automobiles. In France, where auto building was happening at the quickest pace, the aristocracy took a keen interest in the machines and competitions between them to see which could go faster and most reliably. Two nobleman members of the Jockey-club de Paris, the Count de Dion and Baron de Zuylen, joined journalist Paul Meyan from the *Le Figaro*, who was also editor of the newsletter *La France Automobile*. The men formed the first automobile club in 1895, the Automobile Club de France (ACF). The ACF organized international races with the help of the International Association of Recognized Automobile Clubs (Association Internationale des Automobile Clubs Reconnus, AIACR), formed in 1904. Even today, the ACF office is located next door to the AIACR's, at 8 Place de la Concorde in Paris. The groups shared presidents until 1963. Essentially, the ACF could be considered the early organization that led to the development of the current Fédération Internationale de l'Automobile (FIA), founded in 1947. The FIA remains the world's governing body of motor sport to this day. Several of its presidents have been noblemen, fostering the early tradition of international motor racing's connection with European gentry.[9]

The city-to-city races held by the ACF each year built to a crescendo in 1903 when the Paris-Madrid race attracted two hundred thousand spectators, with a reported two million in total watching along the roadside between Paris and Bordeaux. The race took off from Versailles on

May 24, 1903, but unfortunately, the world's largest sporting event to date was fraught with accidents, signaling one of the major problems—and perhaps lurid appeals—of the sport for decades to come.

During that race, Marcel Renault, brother of Renault car company cofounder Louis, died when his car overturned. Other victims included one riding mechanic whose car hit a tree, breaking apart with such force that fragments of the vehicle lodged in the tree's trunk. Another mechanic died when his car hit a wall; yet another mechanic and a soldier died when a car drove off course into the crowd. The French government put a halt to the race and ordered that the cars be taken back to Paris pulled by horses or on vehicles drawn by horses. When this became too problematic, the cars were allowed to return under their own power but at a reduced speed. However, even then, one car injured a woman on the way.[10]

Despite the fatalities and casualties, those involved in the new sport would not be deterred. As technology and increasing land speeds grew well into the twentieth century, so did the venues and opportunities where cars could be tested, modified, designed, and raced against each other. Move many decades ahead to the middle of the twentieth century, especially before and after World War II, and history shows that several professional series had evolved where cars of similar type and horsepower raced against each other and still do today. These series include Formula One (F1), the "pinnacle of the sport" at the height of expense, engineering, and experimentation; IndyCar, the American open-wheel series; NASCAR, the American stock car series that uses cars similar to those most people drive on the highway; and sports car endurance racing—high-tech "prototypes" and various other classes of automobiles competing in six-, eight-, and twenty-four-hour competitions at the World Endurance Championship (WEC). There are many more series run at both the professional and amateur levels, including truck racing, drag racing, and even historic racing, the latter recycling retired professional race cars from the different series to be collected and raced against one another by amateurs and a few retired professionals.

As anyone who watches a Formula One, IndyCar, NASCAR, or WEC race today knows, commercial promotion did not end with auto manufacturers and newspapers in the very early days of racing. In fact, commercial advertising in racing has not only stayed with the sport but become an even bigger part of it. In the 1970s, race teams seeking financing for the expensive sport realized that people watched race cars for hours at a time. The sides of race cars were like blank slates, moving billboards waiting for something to be advertised on them. Soon, space on the sides of the cars began to be sold, ruining the more nationalist look, created by colors representing certain countries (for example, "British green"), that international Formula One, for one, had enjoyed in the years before that. Eventually not only the cars but also drivers' racing suits and helmets were affected. Now, products from crackers to shipping companies, from motor oil to candy to fast food, cover nearly every visible spot on cars, racing suits, and helmets. Not only individual races but even entire professional racing series are named for, and become promotional vehicles for, entitlement sponsors. It costs big money to race, and it has always been that way. Business and the media have been involved in racing and keeping it going in an integral way from the beginning. Some things change as much as they stay the same.

At the same time as it became a means to an intense personal experience for the individual to drive fast and watch racing, and as much as it turned into an advertising medium for commerce and the press, motor racing has other important components that have kept interest in it moving forward. Alongside the sport aspect—teams from countries around the world entering cars in competitions, almost like for the Olympics, to showcase their design and engineering skills—testing is another key element of the sport and its history. While private testing by manufacturers did take place years ago, racing provided another form of testing for auto and tire companies and others. If you own, drive, or ride in an automobile today, you may have racing teams and race car drivers to thank for some of the developments in technology that both keep you safe and get you where you want to go more efficiently. Rearview mirrors, disc brakes, and aerodynamic body designs are among the developments tried out in motor racing before they arrived in road cars and on highways.[11] The testing heritage of motor racing goes all the way back to the reliability tests of early automobiles in the late nineteenth century and progresses through World War II test pilots who came home to take up race car driving to today's designated test drivers employed by teams to not only try out new equipment and ideas for increasing speed and reliability on the track but to also feed information back to the factories building road cars that are still involved in high-level professional racing. Such companies include Mercedes, Ferrari, Porsche, Audi, Renault, McLaren, Ford, Honda, Toyota, and others.

With all these forces motivating racing as a sport, hobby, and business, automotive performance and design improved exponentially. Fans paid for races, and races paid for development, and development fed back into the cars to make faster races. The wheels kept turning. The decades of the mid-twentieth century—between the early races and those of the early twenty-first century—were an especially dangerous period, when advances in the speed of the cars outpaced the support structure for organized racing; that is, cars could go faster than the tracks on which they ran were equipped to handle. Medical staffs were not trained, or even available, to help with crashes. Safety equipment was either not thought of yet or not yet invented or was not yet required by the rules. There was a bit of a Wild West mentality in the sport—brand-new territory where all the dangers were not even identified. The new sport depended not just on the human being and his or her physical strength, finesse, and endurance but also on the extension of that athlete's prowess in the form of handling a powerful and continually developing machine—a machine that could behave as unpredictably at times as an entity existing somewhere between Frankenstein's monster and a rearing, snorting stallion.

"Warning: Motor Sport Can Be Dangerous," reads a sign commonly affixed to chain-link fences, poles, and other places around racetracks where cars and drivers compete. The words typically appear in bold face inside a red triangle with a large exclamation point inside the angle at the top. Other words below usually include some variation of this statement: "Despite the organizers' taking all reasonable precautions, unavoidable accidents can happen. In respect of these, you are present at your own risk." In other words: fair warning—if you are there, you may get hurt; if you stay there, you are accepting this risk and its consequences for your own safety and well-being.

Despite the danger, and many admit because of it, millions of spectators go to watch professional and amateur automobile races around the world each year. Others watch races on television or, more recently, via electronic streaming media. The Indianapolis Motor Speedway holds the distinction of currently being the largest sporting venue of any kind on earth. With a seating capacity of 250,000 in its sweeping, voluminous grandstands, and with standing room on the grounds for 150,000 more, nearly half a million people can witness in person a single race on a single day at IMS. That is approximately four times the size of a crowd at a large American pro or college football stadium.

According to *Forbes* magazine, the Formula One international motor racing series posted a 2014 network television viewership of 425 million people. *Forbes* maintains that F1, broadcast in two hundred countries and territories, is "still the world's most watched annual sports-series." It has been claimed that only the Olympics or the World Cup, which do not happen every year, can boast higher global viewership of a sporting event. In the United States, the NASCAR premier stock car series (called the Monster Energy Cup in 2017) drives thousands of spectators to the nearly two dozen tracks it races on around the country between February and November each racing season. Online and other ways of watching races remotely only expand the 23.5 million American television viewers who watched all or part of the Daytona 500 in 2015. In France, arguably the world's most iconic annual sports car endurance event, the Le Mans 24 Hours race, reported 245,000 spectators on the grounds of its general enclosure in 2013. In 2015, Le Mans released an official attendance figure of 263,500, a new record, which was met again in 2016.[12]

Numbers like these from some of the world's largest race events do not take into account the millions of people who participate in or watch a wide range of amateur auto racing around the world as well. While organizers and analysts of professional series compare spectator figures up or down from one year to the next and comment on the reasons for the fluctuations, it cannot be denied that, overall, motor sport is widely popular around the globe, despite the fact that the sport is still dangerous and relatively young at only about 120 years old.

A race car driver knows the risks. What is curious to so many people is why or how he or she accepts those risks to climb into that car like other people insert a key into their office doors each morning. Like most of those office workers, professional racers take their work seriously, and most want to do it well. Doing it well means going faster and beating the competition without hurting themselves or damaging the car. This is what drivers say they are wired to do. Driving the car is what makes them happy. When they retire, they may miss the crowds, the accolades, and the lifestyle of the professional athlete, but they almost always say they most miss getting in the car and having a quick go around the track. They are chasing that perfect lap, or that place of wild beauty they know they have been to before, however briefly.

The number of people who have died in the sport of motor racing, including amateurs and professionals around the world, stretches into the thousands. Three-time Formula One world champion Sir Jackie Stewart claims that at the height of his career from 1968 to 1973, the chances of a driver dying during a typical racing season were two out of three.[13] He said that over the course of his career he and his wife, Helen, had fifty-seven friends who raced but died while doing so. Stewart's own crusade in the name of safety as a world champion is well documented and appreciated. Even with many more safety measures in place since that most dangerous era, however, drivers and others in the sport continue to die on rare occasions and certainly with more frequency than athletes in other sports.

* * *

This book presents a selection of stories from some of the more well-known individual and collective losses in the sport from 1955 to 2017. Out of the many possible engaging stories from the sport, final selections were based on three primary criteria: (1) a notable legacy left either for the sport or the world at large, or both; (2) the interest perceived by the author that each story might have for a general reader who is not necessarily a motor sport fan; and (3) representation, either through descriptions of individual racers or race events, of four of the major series in auto racing—Formula One, IndyCar, NASCAR, and world endurance sports car racing. The use of the phrase "fallen heroes" in this context of sport, by the way, in no way means to compare these losses, as horrific as they are, to the sacrifices made by men and women in uniform, serving others at home or abroad and protecting their homelands and loved ones.

The people in this book were taken, in both senses of that word, not by a mission they were sent on to protect others but by speed. They were "taken" by the wild beauty of speed that enticed them into racing in the first place, and then, in tragedy born out of that love and passion, the cruelty of speed stole them just as quickly away from life itself. The stories here are compelling whether the listener is a motor sport enthusiast or not, simply because we are all human, and all human beings look for intensity, beauty, transcendence. Some are just luckier than others in where they go to find it.

This book is also a bit unusual in the motor sport genre. It is not, for example, where you will find hundreds of brief biographical profiles of racers from around the world, or race-by-race, lap-by-lap career statistics, or even, for that matter, much detail about race cars! There are several other books out there where interested readers may find that kind of detailed information. *Taken by Speed* is instead a series of chapters that look at some of the more dramatic stories in the sport within a bigger cultural framework. Racing is, after all, a passion, and many of us have a passion for something or someone—our families, our work, art, music, a hobby, a place or activity, and so forth. The book frames the sport of motor racing within the larger setting of people giving their all in the pursuit of a passion in life, no matter what that passion might be. What happens when someone gives his or her all in the pursuit of a chosen interest? What happens if one loses his or her life in the process? Racing just happens to be what these people dedicated their lives to doing.

In the broadest sense, the book is a reflection on passion in life. Perhaps, for example, finding one's passion can also be a kind of curse as well. If you are willing to die to do whatever it is that you love most in life, some people will see that and admire your courage. They see dignity in people who seemingly having a single purpose in life, knowing who they are and what they think they are here to do. Others will view these people as selfish, thinking only of themselves and risking leaving behind loved ones or others who may need them. At times, in perhaps an extreme or misguided way, a strong passion can lead people, believing in causes so strongly and seeing their missions as noble or even divinely inspired, to do harm to others. Others operate at the completely opposite end of the spectrum: they do what they do because they wish to help others—firefighters and police officers, for example, routinely rush into danger rather than away from it, all in the name of protecting other people in their communities. Such folks have a passion for their work; they see their lives as having a directed purpose. They do not take risks for their own enjoyment, however, but instead lay their lives on the line for the benefit of other people. In talking about astronauts, who also seem to feed on adrenaline that fuels them to go further and faster into the unknown world of exploration, author Tom Wolfe wrote that they appear to have an "uncritical willingness to face danger" and characterized them as "those who, in short, had the right stuff."[14]

In some ways, to consider those who gave their lives for a sport such as motor racing is to contemplate what is good and maybe not so good about being absolutely dedicated to a pursuit, whatever that chase may be. Is there a time when unending dedication is too much, even if it is not harming others, or is there a time when it is the best we can be as human beings to give all we are and all we have to the pursuit of excellence in a goal we set out to accomplish?

Generally speaking, though there are exceptions of course, professional and amateur racers don't tend to philosophize too much about their occupation or hobby. Other than possibly the pros who are required to devote some of their time to sponsors or the ticket-paying fans in the stands, they don't ask why or ponder much about what their work or amusement might mean to other people or society at large. Most racers are people of action rather than prolonged reflection; they are too busy finding fractions of time by increasing speed, positioning their cars for the next split-second move on the track, or strategizing with their teams about their cars' setup for the next circuit. This does not mean that they do not have keen intellects, however, any more than an astronaut or a jet pilot or an engineer would be said to lack that asset. They simply see motion as the way to express themselves.

"Movement is tranquility," said famous 1950s and 1960s British racing ace Sir Stirling Moss.[15] Frequently racers will tell you, counter to what many observers believe, that going fast does not blur drivers' sense of reality like the scenery that appears to fly by as they shoot past; instead it seems to clarify their thinking, to actually slow things down. Racers tell you that the act of motor racing temporarily pushes most of the other distractions of life from their thoughts and allows them to focus on the intensity of existence, the here and now. There is not much room to think of anything other than the task at hand as they hurtle down a straightaway, or brake as late as they dare to quickly negotiate a sharp turn as fast as possible, or make that move to pass the driver in front of them. It's about an efficiency of movement, expanding space and compressing time, feeling the car with their bodies and experiencing a sense of becoming one with the vehicle so that human and human-made machine move together to do what one human alone cannot.

More than one racer, professional or otherwise, will tell you that the experience of motor racing, for them, is not that unlike making love.

One would have to drive a race car fast to know exactly what draws amateurs to pour their hard-earned money into taking a car to the track and racing it for a weekend, only to crash it and tow it home with a heavy heart and a heavier repair bill, or why a professional will climb back into a car immediately after losing a friend who crashed right in front of him on the circuit. However, listening to drivers who have had a good run, one can gather some clues of what it is like. At its best, in some small moments of time when things are going well, it seems that racing can be transcendent—like creating or enjoying art, or poetry or music, like anything one really loves to do. When it is going not just well but supremely well, all else falls away, and the person involved in it can feel like she or he has entered a different place or state of being, a kind of zone.

One might ask, however, is even a sense of transcendence worth death?

Here is where perhaps racers and others who passionately love what they do—artists, for example—may or may not part ways. One reads about artists who are never pleased with their work. The actual piece they produce does not come close enough to the vision they hold in their minds to ever satisfy them. They say they never quite finish a piece but instead resign themselves to "abandoning" it, knowing that they have given all they can with the skills they have for that particular moment in time and must move on and start something new. Typically, though, painters or musicians or writers are not in physical danger from doing the very work that thrills them and gives their lives meaning. The thrills they seek are on a different plane than those of someone who thrives on speed and pushing the envelope between what human beings are capable of doing alone and what forces of physics they can push against with machines other people have made.

Perhaps that's one thing that a consideration of race car drivers who have given their all can teach us about ourselves, or at least offer us to think about. How far should human beings be willing to go to feel complete, to go to a place beyond their dreams?

Is there an authentic answer that exists anywhere outside the individual human heart?

FATHERS AND SONS, SPEED AND SUPERSTITIONS

Alberto Ascari

A husband married for sixty years dies within a week of his wife's death; both pass away from natural causes. An adult twin gets sick eating fish at a sea shack while on vacation on the West Coast. Not knowing about it, her twin sister, playing with her child at home on the East Coast, feels nausea at just the same time; yet she is not ill. A house catches fire in the middle of a weekday. No one is home, and all the neighbors are at work. A retired firefighter chasing his loose dog wanders into the backyard of the house and manages to start putting out the fire just in time. A tornado spins its way across an open field. A young family's house lies right in its path. At the last minute, the storm shifts course and whirls away from the house until it spins itself out. The home in danger belongs to a meteorologist.

There are people who do not believe in coincidences. They think that events happening at ironic times or chance encounters with people who end up playing important roles in their lives, or freak accidents, or falling in love at seemingly the wrong time are the result of some unknown power or fate, or signs from a spiritual place, or some kind of alignment of forces that have a grand design behind the scenes of life. Other people chalk up such strange encounters or occurrences to simple luck or, in more analytical terms, perhaps to the likelihood of statistical probabilities over time. Whether believed to stem from the unknown or to be a simple matter of probability, when similarities involve close members of a family, the mysteries of coincidence become part of that family's history and lore. This is no less true with racing families.

Many fans and participants in the sport of motor racing describe fellow enthusiasts as family. In many instances, the comparison is quite literal. Racing does, in fact, tend to run in families—boys and girls tinker with their parents' cars in garages, then join them at the track on the weekends. Teens watch a relative running a car around a track and become enthralled enough to ask to drive the next thing they find that moves. Eventually, these young people earn what they may see as the privilege of themselves climbing into a car at the track and giving it a go. Families with means, since racing takes money, support a promising niece or nephew in local races, providing funding for a car, parts, tires, maintenance, racing helmets, suits, gloves, entry fees, insurance, fuel, transportation, car repairs, paint jobs, and everything else.

If a professional racer is in the family, that family's livelihood has been, at least in part, dependent on that racer's winnings and sponsorships. As with acting or other entertainment professions, perhaps, the lifestyle seems to get into the blood of the offspring, and a few of the sons or daughters growing up at the track just naturally gravitate toward taking their own chances behind the wheel. Some successful racers believe that the skill of having a particular sensitivity or feel for the handling of a motor car may actually go beyond environment. Though he says there is "no particular breed" of person one can predict will become a racing driver, five-time Le Mans winner Derek Bell, for example, commented in a recent interview, "I think a lot of it is genetics. I've got two sons—you watch them drive. I watch Sebastian, and he's so calm. He's always quickest in karting." Already having one son, Justin, become a racing driver, Bell described himself watching his younger son, Sebastian, drive a kart and wondering how the lad could go so fast with so little experience at that point in time. Then he described the notion as it dawned on him while he watched. "Actually, it's genetics; it comes through the family."[1]

There is a good argument through example for genetics. Family dynasties in motor racing exist on both sides of the Atlantic. Family names like Andretti, Rahal, Unser, Petty, Earnhardt, Villeneuve, and others are well known in North American racing history. Prominent European racing families include the father-and-son pairing of Formula

One world champions Graham and Damon Hill and Keke and Nico Rosberg, among other related racers.

Alberto Ascari was the son of Antonio Ascari, an Italian racing driver in the early years of the sport. The elder Ascari was named after St. Anthony of Padua, a fact that meant a great deal to both men, especially later in their eventual destinies. St. Anthony's feast day is June 13, as he died on that date in 1231 at the age of thirty-six. He was canonized by Pope Gregory IX just one year later. The saint is often called the patron saint of lost objects, and his believed intercession (advocating with God on behalf of the living) is frequently invoked by faithful Roman Catholics when they lose something, whether it be a common object such as a pair of eyeglasses or a sentimental one, like a wedding ring.[2]

Antonio Ascari was born near Mantua, Italy, on September 15, 1888, at the dawn of the automobile era. In his career, Antonio was successful racing for Alfa Romeo. His victories included the Italian Grand Prix in 1924 and the inaugural Belgian Grand Prix. In one race, he was so far in the lead he could take a fairly leisurely pit stop that even included a snack and a drink. He did this without losing the lead when he went back out. By 1925, having shown spirit and determination while racing Italian cars against automobiles from other countries, Ascari had become an Italian national motor racing hero.

Hours before the 1925 French Grand Prix, Ascari seemed unsettled. He was not sleeping well and went to the track unshaven and, also uncharacteristically, wearing sandals. The sandals, he said, were in case he needed to exit from his car quickly in an emergency. Unfortunately, after protesting about wooden fencing connected by wire that he thought was too close to the track, Antonio suffered a tragic accident that day after swerving on a left turn that involved the very fencing he did not like. His car uprooted the fencing and dragged it several yards. The date was July 26, 1925, and Ascari had been leading the French Grand Prix at Montlhéry at the time of his crash. No one knew what caused the initial accident—rumors flew that a French nationalist did not want the Italian to win the French race and threw barbed wire into his path on the track, but no one could say for certain. If St. Anthony is the patron saint of found objects, this was certainly one object that Antonio would rather his car had not found.

Ascari tried to climb out from under his car despite having one leg nearly severed and the other one broken. The driver also suffered a broken arm; bloody wounds covered his head and body. Medical help took longer to get there than required; one report said that doctors did not arrive on the scene for an hour. As he rode to the hospital in the ambulance, doctors determined that Ascari's one leg would need to be amputated. His body jerked while the ambulance increased its speed. As the car sped through the town of Linus, Ascari's body gave a final jolt, and he died. His body was taken to the villa of Alfa Romeo, where a mortuary room was set up. Strangely, like his namesake, St. Anthony, Antonio was thirty-six years old when he died, having not yet had his thirty-seventh birthday that year.

The sudden death of Ascari, a native son driving for an Italian racing team, was taken hard by his countrymen and -women but also by the French. In the mortuary room in Linus, the local people filed by his casket, viewing his body, which lay on white cushions, dressed in a red Alfa Romeo racing shirt. The lower portion of his body was covered by a tricolor flag. Later, when his body traveled by train from Montlhéry, about fifteen miles south of Paris, to Milan, Italy, men, women, and children added flowers to the car carrying his oak coffin. At each stop of the train, people added more and more fragrant blooms to his coffin car as well as ribbons with the tricolors of France and Italy to that car and the compartments next to it.[3]

Alpine flowers were added at a stop at the border; even the new Italian dictator, Benito Mussolini, sent a wreath of colorful blooms with a note reading, "To the Intrepid Ascari."[4] From the train, and followed by a crowd of people, the coffin was taken to the Alfa Romeo building in Milan, Portello House, where it lay in another mortuary room adorned with a silver cross, black velvet curtains with silver fringe, and a large flag of Italy. The room was opened to the public for the masses of Milan to file past, paying their respects. A cortege made up of a stream of black cars then accompanied the casket to Monumental Cemetery. Thousands of mourners lined the route to where Ascari was laid to rest behind the opulent monuments of the wealthiest deceased of Milan.

The accident, funeral, and outpouring of international grief would stick in the mind of anyone there, let alone a small boy. One such lad witnessing all of this up close and firsthand was Antonio's son, Alberto. Alberto was only six years old at the time of his father's quick passing at the wheel of a race car. Born on June 13, coincidentally the Feast Day of St. Anthony, Alberto Ascari, just like his father, lit candles in church in front of images of St. Anthony in tribute to his father and his father's namesake all his life.

Despite his own father's death in a race car, Alberto began racing Bianchi motorcycles starting in 1937. Perhaps the memories of watching his father's victories and the adulation that came from them drew the boy to the sport. No doubt, others would pat the youngster on the head and ask if he might try racing himself one day, like his father. In any case, by 1940, Alberto Ascari was well into the pursuit of racing cars. He and a cousin, Minozzi, took the first Ferrari T815 sports car out to compete in the famed Italian thousand-mile race called the Mille Miglia. The pair led the race in their class before mechanical problems forced them to retire.[5]

World War II interrupted the younger Ascari's racing, but once racing came back, Alberto won the 1949 Buenos Aires Grand Prix for Maserati, another of the famous Italian car manufacturers, then soon left that team for Ferrari, where he made his career and name in the sport. Soon, his career performance surpassed even his famous father's. In 1950, Ascari won the Swiss, Italian, and Perón grands prix in a T125. Competing against the Argentine mega-star of the era, Juan Manuel Fangio, who often drove superior race cars, Ascari won the world championship in the Formula One motor racing series not once but twice—in 1952 and 1953. The dominance of Fangio in this period is well illustrated by the fact that Fangio took world championship victories on either end of Ascari's—in 1951 and 1954—then also in 1955, 1956, and 1957.[6]

During 1952 and 1953, Ascari won an unprecedented nine consecutive grand prix races—a world record not matched since and unlikely to be met again.[7] By now, Ascari was a full-fledged sports icon in Italy in a sport that had grown in popularity several times over since his father had raced thirty years before. The second Ascari, with the famous racing heritage, impressed young fans of the 1950s who went to watch him drive a race car. His speed, it was noted, belied his rather expressionless face while driving. None other than future émigrés to the United States Mario Andretti and his twin brother, Aldo, were among the teen fans of the day drawn to the sport by the allure of Ascari's moves and his cool persona on the racetrack.

Reflecting on his early influences in the sport in a recent telephone interview, Mario Andretti commented that observing the successful

Alberto Ascari at the European Grand Prix, Reims, France, July 1, 1951. *International Motor Racing Research Center.*

Italian driver in his youth back in Italy was a critically important factor. "When I was growing up in Italy, motor racing was more popular than any other sport," he said. "In 1954, my brother and I went to Monza, where we saw the Italian Grand Prix. My idol, Alberto Ascari, was driving for Ferrari. It was fascinating for me to watch Ascari battle Juan Manuel Fangio in his Mercedes. I was totally mesmerized. Even though I was only 14 years old, that's the day I decided I wanted to be a race car driver."[8]

Nicknamed "Chubby" ("Ciccio") because of his physique, Ascari was full muscled with a thick neck like a rugby player or wrestler. The neck is an important area of the body to strengthen for success in motor racing. This is due to the need to withstand several g-forces on winding turns and sharp corners. Racers today still develop neck muscles to withstand the even higher g-forces that exist in a sport with faster cars. The idea is that racers must try to hold their heads upright against these forces not only to see and think clearly but also to help them feel and discern how late they can brake and make their quickest getaway out of a turn.

Despite his talents, which took championship victories away from the dominant Fangio in the 1950s, Alberto Ascari was widely known to be superstitious. Undoubtedly because his father had died on the twenty-sixth of the month, Ascari neither liked that number nor its multiplication factor, the traditionally unlucky number thirteen, even though that was the date of his own birth and the date of the beloved St. Anthony's feast day. Alberto reportedly did not like black cats, especially after encountering one on the day of his first bad accident in a race car. He was also fussy about his racing equipment to the point that he did not want anyone else touching it. Ascari wore a specific light-blue helmet that he seemed to feel was a lucky charm; perhaps he believed it served him like a St. Christopher's medal, mysteriously warding off danger for travelers. So known for his superstitions was this champion racer that his archrival Fangio once pointed out this trait as Ascari's only weakness.[9]

Though his place in racing history was already firm, Ascari had experienced quite a streak of bad luck since his Ferrari drive for the 1953 world championship. In the next season, he drove several races for Maserati. In eight races out of nine between the Swiss Grand Prix of 1953 and the Monaco Grand Prix of 1955, he ended his race with a DNF ("did not finish") for mechanical problems. In fact, in all of 1954, he had not completed the French, British, Italian, or Spanish grands prix and placed a dismal twenty-fifth in the overall rankings for the season. In 1955, the year after he had defeated the great Fangio for two straight years, he did not even finish the Argentinean Grand Prix, Fangio's home race.[10] Only a defending champion running into that kind of streak of bad luck in the very next season of his career can understand the disappointment that it must make a racer feel or what it does to a driver's psyche, temperament, and personal will to go on.

For decades, the Monaco Grand Prix has been arguably the most beautiful, glamorous, and skill-testing race on the racing calendar; with the dawn of the Formula One World Championship, it quickly became the hot spot on the F1 schedule as well. Its history as a street race goes back to 1929, and, along with the other two races in what has come to be called the "Motor Racing Triple Crown"—the 24 Hours of Le Mans and the Indianapolis 500—Monaco is considered the race most drivers dream of winning at least once in their careers.[11] As a race run through the streets of Monte Carlo, its path winds up and down hills, through a long tunnel and out into the bright sunlight again, along the edge of the blue Mediterranean with its harbor full of large, expensive white yachts and other pleasure boats of the rich and famous, and on through extremely narrow streets with walls and buildings on both sides. There is no room for error on such an intricate street circuit, and the driving, obviously, must be precise.

The glamor of the event is heightened not just by its taking place in a small principality where a prince or princess hands out the trophy and where extremely wealthy people live or relax year-round but by the fans who come to the race and are themselves often among the world's most well-appointed. Serving as casual spectators, they watch occasionally during parties from elaborate, wrought-iron balconies overlooking the scenic harbor, sipping champagne as the fast, sleek cars speed by them on the narrow, twisty streets below.

In May 1955, Ascari was running a Lancia in the Grand Prix of Monaco when his car, like more cars in the years afterward, careened right out into the water instead of staying on the narrow street track. Ascari was all right after the spill but did suffer some facial wounds.[12] Doctors wanted to check out his spine for injury, but Ascari walked away, saying that he was fine. The spill made it all the more surprising when four days later he turned up at Monza, the track where the Italian Grand Prix was held, on the premise of watching another driver, Eugenio Castellotti, perform a test drive of a Ferrari 750S. The Ferrari was so new that it had not yet been painted.[13]

WHAT HAPPENED

Ascari had received an offer to share a drive with Castellotti in an upcoming race called the Supercortemaggiore, but the two-time world champion turned down the opportunity. On this particular day at Monza, less than a week after his spill in the Mediterranean during the Monaco Grand Prix, Ascari stood watching the test in a suit, shirt, and tie. He said to a colleague, "You . . . know that after a crash it is better to put yourself back behind the steering wheel as soon as possible."[14] He did not have to do so; no one expected him to drive that day, but he requested a go behind the wheel. As a star and double world champion, he was allowed to remove his jacket, tuck his tie into his shirt, climb into the new Ferrari, and take off.

Over sixty years later, it is still not known exactly what happened to cause the accident on the third lap that day. No other car was on the track. Dark tire streaks marked the surface at a left-hand corner called the Curva Vialone (now renamed Ascari). The marks showed that the car had gotten sideways in the turn, something a driver of Ascari's skill, even on a fast corner such as that one, should not have experienced. The Ferrari turned sharply and somersaulted, crushing the Italian driver in the process, throwing his near-lifeless body out onto the track.

Speculation about causes later included Ascari's possibly trying to avoid hitting something or perhaps someone running across the track or his tie maybe coming loose in the breeze and blocking his vision. Fellow racer of the period Mike Hawthorn (UK) conjectured the choice of tires was wrong for the combination of that car and that corner, as Hawthorn had determined when he tried driving it himself. Still another driver pointed out that the corner handling of the Ferrari 250 Monza, as the car came to be called, was not forgiving of any errors; in his experience, when he took a corner just a bit too fast, the car swung around from the back, and he lost control. Whatever the cause, the combined sounds of the crash and the silence of the engine gone quiet in the distance sent Castellotti and others rushing out to the scene on the Monza track. Ascari was close to death when they found him; it turned out he could not be saved.

AFTERMATH AND LEGACY

So big a star was the younger Ascari by this time in Italy that one million people lined the streets as his funeral cortege rolled through his hometown of Milan to the church of San Carlo al Corson. He is buried near his father. The city, in a country that values its strong motor racing history, virtually shut down for the day. The Argentinean ace, Ascari's rival Fangio, later said, "I have lost my greatest opponent." Fangio noted that his world championship in 1955 was somehow less of an accomplishment without Ascari around to challenge him. Ironically,

Ascari's death happened just days before Mario Andretti, a future world champion in Formula One himself, left Italy with his family to settle in the United States.[15]

Andretti has described losing his motor racing hero as one of the worst days of his life. Although he had never met the racer in person, he said, "he had a greater influence on my life than anyone else."[16] Perhaps one of the most significant, visible legacies of Alberto Ascari within the sport could be this model he would serve as for Andretti, who, unlike his hero, did not grow up in a racing family. Andretti, to date, is the last American to win the Formula One World Championship; he is also the patriarch of a racing dynasty that continues to this day. In a recent e-mail interview, the Italian American further described the effect of watching Alberto Ascari racing for the iconic Italian racing team of Ferrari when Andretti was a teen growing up in Italy in the 1950s.

> My admiration for Alberto Ascari began when I was a child growing up in Italy. I was a *true* fan. He was world champion, driving for the Ferrari team. He was always so cool and calm, even at high speeds. It was almost like he had ice in his veins. I watched him go around the race track and I was impressed. His every move, every turn of the wheel; I never took my eyes off of him. I didn't just want to be *like* Alberto Ascari—I wanted *to be* Alberto Ascari. And I also loved Ferrari. In fact, I had pure love of Ferrari. Later in my life, when I had the chance to drive and win for the Ferrari team—as well as have a personal relationship with Enzo Ferrari—it was incredible. Today, Ferrari is at the top of the list of unforgettable experiences in my life. I don't think there is anything more prestigious for a professional racing driver than to say you drove and won for Ferrari. It has extreme special meaning all across the globe. You can talk about Ferrari anywhere in the world, and everyone knows the esteem.[17]

The scope of one athlete's influence on the many others who came after him or her can of course never be fully realized. Though Andretti was born in Italy, because he became a U.S. citizen a bit later, he is listed as an American throughout his racing career, not an Italian. This makes writer Nigel Roebuck of *Motor Sport* magazine's claim perhaps all the more appropriate. Roebuck has called Alberto Ascari "the last great Italian Grand Prix star."[18]

COINCIDENCE AND SUPERSTITION

A father and son both die tragically while participating in motor racing. Some people might call that a coincidence, or they might call it fairly logical, given the times in which both men raced. What about coincidences and superstitions? Strange facts were noted about the day of Alberto Ascari's death. For one thing, the younger Ascari had not worn his lucky light-blue helmet that day. Instead, he had borrowed Castellotti's white helmet. His own blue helmet was getting repaired from the spill at Monaco. Also, Ascari was not dressed for racing in his usual attire. Instead of wearing his racing clothes, when he went to get in the car, he was wearing a dress shirt and tie.

Perhaps most startling to think about now, and a fact that has not gone unnoticed in the motor racing community, is the fact that Alberto Ascari died on May 26, 1955. This was the very date of the month when his father also crashed and died almost exactly thirty years before on July 26, 1925. Not only that, but Ascari's father was thirty six years old when he died, as was his namesake, St. Anthony. When Alberto died, how old was he? Thirty-six.

Why Ascari, typically so conscious of these numbers and factors throughout his life and racing career, did not apparently listen to his normal sense of premonition on that day remains a mystery. He certainly knew what the date was. Was the whole thing a coincidence? Had the many recent losses after two consecutive world championships and then the failure of driving out into the Mediterranean in front of thousands of people four days before at Monaco set some kind of inevitable, tragic finale in motion in Ascari's mind? Another fact that adds to the overall tragedy of motor racing in this period is that Ascari's death occurred just a little more than two weeks before what would become the catastrophic events of the 24 Hours of Le Mans in 1955.

It is interesting today to ask drivers whether they have certain superstitions about the way they approach their sport. Some may wear a good luck charm, for example; some may go through a certain routine the night before or morning of a race day. One racer may want a certain family member or friend to be in attendance at the race; others want certain people not to attend their races to avoid a kind of bad luck they don't want to risk. Some step into the car from the left or right side, each time they get in. Others put on their racing gloves with a ritual of the right one first, then left, or vice versa. Some pray, cross themselves, or keep a Bible verse taped to their dashboards; others kiss their wives or other loved ones.

What role does luck play in sport? What role does it play in life? What energies exist in events that seem like coincidences? Are they only that, some wild mixture of chance and circumstance that just turn out in such a similar way that those involved and some observers tend to notice them and wonder? Are they signs of a spirit or an intelligence that sees all and is trying to communicate with us?

Of course, it is highly unusual for a parent-child duo of racers in motor sport to meet the same end, both dying tragically while driving. High-profile parent-child racers today, including third generations and those who are retired, deceased later in life, or now occupying other positions in the sport, continue to exist and grow. These family dynasties have racers alive and well today. They include names like Andretti, Rahal, Unser, Petty, Bell, Hill, Rosberg, Force, Brabham, Stewart, Prost, and many more. As has been mentioned, motor sport tends to be a family business.

Coincidences can be just that, or they can be interpreted as something more. Either way, they are as curious a phenomenon in motor racing as they are anywhere else in life. When a coincidence or a superstition relates to matters of life and death and even gets handed down as legend, it becomes more curious still. Why did the normally superstitious Ascari go against his premonitions on that day? Why do racing drivers, who know the high risks of their sport, even to the point of losing a family member to it, continue to engage in it anyway?

—⁓∽∾—

Racer: Alberto Ascari (Italy), age thirty-six; b. July 13, 1918, in Milan, Italy; d. May 26, 1955, at Monza, Italy.

Career Highlights and Honors: Two-time Formula One world champion (1952 and 1953); holds several records in Formula One, including highest percentage of wins in a season (75 percent in 1952), highest percentage of fastest laps in a season (75 percent in 1952), most consecutive fastest laps, and most consecutive laps in the lead (304 laps between the 1952 Belgian Grand Prix and the 1952 Dutch Grand Prix); shares record with Jim Clark for highest percentage of possible points (100 percent) in a championship season (Ascari in 1952; Clark in 1963 and 1965); shares record with Michael Schumacher for most "hat tricks" in a single season (pole, win, and fastest lap in the same race) with five in 1952 (Schumacher had five in 2004).

Among His Legacies: Dubbed by at least one journalist the "last great Italian racing star" to date; nationalistic and local pride; strong influence on future Formula One racers such as Mario Andretti.

2

THE FOG OF WAR AND MOTION

Le Mans, 1955

"War is the realm of uncertainty; three quarters of the factors on which the action in war is based are wrapped in a fog of greater or lesser uncertainty." —Carl von Clausewitz, *On War*[1]

Uncertainty is not something with which many human beings feel comfortable; yet it is a part of life, and certainly we encounter it more often than most of us would like. If we knew the causes or outcomes of many of our actions or troubles, perhaps we could avoid more of them than we do; perhaps not. If we knew for sure the outcome of a job decision, our choice in a marriage partner, a house purchase, or our selection of the next place to live, for example, it might make the tough decision-making process at crossroads like these easier for some of us. Uncertainty also plays a fuzzy role when we look back. Why did one ancestor prosper and thrive in life, while her sibling struggled? What made an active person who ate healthy foods develop cancer and die young when another person who took worse care of his body lived to eighty-nine? The only thing certain about the "realm of uncertainty" is that it is ever present in our lives and seems to be exacerbated at times of confusion, mystery, or emotion—when we are already at risk of being in a fog, the fog seems to grow denser.

Back on May 7, 1945, a common desire held by many individuals the world over was an end to war. On that day, when Germany signed its unconditional surrender at Reims, France, ending World War II in

Europe, no one could have predicted that other desires entirely, just over ten years later and two hundred miles away at Le Mans, would embroil the British and Germans in yet another kind of battle, one that also used machinery, took place on French soil, and resulted in many casualties—this time, in sport. By 1955, the memory of the long, hard-fought war had not yet faded. The Normandy American Cemetery, with its now famous sea of white crosses just seventy miles north of Le Mans, would not be dedicated until the following year.[2] Both participants and spectators at the sporting venue in question had fought in the war themselves. It is safe to assume that during the conflict none of them had anticipated, ten years later, the possibility of being cut down by a German missile pitching through the air directly toward their heads, especially when that missile takes the form of a race car.

The 24 Hours of Le Mans (24 Heures du Mans) is a sports car endurance race still held each summer near the small medieval town in France for which it is named. The event was then, and remains, an institution in the sport of motor racing—by June 11–12, 1955, the race was entering its thirty-third year. That year brought an enormous crowd, said to number as many as four hundred thousand by the organizing body, the Automobile Club de l'Ouest. The crowds were there to watch superstars from around the world of motor racing compete with and against each other. Argentinian star Juan Manuel Fangio and British ace Stirling Moss were teammates driving one of three German Mercedes-Benz 300SLRs entered in the race. Ferrari (Italy) and Jaguar (Great Britain) also sent three cars each, ready to defend their recent dominance at Le Mans with esteemed drivers such as Eugenio Castellotti for Ferrari and Mike Hawthorn for Jaguar. All was set in motion for a historic European match-up between archrival teams and car manufacturers in a country that had only years before seen German occupation and the heat of battle. In the shadow of the six-year war not long ended, two miles from the site of a former internment camp, feelings of nationalism among the spectators ran high. Though no comparison can be made in good conscience between the horrors of war and any sporting event, some people have since called this particular race "World War II on the track." The terror that would afflict many families that day perhaps makes the comparison, rough though it is, a bit more cogent.[3]

With its six chosen drivers, the German Mercedes factory team (a factory team is one supported and sponsored by a car manufacturer) had covered its bases in terms of considering the nationalistic feelings that were present in the crowd that weekend. Driving car No. 19, the pair of Fangio and Moss were the top drivers of the day from anywhere in the world. Fangio was the reigning Formula One world champion, and Moss had just won the thousand-mile Mille Miglia, an endurance street race in Italy, at a blistering pace averaging 100 mph. They were the car maker's best hope for an overall win. Another Mercedes, No. 20, was driven by Frenchman Pierre "Levegh" Bouillin, who would hopefully win the support of the French spectators, and American John Fitch, who would likely attract American interest in the race, helping with much-desired Mercedes car sales overseas. For the third Mercedes, car No. 21, Karl Kling was initially paired up with Hans Herrmann to form an all-German team; however, the latter driver suffered an injury in a previous race at Monaco, forcing Mercedes to find a replacement. They went with French driver André Simon, thus offering another French driver for the locals to root for in the race.[4]

While Fangio and Moss were the pair to beat, those star drivers' long and varied history of races and victories both before and after this event made the unfortunate Pierre Bouillin arguably the name most associated with this race years later. Bouillin went by the surname "Levegh," an anagram his uncle Alfred Velghe had fashioned from his name many years before. Velghe was an early French racing driver who won the Paris-Toulouse-Paris city race in 1900. It is not known for sure whether Bouillin, born a year after his uncle died in 1904, changed his name legally to Levegh or just started using it, but Pierre Bouillin had been calling himself Pierre Levegh for some time before he drove for Mercedes at Le Mans in 1955.[5] Perhaps out of respect, "Levegh" has commonly been used in writing since then when referring to him.

Bouillin/Levegh was forty-nine years old, much older than most of the other competitors. He had raced in his home country's iconic endurance race a few times before for another team. In 1951, he finished fourth; in 1953, eighth; and in 1954 he did not finish (traditionally listed as "DNF" on motor sport results sheets). Levegh achieved local notoriety at Le Mans in 1952 when he almost single-handedly won the twenty-four-hour race. Four laps ahead, with only an hour left to go, Levegh's car succumbed to mechanical problems. It was thought that he

missed a change in gear, causing the engine to overrev and fail.[6] Levegh's attempt to race the entire twenty-four hours himself received a
mixed reaction in the press and from fans, ranging from those who
admired the effort and Levegh's stamina to those who thought driver
fatigue contributed to the DNF and labeled Levegh an arrogant fool for
not sharing the wheel in strategized trade-offs with a teammate, as was,
and still is, the custom.

Tall and thin as a post, Levegh's teammate at Le Mans in 1955, John
Fitch, hailed from New England. European car manufacturers coveted
U.S. car sales then as now, and racing was used then, perhaps more
than today, as a way to profile and promote car makers' wares and
capabilities. The saying went, "Race on Sunday; sell on Monday," so
having American Fitch in a car in a globally high-profile race was another strategic choice for Mercedes in terms of selling its German cars
in America, especially after the war. In a twist of irony, Fitch had been a
fighter pilot in World War II and told at least one journalist that he
believed he was one of the first Americans to shoot down a German
Messerschmitt Me 262 jet fighter.[7] Three months before the end of the
war, Fitch was attacking a train in Germany when he was shot down
himself and taken prisoner. Now, this former POW raced automobiles
for a car manufacturer based out of his former enemy's country. World
War II on the track, indeed!

With Mercedes as the overall team to beat, Great Britain's three
Jaguar factory teams were racing cars No. 6 (driven by Mike Hawthorn
and Ivor Bueb), No. 7. (Tony Rolt and Duncan Hamilton), and No. 8
(Norman Dewis and Don Beauman). Hawthorn had replaced Moss
earlier that year at Jaguar when Moss went to Mercedes. Nicknamed
"the Golden Boy," Hawthorn had won the French Grand Prix driving
for Ferrari two years earlier in Reims, beating Fangio, who was regarded by many then and now as arguably the best race car driver in
history. Now, Hawthorn had his sights set on beating Fangio again
when he climbed into his mother country's Jaguar D-type that June day.
Another driver who would play a key role in what happened at Le Mans
on this particular day was Lance Macklin of Great Britain, piloting the
Aston-Healey 100S, No. 26 car, with teammate Les Leston. Aston-
Healey was another British team, and Macklin, like Fitch, was also a
WWII veteran. Macklin had commanded his own gunboat, becoming
the youngest lieutenant commander of the Royal Navy. Macklin had

started his racing career in 1948, but later observers would note that he seemed to offer the sport more promise than dedication.[8] Bouillin/ Levegh, Macklin, Hawthorn, and to some extent Fangio would be the key players in the incident that would change motor racing from that day forward.

Notably, sixty cars were entered in the 24 Hours of Le Mans race in 1955, though only fifty-eight took part. So much interest did car manufacturers have in motor racing at that time that only thirteen of these cars were not running for factory teams. Also interesting was the fact that none of the cars running had a roof.[9] Not only is Le Mans a grueling race for the length of time the cars and their pilots race, but it is also a test of endurance in terms of distance. The Le Mans circuit was then, as now, approximately 8.5 miles long; as such, it is one of the few tracks in the world where some of its drivers today say they feel like they are actually "going somewhere" when they set out on it. Perhaps it feels a bit like driving to town from out in the countryside to buy a loaf of bread, but at an exceptional rate of speed. (Compare the length of the 8.5-mile circuit at Le Mans, for example, with the 0.5 mile NASCAR oval tracks at places like Bristol or Martinsville.)

In 1955 the winning speeds at Le Mans were well over 100 mph.[10] At that rate, it could take just over five minutes to complete one lap of this long course. As any driver of the racing or daily commuting variety knows, a lot can go wrong when driving a car on any street or highway. Push a specially designed racing car at the top speed it is mechanically capable of for twenty-four hours, and the chance of malfunction or breakdown increases even more. Add to that the fatigue of weary human beings trying every second to outrun their closest competitor while staying awake in the dead of night, and this magnifies the achievement of not only those who win the race but also those who simply manage to finish this twenty-four-hour endurance extravaganza of human and machine. "To finish first, you must first finish" is a well-known motor sport maxim, and nowhere is it more apropos than at Le Mans.

Fifty-eight cars and teams of drivers lined up to start the race on that warm June day.[11] By tradition, the race starts at 4 p.m. local time. The drivers stood on designated painted circles on the track, lined up across from their cars. When the French tricolor flag was waved, the drivers ran across the track, jumped into their cars, and started off, a feature known as the famous "Le Mans Start."[12] (The "Le Mans Start" was stopped decades later when it was deemed too unsafe.) The race then went through the night until the same hour the next day. It ran nonstop except for pit stops for fuel, tires, minor fixes, and changes of driver. Even for such a long race, quick pit stops are both desired and expected, so the team of pit crew and mechanics is in many ways just as important as, if not more so than, in some aspects, the driver who jumps into the car and takes it away again. Though the driver typically gets either the credit or the blame with the public for the outcome of a race, those involved know that motor racing is a team sport. At Le Mans, everyone on the team must stay alert and play an A game for twenty-four hours straight.

WHAT HAPPENED

At the start of the 24 Hours of Le Mans in 1955, the German Mercedes cars got a slow getaway compared to the British Jaguars. The great Fangio, in fact, underwent some unwanted fumbling when he jumped into his car in such a way that his pant leg went straight down over the gearshift. The cars charged away, Ferrari's Castellotti's getting away first to an early lead. By the end of the first lap, even with Fangio getting such a late start, the order of the drivers involved in what was to come was Hawthorn, second; Levegh, seventh; and Fangio, fourteenth. By the third lap, Fangio had made it up to third place, and the racing, especially for this early in the contest, was ferociously fast.[13] Fangio and Hawthorn were setting lap-speed records as they traded places back and forth for second and third, with Castellotti ahead of them.

Motor racing, in many ways, involves more strategy than the flat-out speed that casual observers may notice most. In endurance races, for example, drivers need to take breaks; tires wear out and must be replaced; engines fail if pushed too hard too early or too long, so must be selectively nursed along by a driver who can not only maintain a high speed but also finesse the equipment and not run it too hard. At Le Mans, all of these factors get magnified by the length of the circuit and the duration of the race. Drivers also look for weaknesses in their opponents—any tiny mistake that affects pace from which a competitor might gain an advantage. In 1955, the question became why Fangio and Hawthorn were tearing up the track so early in the race. Surely they knew they risked burning out their cars, if not their own energies, hours before the finish. One train of thought has it that Hawthorn knew he could not beat Fangio on speed alone over the twenty-four-hour period, so the Jaguar team strategized that he would go fast early on to try to force the Mercedes into a mechanical failure.[14] Another theory holds that Fangio and Hawthorn, whether consciously or unconsciously, were dueling a kind of rematch of the French Grand Prix of 1953 that had been so close between them, running their own grand prix sprint race in the middle of the endurance trial of Le Mans. Whatever their reasons, neither driver was letting up, and each was racing as though he were in the closing minutes of the daylong contest instead of at the beginning of a twenty-four-hour marathon.

It is also a custom in racing that "back markers," as they are called—the cars at the back of the pack in a race that are clearly not in contention for the lead—move over or slow just a slight bit to allow the front-runners to pass, whether they are teammates or not. The faster cars thereby "lap" the slower ones. Another indication of how fast the leaders were going in the 1955 Le Mans race was the fact that they were already lapping the back markers by their fourth lap around the 8.5-mile circuit.[15] Meanwhile, the pace between Fangio and Hawthorn was taking its toll on Castellotti's ability to hold on to the lead for Ferrari. At one point, the Italian's foot slipped on a slick brake pedal, and Hawthorn shot in front of him, with Fangio close behind. Soon, the strategy for many of the teams was to pit and change drivers. With signs of Castellotti's car slowing, the Italian pitted. Moss was preparing to take over for Fangio in the No. 19 Mercedes, Fitch for Levegh in the No. 20, and Simon for Kling in No. 21. Levegh would soon be lapped by Fangio in front of the grandstands, but this did not concern their team, according to Fitch. Fitch contended the strategy of the No. 20 car had been to save their push for the end of the race.[16] Hawthorn, in the Jaguar, was also due to come in and hand over the wheel to his teammate, Bueb.

What took place at the end of the thirty-fifth lap of the race was a chain reaction on the surprisingly narrow portion of the track between the main grandstands and the pits. It happened so fast that it wasn't until film footage from a spectator surfaced and was restored decades later that the individual actions could be more closely examined. This narrow straight with a white line down the middle, which slower cars were told to stay to the right of and not cross, was only three car widths wide, not quite twenty-three feet, and had no separate area for the pits. This meant that speeding cars going as fast as 150 mph, parked cars with drivers getting in and out of them, mechanics working on cars, other team members standing around, and so forth, all occupied a space of road that was not much wider than a typical American two-way road. In addition to this tight squeeze, right before it was a small kink in the track. The small turn was not too perceptible at normal driving speeds, but at racing speed, the kink affected where the drivers would position the cars on the track hurtling toward that section, making the usable width that racers would travel on the course even narrower. The main grandstand was packed. Only a chest-high banking and hedge fronted the grandstands against the track, separated by, of all things, a low white picket fence.[17]

From what can be seen in the spectator's film footage, at the end of lap thirty-five, Hawthorn was leading Fangio and lapped Levegh, who was also likely expecting to be lapped by the great Argentinian. According to the custom of the day, it is likely Levegh would have wanted to stay out of the way to allow Fangio by him, since he would be expected not to hinder his faster teammate's progress in the race. Just as Hawthorn got around Levegh, Hawthorn came up upon Macklin, a back marker then, who was going slower. In a split second, Hawthorn made a move around Macklin and to the right, cutting Macklin off, as though Hawthorn were going to pit. To avoid hitting him, Macklin slammed on his brake, and his car swerved left. In doing so, it crossed the forbidden white line and moved into the path of the two oncoming Mercedes driven by Levegh and Fangio. Macklin would get blamed later for moving out in front of the oncoming Mercedes, though further explanations speculated that his braking mechanism and the force of his effort to avoid a collision with Hawthorn in front of him may have made the car shift uncontrollably to the left. Raising his arm in a gesture that Fangio took as a warning and claimed later saved his life, Levegh, going about 150 mph, had no time to swerve around Macklin. Instead, he found himself riding up the back left of Macklin's car as though flying up a ramp. Levegh's Mercedes launched an estimated twenty feet into the air, at one point nearly vertical, and flew straight toward the banking in front of the packed grandstands, where it hit and launched again. The incredible momentum and weight of the car kept the vehicle flying through the grandstands until it hit the concrete wall of a tunnel entrance to the track. Here, it exploded and broke apart, parts flying everywhere. Levegh is presumed to have been shot out of the vehicle at that point. His lifeless body was found eighty-two yards away.[18]

Car parts, scattered and on fire, flew and fell into the crowd. People standing on trackside platforms to see the race better were killed instantly, some decapitated by flying machinery. What remained of the larger part of the car was also on fire, the magnesium body resisting efforts to extinguish the flames. In all, even today, the exact death toll from this catastrophic crash remains uncertain, but numbers from most sources range from eighty to ninety, with over one hundred more reported injured. It is by far the largest death toll at a single racing event in motor sport history anywhere in the world. Many who were there likened the scene to a battlefield. People screamed and dropped to the ground; others ran. Still others tended to their loved ones or covered the dead. Priests moved among the crowd administering last rites; the staff of on-call doctors ran to the scene and tried to treat or save as many of the injured as possible.

It is difficult to understand why more people at the track were not aware of the severity of this crash, especially with it taking place at the main grandstands across from the pits and near the start/finish line. Certainly, this is the central focal point on the track. The enormous extent of what happened would not have been immediately known by everyone around the entire 8.5-mile circuit, given the more limited communication systems of those days, but even spectators yards away who could see the smoke from Levegh's burning car did not fathom what had happened. Just like in the fog of war, confusion reigned over magnitude, and numbers were not yet counted because the numbers kept rising. There were no jumbotron screens, cell phone apps, or instant replays back then either to communicate or to help people understand or receive updates.

Unbelievably, to many now and back then as well, the race continued. The reason given by the organizers was that if the race had been stopped, the access roads would have become congested with thousands of spectators leaving the track grounds. If the race continued, spectators, most of whom had no idea how severe the accident or death toll was at the time, would stay in place, watching, and ambulances could move out the fallen and the injured with less interference. The individual teams involved had another issue to deal with, however. A

French driver in a German car had just mowed down several dozen mostly French spectators and ended up dying himself. Given the postwar nationalism in the air at this event, public relations over a likely German win with the star Fangio-Moss team began to chip away at Mercedes's resolve to keep going. At one point, Mercedes asked the Jaguar team to stop racing out of respect for the fallen; if Jaguar would stop, Mercedes would too. Jaguar, in the lead at the time with Hawthorn, refused.

Both teams continued racing for several more hours as officials in the Mercedes camp tried to contact team officials away from the track to decide what to do. Finally, at 2 a.m. Sunday morning, Mercedes received the word that the decision had been made to withdraw the team from the Le Mans competition. Their cars were called in and did not go back out.[19] With this happening under the darkness of night, the changeover was less noticeable among the fans when it happened, since many of them were sleeping. They awoke to find Jaguar handily winning the race, now with little to no competition at the front. In fact, at 4 p.m. Sunday afternoon, Mike Hawthorn did take the tainted win, the celebratory wreath hung around his neck in victory lane. Though some have said his reaction has been overblown and that Hawthorn was indeed still upset, at least one photo caught him smiling broadly, looking to an objective observer even years later as though he thought nothing unusual at all had happened.

People not interested in motor racing might quite reasonably say that the sport as a whole caused the demise of innocent human beings that day; they might say that the accident proves just how foolish and dangerous motor racing is. By contrast, within the sport, there were many fingers pointing in different directions to pass the blame around. Even in death and thereby unable to defend himself, Bouillin/Levegh, who drove the car that flew into the crowd, inflicting the carnage, was blamed. Was he trying to avoid being lapped by Fangio by outrunning him? Was he too old to be driving that fast? Was the powerful Mercedes car too much for him? Was there anything he could have done to avoid hitting Macklin's car in front of him? Going further up the chain toward the front of the accident, Macklin was blamed for crossing the white line and veering left in front of the oncoming speeding Mercedes cars of Levegh and Fangio. Looking at the trigger of the events, blame fell on Hawthorn. Had he not suddenly moved right, cutting off Macklin, none of the subsequent chain reactions behind him would have taken place. It did not go unnoticed as well that instead of coming in after the incident, Hawthorn drove another lap and came into the pits the next time around.

Levegh's teammate John Fitch said for years afterward that when Hawthorn initially came into the pits after the accident that day, he was a broken man. Hawthorn, shaking and in tears, had taken the blame. Fitch does not know what changed Hawthorn's public response in victory lane and in his subsequent autobiography, where readers, including Lance Macklin, whose car had evaded Hawthorn's and moved into the path of Levegh, perceived him as not taking responsibility. (Macklin felt that he was being blamed through implication by Hawthorn, an impression that caused Macklin to file suit for libel against Hawthorn.) Fitch speculated that, perhaps as a defense mechanism against the horror, Hawthorn may have buried his involvement in his own thoughts and instead lashed out at the Germans, riding on lingering anti-German sentiment from the war. Whatever his true thoughts and feelings, Hawthorn continued his racing career after the incident, in 1958 becoming the first British driver to win the Formula One World Championship.

Fitch thinks the Le Mans tragedy continued to play on Hawthorn's mind, whether it directly affected his racing career after the disaster or not. In Fitch's view, Le Mans 1955 perhaps worked on Hawthorn's conscience all the way to Hawthorn's own death in 1959. Out driving on a wet night in his (of note) Jaguar, Hawthorn attempted to pass (also of note) a Mercedes and hit a tree.[20] The recently retired world champion driver had simply been on his way to pick up fish and chips. The 1955 winner of the 24 Hours of Le Mans race, whom the public learned later was also by then suffering from a terminal illness, was twenty-nine years old when he died. Hawthorn's death also effectively put an end to Macklin's libel suit.

Though Fitch, who admits any change of circumstances could have put him in the Mercedes at Le Mans instead of his teammate Levegh, points at Hawthorn as making the initial move in the chain of events on that horrible day in France, he also says it is "unfair" to lay blame on any one of the three implicated drivers—Hawthorn, Macklin, or Levegh. "If Mike Hawthorn could be said to have caused the accident," Fitch writes, "he cannot be said to have caused the tragedy." He says the entire catastrophe was as unlikely as a jet plane "falling on a schoolhouse,"[21] saying that society would not abandon use of airliners or schools if such a freak accident were to occur, so neither should the world give up on the sport of motor racing. Fitch's own engineering legacy afterward illustrated the lasting effect the incident had on him personally.

AFTERMATH

As one might imagine, the magnitude of the disaster at Le Mans in 1955 had an impact throughout Europe. Motor racing was banned or suspended pending further investigation in several countries. Sweden cancelled its planned grand prix in August and, in fact, banned all motor racing, a rule that held for generations. France suspended both motor racing and bike racing for a time. Spain's grand prix was removed from the calendar that year when officials did not feel confident that they could protect spectators. Italy also banned the sport for a time, then agreed to hold races again when the view was taken that Le Mans was more of an anomaly than the norm. Saying that needed improvements to its Nürburgring track could not be made in time, Germany also cancelled its grand prix that year.[22] Though the sport may have been in limbo for a time following the disaster, to the surprise perhaps of some non–motor sport fans, it was not long before racing was back on fans' agendas.

Mercedes not only withdrew from the 1955 Le Mans race but also left motor racing competition altogether, a status that it maintained for decades. The company received several letters from victims' family members, fans, and others praising its decision to withdraw from a major race it was winning out of respect for the fallen. Decades later, Fangio's Mercedes teammate Stirling Moss would say in public in front of John Fitch that he thought the team should have stayed in the race, since the race had continued after the tragedy. In his book *Racing with Mercedes* and in interviews, John Fitch admitted that his role at the time was to convince the team to withdraw as the best course of action not only for decency's sake but also for public relations concerns. He knew a German car killing a French driver and dozens of French spectators only a few years after World War II would generate bad press, to say the least. Perhaps surprisingly to people who are not fans of motor

sport, despite Mercedes's withdrawal from competition and several other major changes that rippled throughout the sport, the 24 Hours of Le
Mans endurance race was still held the next year. As Le Mans historian
Quentin Spurring notes, "The commitment to Le Mans by the passenger car industry remained strong, despite the events of the previous
June." The next race was held with a delay on the calendar due to
significant changes made to the French facility.[23]

Before the race in 1956, the pinched area in front of the pits was
widened by thirteen meters, and the kink leading to that area at the
start/finish line was removed. The grandstands opposite the pits were
taken down and replaced with a viewing area separated from the track
by a ditch. The pits, though only seven years old at the time, were also
demolished and rebuilt to include a deceleration lane and more room
for crews to work. Other areas of the circuit were widened, realigned,
or otherwise modified with safety and the growing speeds in car technology in mind. Some of the track was also repaved. By July 1956, Le
Mans had forty-nine cars start the race. Jaguar once again won the
overall event, with two British drivers taking victory in the D-type. This
time Stirling Moss, in an Aston Martin DB3S, came in second with his
fellow British teammate, Peter Collins. Mike Hawthorn and his 1955
teammate Ivor Bueb came in sixth in their Jaguar D-type.[24]

Did anyone die in the 1956 Le Mans twenty-four-hour race, one
year after eighty to ninety perished in the same event? Unfortunately,
during the second hour, on a rainy track, Frenchman Louis Héry suffered fatal injuries when his car flipped over at the Maison Blanche
section. He had raced in the 1955 Le Mans but was not involved in that
horrific crash. In 1956, he died on the way to the hospital after his own
accident.

Despite safety improvements, the sport continues to be dangerous.
The last driver death to date to occur from a crash during the 24 Hours
of Le Mans was that of Allan Simonsen from Denmark in his No. 95
Aston-Martin Vantage GTE. Nine minutes into the race, on his fourth
lap of the circuit, his car spun off the curb at the exit of the Tertre
Rouge corner just before it connects with the Mulsanne Straight. Simonsen hit the Armco barrier along the side of the track. The car hit with
such force that it kicked back out onto the main part of the track, where
it stopped. The impact crushed the roof and supporting roll cage. No
one else was involved or injured. Simonsen was treated on the scene,

then moved to the circuit's medical center, where he died a short time later.[25] The day was June 22. The year was 2013. At the time that this sentence was being written, Le Mans was preparing for its eighty-fourth running with an expanded list back to sixty cars in four classes expected on the starting grid.

LEGACY

Many of the world's passenger automobile companies continued to use racing to test and develop car technology, even at high risk to drivers. The continuation of the sport allowed for several developments in technology used by everyday drivers on the roads today. The events of Le Mans 1955, however, also prompted safety measures beyond the auto industry or the sport of motor racing. John Fitch, as one example, came home to the United States to invent what later came to be known as the "Fitch barrel." The barrier systems are comprised of a barrel-shaped object made of several parts that is filled with sand and engineered to absorb the impact of vehicles on everyday highways. The barrels are frequently placed near bridges or construction zones. By this point, the barrels are known to have saved thousands of lives in auto accidents. Fitch, a former WWII POW who was affected by the events at Le Mans 1955, turned his tangential involvement in such a horrible civilian event toward developing a positive outcome for the greater public good.[26]

A legacy, of course, need not always be positive like Fitch's. One can only imagine the permanent impact on the families, friends, colleagues, and others who knew the eighty to ninety people who died as a result of going out for a day of fun watching an automobile race. Families were left without loved ones, breadwinners, and children. There are survivors among the spectators who still remember the horror of that day and will never forget living through what seemed like a war zone at the racetrack. Their legacies, the memories they have shared, and their changed lives, as well as those of their loved ones, friends, and descendants, can and should never be forgotten.

Then there are the fans who demonstrate another kind of legacy from Le Mans 1955 any time a spectator is injured or worse at a motor racing event. Motor racing did not stop after the worst disaster in its history. One might expect the car manufacturers, drivers, crew, mechanics, and others with livelihoods and reputations at stake around Le Mans to want it to continue. However, Le Mans would not have returned if not for the fans, those who bought tickets and came back to the racetrack after the carnage of Le Mans 1955. The fans—the fallen, the injured, and those who came back—are arguably the heroes of this horrific event in terms of the sport's survival. Returning spectators ultimately make the decision whether motor racing in public venues will continue around the world. Despite the difficulties and risks involved— some say maybe even because of them—they have so far chosen that, for good or for bad, they love the sport and will not stay away.

The fierce and hard-fought battles of cars hurtling around a racing circuit are not war, of course, but accidents in the sport may be said to cause a related, if sometimes unexpected, sense of confusion. The physics of any accident—the conditions of the car or the surface of the track, the weather, the functioning or performance or failure of individual components in the car, the driver, the landscape, or changing conditions of the track in a particular spot, fallen or accumulated debris, what is happening with the cars and drivers nearby—all of these elements, added to the quickness of everything moving simultaneously, contribute to what this author would call a "fog of motion," a level of uncertainty that can result in pointing the finger of blame for many racing incidents in a number of potentially reasonable, arguable, but different directions. Several accidents in the sport dramatize this observed phenomenon.

What results from a fog of motion in racing accident investigations? Despite detailed and careful analyses by experts, a margin of error may exist that cannot be narrowed enough to quiet debate in some cases. Some factors may simply remain unknown; questions go unanswered. People who were there will give conflicting testimonies about what they saw, some honestly, some out of fear or politics. In short, motor racing crashes have results that are definable and undeniable, but the causes can be debated and studied for years. The fog of motion is like life that way—perhaps, ironically, this is one of the reasons why people who enjoy the sport embrace it with such enthusiasm and devotion. The fog of motion in motor racing replicates the uncertainties we all face in life.

—◦◦◦—

Event: 24 Hours of Le Mans of 1955, Le Mans, France.

Elements of the Tragedy: Pierre "Levegh" Bouillin (France) and more than eighty spectators die; more than one hundred are injured; Mercedes team withdraws from the race out of respect for the dead; Mike Hawthorn (UK) wins driving for Jaguar (UK); tragedy goes down as, and remains, the most catastrophic event in motor sport history.

Among the Legacies: Safety improvements to the circuit at Le Mans; Levegh's teammate, John Fitch (U.S.), invents several safety devices, such as the "Fitch barrel," that are used on everyday highways and have been shown to save lives; Mercedes leaves racing for several years.

———*ᴕᴕᴕ*———

3

SMOKE OVER THE HEARTLAND
1964 Indy 500

In 1964, the United States was still reeling from the previous November, when its popular thirty-fifth president, John F. Kennedy, was assassinated. Some say that is one reason why the Beatles' installment of the so-called British Invasion in popular music took such a firm hold on the nation's popular culture. When on February 9 the Fab Four performed live on American television for the first time on *The Ed Sullivan Show* in a studio theater full of screaming teenage girls, the country was captivated—it needed something to feel good about again. After Memorial Day weekend that May, when nearly a half million people headed to Speedway, Indiana, to watch the annual tradition of what has come to be called "the Greatest Spectacle in Racing," the Indianapolis 500, it could have only felt like tragedy had proven once again that it had moved into the American landscape to stay. Certainly, the 1960s in general would turn out to be a turbulent decade for the country both socially and politically. Motor racing in the United States proved in no way immune to the dangers the sport was going through in Europe and elsewhere during the mid-twentieth century. With the American automobile manufacturing center of Detroit situated just three hundred miles north of Indianapolis and tire manufacturers Goodyear and Firestone headquartered in neighboring Ohio, the connection between car racing and sales of automobiles and their components was perhaps more than obvious. Car sales still drove the sport and vice versa.

Indeed, the now famous Indianapolis Motor Speedway (IMS) began, at one level, as a testing ground for car and tire manufacturers. Men like Louis Chevrolet, Ransom Olds, and Charles Goodyear were associates of the track's founders in its earliest days, when thoughts of purchasing the old Pressley farm property on the west side of downtown Indianapolis were germinating. Historian Ralph Kramer describes a P. T. Barnum–esque promoter by the name of Carl Fisher spearheading the effort. A salesman and a showman, Fisher turned from bicycle racing to cars and is said to have been one of the first people to drive a self-propelled four-wheeler through the city. Soon he was challenging county fairgoers to race "any horse you want to run against me" in his Winston race car. He became one of the country's first car dealers and perhaps helped launch the outrageous advertising and publicity stunts that are still the hallmark of U.S. car dealerships today. Once he pushed a car off the roof of a seven-story building. When it crash-landed on its four wheels, he said he did it to show how rugged it was. In 1908, he and a partner rode in a new model Stoddard-Dayton touring car high above Indianapolis and on over the countryside, floating over the gawking onlookers under a huge, gas-filled balloon.[1]

Fisher visited Brooklands in 1907. The new concrete, banked track in Surrey, England, is thought to have made a lasting impression on him. Fisher complained that his own personal automobiles kept breaking down. He is reported to have told a companion in the real estate business that American automakers were using their own customers as guinea pigs. Fisher feared that the better cars being made in Italy and France at the time would take over the market. Something had to be done to improve Americans' ability to engineer their own vehicles before their customers got behind the wheel. They needed a testing ground.

In March 1909, Fisher and three business partners bought over three hundred acres of flat former farmland for $72,000. Construction of the 2.5-mile rectangular track on the former Pressley farm started immediately. A project rising out of the heartland, it was called "Fisher's Folly" by some and took about $3 million, five hundred men, and three hundred mules to complete.[2] Though the land was quite flat already, topsoil needed to be removed and a clay base laid, followed by layers of creek gravel, crushed limestone, hot tar, crushed stone chips, and heavier hot tar, each layer leveled by a fifteen-ton steam-powered roller. Grandstands and bleachers were built to seat twelve thousand and three thousand spectators, respectively. The deadline for all this work was six weeks. Spring rains raised havoc with the construction, however, and the first automobile races were pushed back on the calendar, not taking place there until August 19, 1909. True to Fisher's promotional talents, balloon and motorcycle races took place at the track before the automobiles rolled.

The early days of Indianapolis Motor Speedway auto racing were deadly, setting a trend that would plague the facility throughout its history. On the first weekend of auto racing alone, a combination of mechanical failures and track conditions caused the deaths of four people—two drivers, a mechanic, and a spectator. Wilfred Bourque and his mechanic, Harry Holcomb, were the first people to die at IMS from an auto-racing-related crash. It appears that something broke while they were racing their "Knox machine," sending them into a ditch, where the car rolled over on them and against a fence. Bourque died while being placed into an ambulance; Holcomb died shortly after arriving at the hospital.[3] Like their European counterparts, the Americans did not stop the race, even as medical crews worked to remove the dying from the track.

Problems with early track conditions became more than obvious to all who witnessed the first races. The macadam deteriorated under the load of the heavy cars, and zealous drivers and their mechanics, who rode with them in those days, had to guard against flying stones, dust, tar, and other debris. Soon, the sanctioning of the races themselves came into question, and improvements had to be made if the track was going to continue to offer races to the viewing public.

To help with safety, a decision was made to pave the track, and after some discussion and testing, bricks became the material of choice. It was calculated that 3.2 million bricks at thirteen cents apiece would be required to pave the 2.5-mile course. In September 1909, the bricks came to the track from the kiln at the Wabash Clay Company in western Indiana by way of train. Horse-drawn carts would next carry the bricks, then conveyors, and finally they were piled around the circuit. Workmen made slurry for the bricks and laid them in neat rows. The work was completed in sixty-three days, the last brick being laid shortly before Christmas by Indiana governor Thomas Marshall in front of a crowd of about five hundred spectators. Racers took to the new pavement on that day, too, setting new American records for speed. The famous "Brickyard" was born.

By the next year, all that was needed was a big event to draw larger crowds back to the track after the casualties and messy track conditions that had gone before. The many smaller races, each requiring ticket purchases, appeared to be losing spectator interest fairly quickly. "See what the boys think about one big race a year," Fisher is reported to have said when discussion over falling ticket sales took place at the end of the 1910 season.[4] In his P. T. Barnum style, Fisher talked with his partners about raising the purse for the greatest auto racing show on earth, something that could only be seen at Indianapolis, a five-hundred-mile race. They would hold this extravaganza on "Decoration Day," May 30, 1911, promote the event to the hilt for months beforehand all across North America and Europe, then raise the ticket prices per person. Announcements about track improvements and entries kept the event in the newspapers. Another strategy added was the eye-catching purse of $25,000 (the amount would later reach $27,500). Positions on the grid would be based on entry date, so the first team to sign on to race would get pole position and so forth. Lewis Strang, backed by the J. I. Case Threshing Machine Co., jumped at the chance and signed up first. Fisher's strategy worked. By late May 1911, a reported eighty thousand people clogged the roads on their way to the speedway.[5]

General admission tickets for the 1911 "International Sweepstakes 500-Mile Race" went for between fifty cents and $1, depending on gate of entry; grandstand or bleacher seating cost up to an additional $1.50. Box seats sold from $4 for individuals to $24 for up to six people, and club stands sat twenty people for $50 in addition to the $1 general admission charge for each person.[6] Reserved parking for automobiles cost an additional $2, though other parking was free. For their trouble, the spectators of 1911 got to see what would become the first race of a dynasty event in the world of sport, an annual race lasting over one hundred years now and counting.

To add to the newfound popularity of the first "500," a local Indiana man won the race. Ray Harroun, driving an average speed of 74.602 mph and relieved occasionally by Cyrus Paschke, crossed the finish line first in a yellow Marmon.[7] The day's festivities were, however, marked by tragedy. Driver Arthur Greiner's riding "mechanician," S. P. Dickson of Chicago, died when their Amplex car lost a wheel on the backstretch during the thirtieth mile, causing the car to twist and throw both Greiner and Dickson out. Greiner broke his arm, but Dickson was thrown twenty feet against a fence and died instantly. The *New York Times* reported a rather unsightly scene adding to the tragedy. The crowd on hand had been so large that a militia and special police force had been enlisted for the day to keep order. After the Dickson accident, people crowded so close to the crash site and with such fervor that the soldiers on duty were forced to use their guns as clubs to clear a path for the doctors and ambulance. Meanwhile, the race continued. Riled up from witnessing the first accident, the crowd rushed back and forth across the field to different spots along the inside edges of the track whenever another crash took place. In fact, in the early portion of the race that day, drivers and others were harmed in several crashes, with injuries such as a broken leg, potential internal wounds, and several bruises. The *New York Times* reported a day full of frenzy in the stands as well when spectators there screamed and cheered and one woman fainted and nearly fell out of her seat at the sight of smoke and flames coming out of a car. Another near stampede took place in the stands when a tire broke loose and flew over a retaining wall.[8] If the hardworking people of rural middle America needed something to get worked up about in a collective frenzy once a year, they had apparently found it in their new five-hundred-mile race at Indianapolis. By 1912, the payout for the winner was up to $50,000, and the "500" was well on its way to its current century-plus status as a global institution in sport.

At the first races in the early twentieth century, the sound system was merely a large megaphone that makes today's observers wonder if the commentator could be heard at all by the crowds over the din of the engines. Surprisingly by twenty-first-century standards of nearly instant global communications, the race was not even aired on television when that broadcast technology became available until ABC showed a recorded version of the race in 1965. Even more surprisingly, the complete race was never allowed to be broadcast live via television until 1986.[9] In the meantime, as the decades rolled by and tickets kept selling by the thousands as promoters ensured there was no other way to see the race, radio played a significant role in making the "500" a sporting phenomenon known around the world. The man whose voice told the story of the race while it was happening, allowing millions of listeners not on site at the race themselves to visualize it, was a fellow by the name of Sid Collins.

An Indiana native and a journalism graduate of Indiana University, Collins was "the voice of the 500" to all who listened outside the track from 1952 to 1976. Under Collins's tenure, the radio broadcast went from a schedule of five-minute hourly updates to his proposed "full-coverage concept," and it also expanded from twenty-six radio stations carrying the broadcast to twelve hundred. Collins's talent for describing the race in detailed and colorful language, with an excited tone thrown in, made listeners feel like they were there. From their home garages or living rooms, fans could imagine the race unfolding before their eyes, and soon Collins's voice became synonymous with the "500" for millions of people who were interested but could not physically go to the Speedway. It was Collins who once dubbed the Indy 500 "the Greatest Spectacle in Racing." People believed him, and the phrase stuck. It was also Collins who gave a young Donald Davidson, an Indy fan from England who had memorized an astonishing amount of the track's history, facts, and figures, a few minutes during the broadcast to share his knowledge from the booth. In future years Davidson became the track historian, a position he still holds at this writing. It was also Collins who encouraged a young fellow Hoosier who grew up within earshot of the track, David Letterman, to leave Indianapolis to pursue his desire to go into broadcasting. In 1964, Collins was, as usual, at his post, ready to narrate the story of the forty-eighth running of the famed race. He had no way of knowing when he arrived that day that this "500" would be unlike any other before or since.[10]

As is often the case in this sport so tied to the evolution of engineering, design, and technology, there was a rift going on at the "500" that year having to do with the cars. Someone will often come up with a new design that makes a race car go faster. In the process, the person or team will find a way to introduce this new concept in a race while still fitting in with the rules of the given contest or series, perhaps finding a loophole. Of course, this advantage is met with discord by the other teams, which are still conforming to the older way of doing things and, as a result, are at risk of going slower and losing. Safety is tossed in as an objection to the new car or cars; accusations of rule bending are suggested as another. Sometimes such innovations mark a generational shift in the sport, a time when the new way of going faster is clearly working, and rather than hold on to the old ways and keep losing, the rest of the field adopts many of the same or similar changes, and the playing field levels once again for a while, until the next major innovation by a team arises.

In 1964, the innovator on the racing scene at the "500" and elsewhere around the world was a British engineer and inventor by the name of Colin Chapman. Chapman has been described as a genius. His facial features were not wholly unlike British actor David Niven's or American animator and studio head Walt Disney's, complete with the thin mustache. Chapman often wore turtleneck sweaters and a signature Greek sailor's cap. Chapman designed lighter, more agile cars with a monocoque-style (tub) chassis that replaced the more common tube (joined ladder) design. He founded a race team called Lotus and continued to work on technical innovations to improve downforce (road grip) on his cars.

Chapman's key racer in this period, a Scot named Jim Clark with whom he had a close, nearly fatherly relationship, was running away with races in the Lotus. The distinctive, small, cigar-shaped race cars, painted British green with a yellow stripe, were quick and beautiful to watch. These vehicles of "elegant simplicity" also, however, had a reputation among competitors and some of their racers at the time as fragile, unreliable, and unsafe. Chapman as a man was reputed, like Enzo Ferrari, to perhaps harbor a preference for the future life and well-being of his cars over those of his drivers.

Chapman and Clark had, in fact, just come in second in their first Indy 500 in 1963 with a Lotus 29. They were back in 1964, riding on the wave of Clark's first Formula One World Championship the previous year. Clark put the Lotus 34 on pole (first place on the starting grid), and the American crowd once again had to wonder what was happening with this light, agile, mid-engined machine from Great Britain, which seemed so close to taking over their big and powerful American roadsters.

Two other men arrived at the track that day who would be particularly relevant to the events that unfolded during that year's Indy 500. Writer Art Garner calls Dave MacDonald "the hottest driver most Americans had never heard of" in 1964.[11] Born in 1936, MacDonald had found success racing Corvettes on drag strips in Southern California and then elsewhere around the country. MacDonald was known for driving with lots of oversteer, letting the back end of the car slide around while keeping the front tires under control. It wasn't long before people were paying to have him show up at races, just because he was so much fun to watch. He drove aggressively, taking most corners sideways in the car. He could take the lead so easily that even when he put the car on pole in qualifying, he would still start at the back just to give the spectators a show—and presumably himself a challenge in the race to make it to the front again.

Like many other drivers, MacDonald showed most of his personality on the track. Out of the car, he was quiet and shy. At victory parties in his honor, he was not the guy in the center of the room eating up attention or telling exaggerated, colorful stories to make his supporters laugh. MacDonald would more likely be found in a corner of the room, talking with his young wife, Sherry, who was a big supporter of his racing.

If Chevy had its Corvette and MacDonald had come to be regarded as one of the fastest drivers of the 'vette in the country, if not the fastest, Ford has its own ideas in mind for a sports car that it wanted to compete at races. Carroll Shelby, with his infamous Cobra, was just entering the scene with a debut at Riverside. Shelby saw how MacDonald handled his Corvette, and the car designer was soon on the hunt to acquire his services for the Cobra.

MacDonald was loyal to Corvette. He knew the cars; he had had success in them, and they were making his name in racing at the time. However, he was competing in club racing—amateurs racing against each other—and taking on the Cobra for Shelby would mean a big jump in his career: it would turn him into a professional driver, which was a move that he wanted to make. It became clear to the young couple and even to MacDonald's supporters with Corvettes that the move to driver for Shelby was one he had to take to advance his career.

"He's out of control half the time, but most race drivers are when they start," Carroll Shelby said about his new driver. "If I can get him to be more cautious, he'll be some driver."[12]

Shelby put another California racer, Ken Miles, on the case of taming MacDonald a bit so that he drove with more control. Miles had been a tank commander in the British army in World War II. He soon found, though, that he did not need to be too tough with MacDonald. The young driver was quiet and eager to learn. MacDonald won eight of their first twelve races. He might still be using some of his popular sliding technique around the corners, but the wins made it harder to demand that the driver drop his oversteer technique entirely.

Though doing well racing for Ford and Shelby, MacDonald remained a fan of his beloved Corvettes. He helped his competitors set up their 'vettes and still drove his on his own time, even though Ford had provided him with both a Thunderbird and a Mercury for his personal use. It became a matter of contention when MacDonald would show up for work in his Corvette to race for Ford. Whenever he did that, Shelby required that he park the 'vette across the street.

MacDonald had a chance in late 1963 to test the latest developments he was heavily involved in with a car called the "King Cobra"—a Cooper F1 car with modified body and seats and a 289 Ford V8 engine installed in the back. The October 13, 1963, *Los Angeles Times* Grand Prix sports car race at Riverside attracted the top drivers from many series around the world, since their seasons were winding down. In this race, MacDonald competed against the likes of world champion Formula One drivers, American road-racing stars, and Indianapolis racers. Names on the grid for that race included Jim Clark, Graham Hill, John Surtees, Dan Gurney, Pedro Rodriguez, Richie Ginther, Roger Penske, and A. J. Foyt.

Driving his King Cobra, MacDonald flew past everyone else in the field. A sizable proportion of the eighty-two thousand fans at the race that day jumped from their seats every time the son of Southern California raced by. He ended up winning the race, taking home not only more than $14,000 in prize money but the pace car as well. Carroll Shelby, to say the least, was pleased, saying it was the happiest day of his life and he was glad he took a chance on the kid, whom he called "the greatest."[13]

The next weekend, MacDonald won again at the Pacific Grand Prix at Laguna Seca, again racing against many of the top drivers in the world. Jim Clark had a new engine in his Lotus this time and took pole position, while MacDonald had to start at the back due to engine problems during qualifying. The situation was reversed, however, in the race when Clark's Lotus had mechanical issues and MacDonald shot ahead, winning the United States Road Racing Championship in the process. The drive was not without its difficulties for MacDonald, however. He came away with blisters on his hands from driving with one hand on the steering wheel and the other holding the car in gear via the stick shift.

Just as Ford was putting MacDonald to work also in its NASCAR stock car program, the Californian heard from a former neighbor from his drag racing days, Mickey Thompson. Thompson had been looking overseas for drivers for cars he had built to run in the 1964 Indianapolis 500. When he heard about MacDonald's stellar drive at Riverside, he contacted him. In the meantime, Carroll Shelby had heard about the Thompson cars and did not like what he heard. MacDonald asked his crew chief on the King Cobra what he thought of the Thompson cars, and he didn't like what he had heard about them from friends in Indianapolis either.

The perceived problem was that Thompson was designing and building his cars but not allowing time for the necessary development to test out his ideas. The word was that he was building cars that he would promptly take to the Indy 500 without yet knowing enough about their reliability or performance. Since the Indy 500 did not conflict with his Ford obligations, MacDonald wanted to go, and Shelby was obligated to allow him to race on another team. He nearly begged his promising young driver, however, not to get into the Thompson car. It was soon clear that MacDonald had already committed to Thompson; the lure of the Indy 500 was just too much to pass up.

Early in 1964, MacDonald's career with Ford continued running smoothly. There were lots of events, and he was still racing well. He was in the running for a seat with a bigger Ford presence in NASCAR as well as a potential trip to race for the company at the prestigious twenty-four-hour endurance race at Le Mans. A detour racing for Mickey Thompson in the high-profile Indy 500 would be a quick and pleasant highlight for his career that year. Then he would get back to work racing for Ford. The choice to compete that weekend for Thompson, against the advice of those who knew and cared about him in racing, turned out to be fateful.

Another driver with a completely different personality from MacDonald's took to the grid at Speedway, Indiana, that day in May 1964. While MacDonald would be the man in the corner at social gatherings, likely waiting for the right time to leave without offending anyone, then showing his pizzazz on the racetrack, Eddie Sachs, born in 1927 in Allentown, Pennsylvania, would be the life of the party, situated prominently in the center of the room where the more attention he received, the more he seemed fueled to keep up the show that earned him the nickname "the Clown Prince of Auto Racing."

An outgoing fellow with a sense of humor that sometimes delighted him more than his listeners, Sachs coined the phrase "If you can't win, be spectacular." If he didn't take his racing as seriously as other competitors, he was not about to have any less fun out on the track, whether he was winning or losing. Sachs sat on the grid eight times for the Indy 500 between 1957 and 1964, starting in pole position in both 1960 and 1961.

By 1964, Sachs was concerned about the new kinds of cars coming to Indy. Having been a recent fixture in the race, he had yet to win it, and driving the old-fashioned roadsters with which he was most familiar, he began to wonder if his dream may have passed him by in the name of technology and progress. Indy was the highlight of Sachs's year. Previously, he had joined the navy as soon as he was eligible, but he suffered a back injury while unloading a truck and was sent home. He tried college for a while on the GI Bill, but the classrooms were full of eager veterans out to make successful lives for themselves as civilians, and Sachs, with his medical discharge, did not seem to feel a part of that scene either. He dropped out. When he turned to racing cars instead of finishing college, he lost financial support from his father and now had money strains on top of his other problems in finding a direction in life.

Sachs showed more ability to talk his way into a ride than talent for driving. When he got a chance to race, he would wreck the car in qualifying. He was not particularly well liked off the track either. He was said to be brash and reckless there too. He was also a known womanizer. He turned to several odd jobs as he could find them—taxi driver, night club manager, bellman.

In 1953, Sachs appeared at Indianapolis wishing to take the rookie test and looking for a car in which to do it. Drivers don't just pay a fee and enter their cars in the Indy 500. Among many requirements, they have to pass a strict driving test of several parts. Through slick talking, he got himself a less than impressive car in which to test, but then he took the car out on the track and immediately spun out. The not-ready-for-prime-time driver joked that he had been waving to a girlfriend, then said he was trying to stay out of the way of faster drivers. Needless to say, he was not invited to qualify for the race that year.

Here is where Sachs showed more character, or drive if nothing else. It seems he finally had a goal; instead of leaving Indiana in search of other ways to make money, he stayed in Speedway the whole month of May doing everything he could to make money, from washing dishes and cars to picking up bottles to return for their deposits. Money remained tight; he used his car for a bedroom. Afterward, he tried harder to develop his racing techniques on the Midwest short tracks, where he raced frequently.

Sachs also worked on his ways off the track, putting his extroverted personality to work on sponsors and endearing himself to the fans with quick jokes, poking fun at himself, and standing out in the garages by maintaining a well-groomed appearance in a white racing suit. In short, what he lacked in talent he gained by putting effort into other aspects of the sport that the more talented drivers often ignored. Everyone in the sport knows, however, that no amount of showmanship or charisma replaces driving talent. When he had another chance to test for Indy in 1954, he failed the test again; he was the first driver to fail it two years in a row.

Still, Sachs was not deterred. Instead, he began calling himself "the World's Greatest Racing Driver," apparently thinking that coining a superlative for himself in jest would create a running joke with the fans. The other drivers, however, were not amused. When his mouth got him into trouble at an awards banquet, he was suspended from driving at places like Indy and could not even test for the 1955 contest. By 1956, however, he had had more driving experience and got a chance to test in a better car than before. This time, he passed the test, the first driver to take all four parts of the test in one day. He joked that he had had a lot of practice.

Again, Sachs did not win much support for his persistence at wanting to race in the Indy 500. Just as he managed a step forward, it seemed, his dubious character led him to take two steps back. During qualifying for the 1956 race, for example, it looked like rain was on the way when he was out on the track. Using a trick he later said he had learned from watching the Indiana University basketball team stall for time when leading a game, he remained out on the track after qualifying and did not come in so that the next competitor would have the extra challenge of qualifying in the rain. As usual, Sachs's strategy and apparent lack of sportsmanship backfired. The next racer went out and still qualified ahead of Sachs, even in the wet, and Sachs was bumped out of the last spot on the starting grid. Instead of competing, he went to the race as an alternate, dressed to drive, helmet in hand, hoping that someone would not make the start and he could enter the race after all. It did not happen, and instead he stood listening to the traditional singing of "Back Home Again in Indiana" with tears running down his face.

By 1957, Sachs was used to the drill at Indy. He knew he needed to qualify in a better car. His solution was to sit in the car that had qualified second the previous year and refuse to get out of it. Giving him only one set of tires, its owner, Peter Schmidt, allowed him to qualify in the car. Schmidt was likely as surprised as everyone else when Sachs qualified the car in second place. Finally, Sachs competed in the Indy 500; however, the car retired with mechanical problems about halfway through the contest.

Sachs's racing skill seemed to be developing; at the same time, however, his personal life was still a wreck. Having married another driver's widow who had four daughters, Sachs did not keep up with his child support payments when they divorced. The situation was so dire that his winnings were often impounded, and even Indianapolis police held him at one point for nonpayment.

In 1958, Sachs again qualified for the race and even ran at the front for a time but did not finish due to mechanical problems. Off track, he married Nance McGarrity, a tough woman who knew whom she was marrying and apparently took on the challenge of helping him reform. She enrolled him in a speech class, which she took with him, urging him not to talk so much but instead to present himself through a series of prepared and well-tested stories, more like a politician. In the 1959 Indy 500, Sachs spun out again, but this time he admitted his mistake and took the blame for messing up with a car that could have won.

A break with Schmidt put Sachs in need of a car once again, but now he found that he was a driver who was sought after rather than the other way around. In 1960, he drove for Dean Van Lines, putting the car on pole and setting records for one and four laps before the car retired. In the off-season, he now worked as a regional sales manager for the Dean Van Lines moving company, where he could put to use his newly polished public relations skills. On the track, Sachs may have improved his speed, but he had not bettered his manners or developed much humility with other drivers, so he was still not respected in the paddock. Sachs criticized his fellow drivers for maneuvers he said they made against him. Even fallen Jimmy Bryan was not immune from Sachs's wrath—Bryan was a former 500 winner from Sachs's own home state, who was killed in the 1960 Indy 500.

Sachs almost won the Indy 500 in 1961. He was leading in a tight battle with Texan A. J. Foyt. As he drove the car, he was even preparing his victory speech, until, with just three laps to go, he felt his right rear tire begin to wobble and saw that it was badly worn. Not knowing enough basic information about cars to the level that most drivers did (a criticism often flung at him by mechanics and others within the sport), he pitted to get a fresh tire and allowed Foyt to win the race. While tire experts agreed that the tire would likely not have made it to the end of the race, Sachs's mechanic at Dean, Clint Brawner, thought he should have kept going in any case, that he was so close he should have taken the chance.

Brawner thought that Sachs was losing his nerve. The relationship between the two men, never best friends in any case, grew more and more strained throughout the racing season. In the 1962 Indy 500, a wheel came off in practice. While Brawner was fined for the mishap, Sachs qualified only twenty-seventh after the disturbance. Still, his speed had reached a level where he finished third in the race. Driving the wedge between himself and Brawner even deeper, Sachs complained about slow pit stops in that race and said new cars were needed for the Dean team to stay competitive. When Dean refused to purchase new cars, by the next year Sachs had left not only the team but his job as sales manager for the moving company and started his own franchise of a rival company that he named Speedway Van Lines.

This man's admitted chief goal in life was to win the Indianapolis 500. He said that he thought of it every day of the year, twenty-four hours a day, and that once he won it, he would retire from racing. In 1963, he drove a new roadster for a team called DVS that was little competition for Jim Clark, who appeared on the scene for the first time from the United Kingdom in his Colin Chapman Lotus. Like others, Sachs also got caught up in the oil on the track from Parnelli Jones's car, a source of controversy after Jones's win that year. Sachs finished seventeenth.

In 1964, Sachs—an old hand at the Indy 500 and a popular figure with the fans in the events surrounding it, if not with his fellow racers or the race mechanics—remained determined. For that year's effort, he had convinced his moving company, for which his franchise was doing quite well, to sponsor another DVS new car, and he also secured a Ford engine to put in it. He also went on record saying that he thought the Mickey Thompson race cars were the wave of the future. He continued to appeal to fans, providing a sort of side show to the race. One photograph of the period shows him grinning widely wearing a white Beatle wig and holding a small guitar. [14]

WHAT HAPPENED

On May 30, a sunny Saturday, the stage was set for the beginning of the Indianapolis 500 of 1964. Sid Collins was in the master control tower, ready to call the forty-eighth running and his seventeenth calling of the "500." The reigning Formula One world champion, Scottish driver Jimmy Clark, was back at Indy for the second year in a row, sitting on the grid in the commanding pole position in his rear-engine Lotus 34, car No. 6. Young California hopeful Dave MacDonald, an Indy 500 rookie, had qualified for fourteenth position on the starting grid in his new Mickey Thompson, car No. 83, and Indy fixture Eddie Sachs, the "Clown Prince of Motor Racing," anticipated finally achieving a victory with a new team and a new car, No. 25. Sachs sat undaunted with a seventeenth starting position on a grid of thirty-three cars. None of them knew then that the race that was about to start would be stopped on the second lap.

During the prerace radio show, Sid Collins let the audience know that this was to be the fastest Indy 500 ever, that of the thirty-three qualifying cars, only two had not run at an average of 150 mph or more. The previous year, only five cars could even reach that speed. In qualifying, Clark beat Parnelli Jones's previous year's pole speed record by almost 7 mph, clocking 158.828 mph. Collins also prefaced the major technological issues of the day regarding the engines and other matters. This race, he suggested, would decide once and for all whether the rear-engine cars would make the Offenhauser front-engine roadsters obsolete at Indy. In the field that day, there were twelve of the new rear-engine-type cars and twenty-one roadsters.

Collins announced the names of celebrities in attendance—including Jack Nicklaus, the pro golfer participating with others at a local event tied in with the race. An astronaut or two were also among the 320,000 fans on hand. Racers donned their helmets, which left much of their faces exposed. These were supplemented by strips of white tape across the face in the case of Clark, goggles, neckerchiefs, and other chosen forms of protection. Thousands of balloons were released in the infield, and then it was time for the call for drivers to start their engines. Crew members pushed their cars to start, quickly running out of the way of other crews doing the same. The field followed a new, white Ford Mustang pace car, and when the car left the track and the green flag waved, the race was on.

Immediately, Jim Clark shot out in front of the rest of field, established a comfortable lead all alone out there, and kept it. Collins handed off calling portions of the race at different areas of the track to colleagues who were positioned for a better view. As the cars went around, the commentators handed off the call. MacDonald passed several cars on the first lap, but other drivers later would say they noticed his car was not handling properly. Suddenly, on the second lap on the main stretch, a car went off, hit the wall, and burst into flames. Plumes of black smoke billowed up and over the track; the smoke was so dark and thick that the announcers could not see which car or cars were involved and called to each other to learn who could see the scene better. One said he would try to use his binoculars once the smoke cleared a bit and complimented the other drivers for respecting the caution flag. Collins said he saw several cars on fire, but he would not say how many until he was told officially. Soon all cars stopped, and their drivers got out. Confusion reigned as crews with fire extinguishers battled the fires, one seeming to reignite and billow flames all over again.

It was MacDonald who had gotten loose. Trying to pass two more cars, his car suddenly swerved and hit the inside wall at turn four. When its fuel tank struck the wall, the car burst into flames. The force of the hit sent the burning car back across the track, where seven more cars became involved. Eddie Sachs tried to find an open spot on the outside to miss MacDonald, but the Californian's car swerved right in front of him, and Sachs hit it broadside, causing another explosion. Sachs died instantly. The other drivers involved were not in great shape, but none were in as much trouble as that.

MacDonald was found seriously burned but still alive. He was pulled from the car and taken to Methodist Hospital, where he was treated for pulmonary edema from inhaling flames into his lungs. He died at the hospital that afternoon.

AFTERMATH

It was the first time the Indy 500 was stopped in its long history. However, the race did start again that day. The on-site track announcer, whose voice called the race to the crowd of spectators who were there, delivered the news to his radio audience as well, and Collins reacted to the announcement that his friend Eddie Sachs had died with an impromptu eulogy. In what seemed like an inspired message, Collins spoke words that day and in that moment of collective grief that have been regarded highly by the motor sport community ever since for their eloquence about racers and racing and the risks involved in the sport:

> You heard the announcement from the public address system. There's not a sound. Men are taking off their hats. People are weeping. There are over 300,000 fans here not moving. Disbelieving.
>
> Some men try to conquer life in a number of ways. These days of our outer space attempts some men try to conquer the universe. Race drivers are courageous men who try to conquer life and death and they calculate their risks. And with talking with them over the years I think we know their inner thoughts in regards to racing. They take it as part of living.
>
> A race driver who leaves this earth mentally when he straps himself into the cockpit to try what for him is the biggest conquest he can make [is] aware of the odds and Eddie Sachs played the odds. He was serious and frivolous. He was fun. He was a wonderful gentleman. He took much needling and he gave much needling. Just as the astronauts do perhaps.
>
> These boys on the racetrack ask no quarter and they give none. If they succeed, they're a hero and if they fail, they tried. And it was Eddie's desire and will to try with everything he had, which he always did. So the only healthy way perhaps we can approach the tragedy of the loss of a friend like Eddie Sachs is to know that he would have wanted us to face it as he did. As it has happened, not as

we wish it would have happened. It is God's will, I'm sure, and we must accept that.

We are all speeding toward death at the rate of 60 minutes every hour, the only difference is, we don't know how to speed faster, and Eddie Sachs did. So, since death has a thousand or more doors, Eddie Sachs exits this earth in a race car. Knowing Eddie, I assume that's the way he would have wanted it. Byron said, "who the Gods love die young."

Eddie was 37. To his widow Nance we extend our extreme sympathy and regret. And to his two children. This boy won the pole here in 1961 and 1962. He was a proud race driver. Well, as we do at Indianapolis and in racing, as the World Champion Jimmy Clark I'm sure would agree as he's raced all over the world, the race continues. Unfortunately, today without Eddie Sachs. And we'll be restarting it in just a few moments. [15]

The race did continue without the racers knowing, or wanting to know, the full details of what had transpired. They had their suspicions about what had happened to whom, but they still had a job to do. Jim Clark's dominant start ended after forty-seven laps when the Lotus's suspension broke and he had to retire. That left the race wide open for the remaining players. A. J. Foyt eventually took the 1964 victory, and it was the last time a front-engine Watson roadster would win the Indianapolis 500. Foyt's smile in victory lane became visibly deflated, however, when his wife showed him there the first edition of the *Indianapolis Star* newspaper already announcing in a bold headline on the front page not only Foyt's win but also the deaths of Eddie Sachs and Dave MacDonald.

LEGACY

Someone left a poem on a chalkboard at rookie Dave MacDonald's pit that day. Along the pit wall, the crew had had to correct the spelling of MacDonald's name by adding an *a* with tape to change the "Mc" to "Mac." The fan also committed a misspelling when he or she wrote "To Davie" instead of "To Davey":

> I know a Speedway
> in the sky,—

Where brave young drivers
Thunder by—
And all who love this racing game
Must know that Fate
may call their name.

A photograph of the poem was sent to a journalist along with a letter explaining that the finder of the poem had tried to locate its writer but could not.[16]

A farther-reaching legacy of the accident, of course, was yet another discussion about safety regulations at a racetrack. The kind of fuel used

Poem left on chalkboard at Dave MacDonald's pits, Indianapolis Motor Speedway, May 1964. *International Motor Racing Research Center/National Speed Sport News Collection.*

in race cars was a topic under discussion due to the enormous fires in the tragedy. Fuel tanks had to be made of metal and have a prescribed thickness; they also had to be placed behind, not in front of, the driver. A maximum of seventy-five gallons of gas or other fuel was allowed on the car, requiring two pit stops for loads of forty-five gallons each. The type of fuel allowed was debated and changed. Cars had to weigh a minimum of 1,250 pounds.[17]

Once again, it was the fans who voted with their feet that motor sport would not be stopped, this time at Speedway, Indiana, after the tragedy of 1964. A record four hundred thousand spectators turned up for the next Indy 500 in 1965.[18] Jim Clark would finally win the Indy 500 that year on his third try. It was also the second year Clark won a Formula One World Championship. A. J. Foyt went on to win the "500" two more times, becoming one of the winningest drivers in the race's history. His career four-time wins are currently tied only with Rick Mears and Al Unser Sr.

Sid Collins, the eloquent radio announcer, called the race for remote listeners until 1976. In 1977, at age fifty-four and before he would have called his thirtieth Indy 500 for the radio, Collins committed suicide after being diagnosed with Lou Gehrig's disease.

Legacies are important, of course, and the families and descendants of both MacDonald and Sachs live the legacies of their fallen heroes every day. Perspective is important too. That fateful day in 1964, two men died in the pursuit of speed in a risky sport they participated in out of their own desire. That same Memorial Day weekend across the United States alone, a record number of deaths on the nation's highways was set at 431.[19] The next year, that figure soared even higher.

—◆◆◆—

Tragedy: 1964 Indianapolis 500

Racer: David George MacDonald (U.S.), age twenty-seven; b. July 23, 1936; d. May 30, 1964, in Speedway, Indiana.

Racer: Edward Julius Sachs Jr. (U.S.), age thirty-seven; b. May 28, 1927, in Allentown, Pennsylvania; d. May 30, 1964, in Speedway, Indiana.

Among the Legacies: Improved safety regulations in the sport.

—◆◆◆—

4

NATURAL

Jim Clark

"Well. It's all part of it. If there was nothing to be frightened of there, and no limit, any silly bugger could get in a motor car." —Jim Clark[1]

Stories about inherent talent tend to inspire us. We like to hear about individuals who arrive on the scene of an occupation—be it invention, science, business, entertainment, sport, or whatever—with seemingly no professional training or background of any sort in the discipline, yet surprise everyone by excelling in that activity right from the start. Perhaps we all like to believe that inherent talent exists in all of us, that we only need to find the right luck or insight or discipline to make that important match that will bring our innate talents together with what the world needs or values. We look for that moment when lightning may strike and our purpose on this earth, as we will come to see it, is made abundantly clear.

In the opening scene of the 1984 feature film *The Natural*, based on the novel of the same name by Bernard Malamud, a young farm boy practices throwing and hitting a baseball with his father. The boy dives into a field of tall grain and disappears, only to jump up, having caught the ball. He pitches a ball straight into the center of a chalk circle his father draws on the side of a barn. His father tells him that he is gifted but that having a gift is not enough. His talent must be nurtured and developed for him to be successful in that endeavor. The camera then shows Roy Hobbs's beloved father dying beneath a tree while working.

Lightning strikes the same tree that night, splitting it in two down to the ground. Hobbs hews a baseball bat out of the wood, burnishing it with the name "Wonderboy." The bat sees Hobbs through his professional baseball career, hitting a ball like lightning when his actions and purposes are true but not when Hobbs's intentions become something less than noble. The Excalibur-like bat suggests that exceptional talent, when bestowed freely by nature, comes with an inherent obligation to be used for good. There is a kind of purity in natural talent, we tend to believe; it's a gift that can affect many other people if it is shared in the right way. From what mysterious place does this seemingly inborn talent come, if it is not inherited from one's family?

Unlike many drivers of his or future eras, Jim Clark was not born into a racing family. In the borderlands of Scotland and England, Clark arrived on March 4, 1936, as the youngest of five children—the only boy—born into a sheep-farming family in Scotland. One can only imagine the relief his parents must have felt at the time. In those days, it was the boy who would be expected to take over the family business, and after four consecutive girls, the Clarks now had a boy they could raise and groom for the job of leading the work on two sizable farms. One of Clark's sisters, Bette Peddie, said her little brother "was quite disobedient at times" and shared that her eldest sister, ten years older than Jimmy, "thought he was just a cheeky little boy," to the point where the sister "would reprimand him more than mother."[2] After the birth of four girls, a little boy may have been not only highly welcomed but perhaps indulged a bit to the annoyance of some of his siblings.

In his autobiography, *Jim Clark at the Wheel*, Clark tells stories of his early driving experiences on the farm. He says he was interested in the mechanics of engines from a very early age and jumped on the farm tractors to go from one place to another, knowing as much if not more about how they operated than the farmworkers whose job it was to drive them. By the age of nine, Clark had memorized how his father drove their little Austin Seven and taken it for a safe ride. A bigger family car later on, an Alvis Speed Twenty, proved a bit more of a challenge because Jimmy was too small to both reach the pedals and see out the windshield. A couple of stories grew out of his driving this car. One was about a time when he went to back it out of the garage for his father and his shirt sleeve got caught in the hand throttle. He managed to close the throttle but was not able to reach the brake and clutch quite in time to avoid hitting a wall. He claims no one noticed the negligible damage to such a large car, so he did not tell the story until years later. It was his first shunt. Another story shows again how his parents trusted him with driving when he was a child. His father had some friends over, and they looked out the window with alarm when they saw the Clark family car apparently moving by its own power. Clark's father assured them with good humor that it was little Jim driving, that he was barely big enough to see out the windshield; the boy was not visible at all when people looked at the car from the back.

By his own admission, Clark was a boy who did not take much interest in school. His parents received reports from his teachers that he could do much better if he would only apply himself. Instead of books, young Clark liked action and took to playing hooky outside with some friends if the day were deemed too nice to sit in a classroom. Later, he went away to boarding school, but when he was sixteen, both his uncle and grandfather died unexpectedly, and he was called home to work on the farm. It was said his father felt a little less guilt about ending his only son's formal education to come home and help on the farm because the boy had not found much value in school anyway. This may well have been the layout of Clark's life—working the farm and perhaps meeting a woman with whom he would settle down and have a family—were it not for two things: curiosity and opportunity.

Jim Clark's early exposure to motor racing was fairly indirect and actually somewhat passive. He learned about the sport from books and magazines, and he attended his first race meeting at Brands Hatch during his school days. In his book, Clark describes how he read the three motor racing books that existed in his Loretto boarding school library cover to cover several times. Also while a student there, he eagerly awaited the appearance of the latest edition of his motoring magazine subscription. His brother-in-law, Alec Calder, husband of his eldest sister, Mattie, drove a three-liter racing-type Bentley that drew his attention. The first race he attended as a spectator at Brands Hatch in England was where he saw Stirling Moss race and picked up an autographed photo. He writes, however, that he merely purchased the signed photo as a memento of the day rather than because he was enamored with favorite racing drivers. He was more interested in the cars. Clark describes the day's events as being like watching a "lion-tamer at a circus," something that he never imagined he would do one day.[3]

If Jim Clark were to ever be described as a reluctant hero later in his racing career, perhaps the signs of this were all there at the beginning. At times, it was as though racing "pursued" him, he said. For example, he tells about going home from a cricket match as a youth and coming up on three Jaguar C-types being driven by the Scottish racing team, Ecurie Ecosse. These were the days when racers drove their race cars to the tracks, competed in them, and then drove them back home again on public roads. In this instance, the Jaguar C-types went weaving about while taking a hairpin corner at a quick pace. Clark remembers thinking of the racers as a "shower of madmen" but also recalled feeling a "slight twinge of envy" at their performance.[4] Another example of racing coming close to Clark without his really pursuing it involves the old Scottish airfield, Winfield, which was turned into a racetrack. Winfield was located near the Clark farm. Clark remembers cycling with some friends over to the track one day when they heard that Ecurie Ecosse would be testing there. They snuck inside the fence to get a good look at the cars. When he relates this in his book, however, it is as though it were more of a singular event in his memory than a regular thing he would do. Clark was busy on the farm; he likely did not have time to be a track rat, hanging around racetracks and absorbing the sport from any angle he could. As a young lad he did, however, want to purchase a motorcycle. His parents forbade it, thinking it too dangerous. Like many other racers, Clark ended up competing in events without his parents' approval for quite some time. Besides worrying for their son's safety, they had the farms and his needed work there to consider.

Interestingly, none of these memories of Clark's seem to suggest much more than a steady, if still somewhat casual, interest in the sport. As soon as he turned seventeen, however, he picked up the forms necessary to obtain his driver's license and passed the test. Not long after that, he was given his father's Sunbeam Talbot and "soon became anxious to take part in a competitive event."[5] At the urging of a local garage mechanic, he entered an event sponsored by the Berwick and District Motor Club. He won. However, Clark learned later at Alec Calder's house that he had to be disqualified because he was not a member of the club. The disqualification of his first-ever win in his first-ever meet left a "sore" feeling, and Clark says he did not join the club for more than a year afterward. Not surprisingly, in light of the stellar racing career that would follow, Clark later received a trophy from the club commemorating a lifetime membership.

Even then, nothing so far really suggested the kind of dominating racing career that the future world champion would go on to have. He had moved closer to the sport; his days as an amateur racer were beginning while work on the farms continued. His first major opportunity, however, finally came in the form of a person—Ian Scott Watson. Watson was a fellow farmer and friend and, importantly, taken by speed with a greater level of enthusiasm than Clark at the time.

Getting out and about more now in his Sunbeam Talbot, Clark joined the local Ednam and District Young Farmers' Club, where he met Watson. Watson was actively involved in rallying and amateur racing. In rallying, both then and now, cars race on public and/or private roads, frequently competing in stages of a longer journey over time. The "course" is not always clear to the driver who is concentrating on speed, so a navigator is needed to tell the driver which way to turn to stay on the designated route. The navigator also cues up the next move that the driver must make, thus allowing the driver to anticipate how he or she may want to position the car to brake, turn, accelerate, and so forth, to keep progressing on the route at the quickest speed possible. Watson invited Clark along on these events as a mechanic and also as his navigator. Here is where a map and at least a temporary poor sense of direction may have aided in the creation of a world champion.

Clark himself tells the story of a three-day rally event in northern Scotland. One section of the long route went over "a lot of folds in the map," according to Clark.[6] To navigate, Clark decided to unfold the map in the back seat of the car and kneel in the front seat looking back over it, calling out his instructions to Watson as they raced along. He soon called out to make a turn, but Watson reported there was no turn in either direction. They discovered that Clark had been navigating with the map turned upside down—they had to backtrack, having gone off the course and lost time because of it. After that, Clark reports that he took over driving rather than navigating for many of their subsequent rallies. Watson, in fact, began to encourage Clark to drive and take on more and more challenging competitions when Clark felt neither capable nor ready.

Watson was involved in another unfolding of Clark's eventual talents—this one, finally, related to outright speed with Clark at the wheel. It was perhaps the first indicator that there was something special about this sheep farmer from the Scottish Borders. In 1956, Watson had entered his D.K.W. Sonderklasse in a handicap saloon (sedan) race at the Aberdeen and District Motor Club race meeting. Clark was now twenty. The handicap involved lap times taken during practice and was designed to prevent drivers going slow in practice to throw off their opponents, only to speed up during the actual race. Watson took the "Deek" out for practice and set his times. To Clark's surprise, though, he handed over the wheel to him for the sports car race. The pair knew that Clark's parents were not in favor of his racing, but they thought they could get away with him doing it at this safe a distance from the farms. In practice, Clark went three seconds a lap faster than Watson. Clark remembered the feeling of sitting behind the wheel before the race began. He said that even though he knew the competition was not that strong, he was "terrified" of making a fool of himself. As it turned out, he passed a driver in a faster car but still ended up coming in last in the race. The problem, though, was laid upon Watson when race officials accused him of driving slower in his practice than in the sports car race. Because of Clark's speed, Watson's handicap was recalculated so that he could not compete in his race.

Even with this more exciting race that demonstrated his promise in speed, Clark still did not take his future in motor racing that seriously, but Watson kept after him. Watson was one of the founders of the Border Motor Racing Club and kept involving Clark in racing in his role in that capacity and others. Clark credits Watson, in their years competing in rallying and amateur racing in Scotland and England, with having a great influence on his entrance into the sport. "If it had not been for his pushing I might have retired from the sport long before I reached Grand Prix racing," Clark writes.[7]

Clark's opportunities in motor racing met a second significant juncture with another person who would play a vitally important role in his career and, eventually, his life—innovative British engineer and race car designer Colin Chapman. Chance plays a role again in their meeting. The story involves Clark, still heavily involved in farming, serving as the best man at a friend's wedding. Clark had raced quite a bit by 1958, so much so that it had begun to affect his time at the farm, a fact his

Jim Clark. *William Green Motor Racing Library.*

parents made quite clear they did not take kindly. Several arguments with the young man erupted at Chirnside. In any case, an opportunity came to go to Brands Hatch and drive a Lotus Formula Two (F2) car designed by Chapman. The car was being tested there. A friend of Clark's was thinking of buying one, which was something one could do back then much more than now. Since Clark was going to London for his friend's wedding, he was close enough to the nearby track to visit and give the car a go. Importantly, Clark had never driven, let alone raced, at Brands Hatch, and he had also never sat in a "single seater," the kind of open-wheel race car most people envision when they think of race cars other than stock cars. The Lotus cars were designed by Chapman to be light and quick—however, they would also become known to be quite fragile.

When Clark met Chapman in 1958, he found the designer easy to talk to, a good listener who was ready to hear the opinions of others. Clark described him as "exciting," someone who seemed to be nearly overflowing with creative ideas.[8] When Clark got in the car and drove it around Brands Hatch, Chapman remarked to Watson who was, of course, also there, that Clark was not doing that bad a job of it for never having been in the car before. Watson was perhaps a bit too open when he let out to Chapman that Clark had never even driven the track before, something most drivers with the opportunity to drive a Formula Two race car would have already done (F2 is typically thought to be just one step away from Formula One [F1], which is the highest level of racing in the world).

Clark had a good go in the Formula Two; however, his opinion of the car changed when he saw driver Graham Hill get into the vehicle immediately after he got out of it. Hill took it to the Paddock Bend part of the track, where he promptly experienced a wheel coming off. The car rolled more than once, flinging Hill out in the process. Eerily prophesying what would happen ten years later, Clark writes in his 1964 book, "I remember saying that I was not going to drive anything that broke like that, and wouldn't have anything more to do with the Formula Two Lotus."[9] Chapman had another car, though, the Lotus Elite sedan, which attracted Clark's attention. In December of that year, he returned to Brands Hatch and raced Chapman in that car, having a "whale of a dice" with him and coming in second to him only after getting clipped by someone spinning in front of him, allowing Chapman to skip by.

Chapman did not forget the spirited contest with Clark or the promise he saw in him as a driver. After a series of other events, on June 6, 1960, Clark found himself on the starting grid at Zandvoort, sitting in a single-seater, open-wheel dark green Lotus Formula One car, with its 2.5-liter engine in the back, ready to power him through the Formula One Dutch Grand Prix. On that day, he was filling in for British driver John Surtees, who was also juggling a motorcycle racing career at the time; this was Clark's first Formula One race. Clark got as close to the front as fifth behind Jack Brabham (Australia), the race leader and eventual winner, before the gearbox on his car broke, forcing him to retire from the race. A successful career in Formula One, however, and one of the best-known partnerships in motor racing—between driver Clark and designer Chapman—had been born. By his third year on the team, Clark was winning races; the next year, 1963, he won seven out of ten of them and became world champion for the first time.

Chapman wore a thin mustache and had an appearance much like British actor David Niven or even a young Walt Disney. Photographs and film footage of him show him frequently wearing turtleneck sweaters and a Greek fisherman's cap, which he threw in the air when his Lotus cars won a race. Chapman not only had the intellect to innovate the design of race cars but also the people skills to maneuver his way through situations to help him do it and win. Motor sports journalist Karl Ludvigsen describes Chapman as someone who "could charm the birds from the trees."[10] Chapman valued Clark, the small-framed and soft-spoken Scottish farmer, for his speed and ability to translate to the engineer small nuances in the car's handling and performance.

Clark was quiet and sensitive, a humble farmer who enjoyed machinery. Some said he even seemed a little naive at times, perhaps coming from the country as he did. People around him admired his raw talent and described having a desire to somehow protect him. Perhaps Clark gave off a sense of vulnerability or innocence partly as the cherished youngest son in a family of older sisters, or perhaps it was simply genuine modesty in not recognizing that he was not only a talented, fast racer but a supremely gifted one. Though Chapman was only eight years Clark's senior, some said the pair had almost a father-son relationship. It is possible that, to Clark, Chapman seemed like the older broth-er that Clark had never had.

In any case, Clark helped Chapman in his engineering work on the car, and Clark valued Chapman for his encouragement of the farmer's career and Chapman's own talents in racing car design. Chapman's innovations were not small affairs—they were the kind that changed the sport. One change, for example, was moving the engine behind the driver to the back of the car, a move copied by other race car teams not long afterward. Another innovation involved a "monocoque," or tub, chassis, a design that replaced the ladder-type configuration of other cars. With Clark's driving skills, Chapman kept innovating. Together they made racing history.

In his Formula One career from 1960 to 1968, all driving for Lotus, Jim Clark started seventy-two grands prix races. He won twenty-five of them (35 percent) and took thirty-three pole positions (a driver who achieved the fastest time in qualifying started in first, or "pole," position on the grid). He also ran in the Indianapolis 500 five times, winning it in 1965 and taking second place in both his first try in 1963 and again in 1966. Driving for Lotus, Jim Clark became world champion in Formula One—a feat regarded throughout motor sport as the highest achieve-ment for an individual in racing—in both 1963 and 1965. Throughout all his successes, travels around the world, engagements with the press, social events, and so forth, however, fans, colleagues, and others claimed that Clark never lost his modesty and authentic, country ways (he still returned to the farm when he could to maintain a sense of "balance," he said). For his quiet humility and what proved to be a superior driving talent, he was revered around the world. He never married, but contemporaries on the racing circuit have noted that Clark had his share of relationships and enjoyed the company of girlfriends and a fairly active social life. Other racers trusted him on the track to run a clean race, and that was important, especially during a time when to enter a grand prix, or many other kinds of races, was to risk one's life; many did not make it back to the pits alive.

Clark encountered the tragedies of others many times on the same track and even in the same races that he was running. These instances shook him up. Unlike some other drivers, Clark did not refrain from admitting that he was afraid to race. In only his second F1 race, the 1960 Belgian Grand Prix at Spa, Clark was the first to come on Chris

Bristow, killed in a crash in his Cooper. No flags were waving yet to warn Clark of the scene, and he raced around a corner only to see a marshal dragging something off the track—it was Bristow's body, loose as a ragdoll, from where it had been thrown from his car. When Clark got back to the pits, he saw that his car had blood spattered on it. "I was almost sick on the spot," Clark said.[11] It is a sign of the times that not only did the race continue but yet another racer died in a crash in the same race on the same day—Clark's own teammate, Alan Stacey. Stacey had a freak accident: a bird flew into his face, and he lost control of his car. Helmets in those days did not have as much facial protection as they do now. Stacey died immediately as his car went off in a field, caught on fire, and burned completely. Clark did not see this accident and only heard about it after the race. He said that if he had seen Stacey's crash right after Bristow's, he was certain he would have left motor racing for good right then and there.

There were other accidents during this highly dangerous period in the sport, but the one that affected Clark the most at this time was a tragedy he was involved in directly at the 1961 Italian Grand Prix at Monza. German driver Wolfgang von Trips, piloting a shark-nosed Ferrari, was in contention for the world championship and would clinch it if he won this race. His closest rival that year was Ferrari's American driver Phil Hill. With Hill a few cars ahead of him after getting a good start, von Trips passed Jack Brabham in a Cooper and Jim Clark in his Lotus and was next working on passing Mexican driver Ricardo Rodriguez, also of Ferrari. On the second lap of the race, von Trips went to make his move but did not see Clark close behind him. Von Trips veered in front of Clark, and the Scot remembered in that instant wondering why von Trips had not seen him, mentally shouting at him that he could not do this. Inevitably, their wheels touched. Von Trips's car careened off the course and up an embankment, jettisoning von Trips's body and instantly killing five spectators watching the race along the side of the track. Ten more spectators died later, and dozens were injured.[12]

The investigation afterward deemed the accident a "racing incident" and cleared Clark of wrongdoing; however, both Italian officials and the press dogged him about his role in the crash for some time, looking for someone to blame. Some say that Clark was never quite the same after that, that he got quieter than he already was and would return to the farm frequently to relieve the pressure of scrutiny, perhaps both external and internal. The tragedy in 1961 continued to plague him when he won his first world championship, crossing the finish line with enough points to do so at the same track and Italian Grand Prix two years later. Instead of being able to celebrate his first championship back at the pits, Clark returned to find a crowd of reporters and Italian officials still wanting to question him about the racing tragedy from two years before. Getting out of Italy as quickly as possible, Clark later held a press conference about the Italian request for further questioning, saying it was unlikely he would remember anything more two years later than he had right after the incident, when he gave a full statement and underwent questioning.

Some might think Clark's involvement in such a horrific crash taints an otherwise stellar racing career. Most within motor sport back then as well as today, however, almost universally respect his handling of the issue. They believe that "racing incidents" like von Trips's, while unfortunate, are a risk in the sport—that drivers get into cars knowing the risks and that, even if a driver fully adheres to the rules, mishaps are bound to occur under the heat of competition as one challenges the laws of physics in a motor car. The fact that Clark did answer questions at the time in 1961, held a press conference in 1963 when he discovered that Italian officials and the press still wanted him to talk about the matter, and then also included a chapter about it in his book, published in 1964, indicates that he faced what he thought was his level of responsibility. He would go on to win the Formula One World Championship once more in 1965, and his reputation, among fans and professionals alike in motor sport, as a humble but worthy champion has remained intact for nearly a half century and counting.

What kept Clark driving after witnessing horrific accidents, especially relatively early in his racing career? Why did he not just go back to the farm and stay there instead of visiting only long enough to recharge his spirits and go back out on the world stage yet again? The family farm remained important to him throughout his life because, not in spite, of how different that lifestyle was from his existence out on the international motor racing scene. "Motor racing and farming, to my mind, were in a way two opposites," he said in a recorded interview. "The very fact that they are two opposites helps me enormously to kind of keep a sense of balance."[13]

Jim Clark in his Lotus at the 1967 United States Grand Prix, Watkins Glen, New York. *International Motor Racing Research Center/F1 Collection.*

Clark had several well-timed and perhaps uncanny opportunities to become the racing champion he became, but opportunities are not enough if the individual does not act on them. Clark might tell us that it was his own curiosity that kept him going back to the racetrack time after time. "I enjoy motor racing," Clark said in a BBC interview. "I started as an amateur hobby[ist] with no idea or no intention of becoming world champion, but I was curious to find out what it was like to drive a car fast, to drive on a certain circuit, to drive a certain type of car." One feat or achievement led to another curiosity, and conquering that led to another and another. First it was driving fast; then it was driving on certain tracks; then it was driving certain kinds of cars. The configuration of cars and tracks would continually reshuffle from race to race and season to season. The continuing challenges kept him in it, one might say; they never stopped appearing and were never quite satisfied.

What was so "natural" and superior about Jim Clark's driving, one might ask? The next Scottish racing ace in Formula One to come along, Jackie Stewart, who knew and admired Clark and even roomed with him for a time, has described his idol as having a light touch at the wheel. He credits watching Clark as teaching him all he would come to know about driving a race car. Stewart described Clark as seeming to "caress" the racing car, coaxing it to do what he wished. His driving was "smooth," says Stewart, not rough; he was "not bullying the car."[14] Clark had finesse with machinery; he understood it viscerally and knew what to do to make a car go fast. In short, to most observers, he was a natural.

WHAT HAPPENED

In 1968, Clark was enjoying life. He could return to the farm in Scotland after living for a time in Paris, a self-imposed national exile for the purpose of legal tax protection. Drivers and others often moved their residences out of their home or preferred countries for this purpose. Clark's win of the Formula One South African Grand Prix in Kyalami on New Year's Day 1968 was his twenty-fifth in the championship, setting a new series record. Chapman's Lotus 49 was a winning car. Just recently, Lotus had secured a helpful source of funding by forming an agreement with the John Player Group whereby financial support would be received in exchange for, among other promotional duties, advertising Gold Leaf cigarettes, a product line owned by Player. Ads for Gold Leaf would now appear on the sides of Lotus race cars. The

Jim Clark (standing, second from right) with Colin Chapman (standing, second from left) and Graham Hill (standing, third from left), celebrating Clark's win at the 1967 United States Grand Prix, Watkins Glen, New York, October 1, 1967. *International Motor Racing Research Center/F1 Collection.*

move was unusual for the day in Formula One, and it signaled the dawn of a new phase of commercialization in the international racing series, much to the dismay of fans of the earlier, more nationalistic era. Seeing advertising "clutter" the sides of otherwise beautiful Formula One cars, to the minds of fans, was perhaps not the only negative aspect of this new source of funding for such an expensive sport. In hindsight, it might also be argued that a connection can be drawn from this new era for Lotus and the fact that one of the all-time greatest drivers in the sport may have been in the wrong place at the wrong time because of it.

Part of the deal with John Player was that Clark would not only race in the international Formula One series in the Lotus 49 but also compete in the European series known as Formula Two in the Lotus 48. Formula Two is frequently regarded as a Formula One "feeder" series where up-and-coming racers can cut their teeth in highly competitive open-wheel cars and possibly gain the attention of team owners for a seat in the "big show," to borrow a phrase from American Major League

Baseball. It may have not been as unusual then as it would be nowadays for a world champion like Clark, competing at the highest level of motor sport, to race in Formula Two (back then, F1 drivers frequently competed in these races to keep their skills fresh between grands prix, even though their elevated rank made them ineligible for the F2 championship). Even so, it was certainly not always expected or necessary for an F1 driver to compete in the lower F2 series. In this case, the contract with John Player made it a required race for Clark.

As it turned out, Clark's Lotus 48 retired in a March 31 race in Barcelona when a Ferrari 166 driven by Jacky Ickx struck and damaged his car on the first lap; this left the car requiring quick repairs. Right after Barcelona, Clark returned to Paris, where he had a social dinner at the invitation of a Matra team official, Claude le Guézec. Matra was the team Lotus was competing against closely in F2 at that time. Fellow racer Jochen Rindt (Germany/Austria) also attended the dinner. Clark joked about hoping to see Matra's blue colors in his rearview mirror at the upcoming race in Hockenheim, West Germany, and left the dinner when his roommate in Paris, journalist Gérard "Jabby" Crombac, came to pick him up. In the car, conversation with Crombac turned to Clark reminding the journalist that he had asked about buying his Lotus Elan and that Clark would now sell it since he had a new car lined up for purchase when he returned home. With Clark now also a pilot of his own Piper Twin Comanche, Crombac delivered the driver to an airfield outside Paris, and the racer flew himself to Hockenheim.

Other anecdotes of the weekend have been told since April 7, 1968. One was that on the morning of the race Le Guézec spotted Clark and his teammate Graham Hill rolling Firestone tires toward their cars. Even in those earlier days, Formula One drivers were protected, especially on race day when they needed to focus their attention and prepare themselves for competing in a dangerous sport. They would certainly not be expected to help prepare the car. When Guézec asked why they were moving tires, Clark told him that their mechanics were otherwise busy. In those days F2 teams ran on a scant crew, sometimes with just one mechanic and a few others to tend to the car. Another story is told by one of the up-and-coming racers competing in his first Formula Two race that weekend in Hockenheim—British racing driver Derek Bell.

Bell, age twenty-six at the time, has written that he was looking forward to his first F2 race. He had tried to race a Brabham BT23C, which he had access to with the funding of his stepfather, Bernard "The Colonel" Hender, at Barcelona the week before, but a valve broke in practice, and a spare engine did not get delivered in time for him to race, so they had no choice but to go home. Now, at Hockenheim, the young racer was about to start his first open-wheel European race, which would be far from his last. At this time, though, much was new to him, and his confidence was still developing. Any young driver at this time would know of two-time world champion Clark, and many drivers, especially Brits like Bell, looked up to the Scot as a hero.

Imagine Bell's surprise, then, when not only Jim Clark but also Graham Hill (UK), Clark's teammate and another world champion Formula One driver, showed up at his hotel near the track and sat down at his table to chat. At one point, Clark said to young Bell, "When you come to overtake me, don't get too close because my engine keeps cutting out."[15] In fact, Bell heard the Lotus F2 car outside his hotel at 6 a.m. on race day. Running it along the Rhine River on a tow path, Clark's mechanic, David "Beaky" Sims was working on a misfire with the car—a fuel meter was malfunctioning. With neither time nor facilities available to properly address the problem, Sims was doing the best he could under the circumstances. Bell says that Graham Hill drove them all to the track on that drizzly morning, and each of them got out of the car and went on his way. Given Clark's experience and mature talent, it was perhaps a testament to the condition of the Lotus that fast rookie Bell sat on the starting grid ahead of world champion Clark. One archival photograph shows Bell looking in his rearview mirror at Clark behind him on the grid. Bell says that was the last time he saw the champion.

Clark had made it known he was not happy with the Lotus F2 car that weekend, but Sims says the last concern the driver expressed before he started the race was with the tires. Sims says Clark's last words to him were "Don't expect me to be up there in my usual position. I don't trust the tires"—he could get neither grip nor heat in them.[16]

During the race, Bell had a clutch problem with his car and pitted, so he was not out on the track when the caution flag came down. On the sixth lap, taking a fast turn to the right, Jim Clark's car twitched, then went off the track and hit a tree. The car split in two on impact—the front end went one way; the cockpit, engine, and gearbox went another.

Seat belts were not commonly used back then; Clark was flung out of the car and killed instantly when his head hit a tree. It is important to note that there were no guardrails or other kinds of safety barriers along the Hockenheim circuit in that location in 1968.

AFTERMATH

Not out on the track at the time, Derek Bell heard that Clark had crashed but did not know how badly. In an interview, he said, "Then I saw his mechanic carrying one of Jimmy's driving shoes," adding, "I'll never forget that image."[17]

Lotus withdrew from the race. Chapman, who was on a holiday in Switzerland at the time, later said he "went into shock" at hearing the news.[18] He told Sims to get the car out of Germany and back to England as soon as possible. The engine was sent to Cosworth; the gearbox went to its manufacturer; other parts went to Farnborough, where aircraft accidents were investigated; the tires went somewhere else. The assumption was that there had been a tire puncture, and one was indeed located on the right rear side. After no other problems were found in other parts of the car, the tire puncture was settled on as the official cause of the accident, though, yet again, no definitive cause was ever quite determined.

Bell said that he remembers the misfire he heard outside the Hotel Luxoff early that morning and has said that, to him as a driver, that makes more sense as a cause than a tire puncture, especially a right rear puncture on a right-hand turn. Bell said in a recent interview that he talked with Sims at the 24 Hours of Daytona in 2017, and Sims confirmed the misfire that Bell heard that morning. When asked, Jackie Stewart said Clark "died almost certainly by a vehicle failure of some kind."[19] While the declared cause was a tire puncture, such a defect could have happened as the car wheeled out of control through the brush and into the trees alongside the track. It seems no one will know for certain what took the car out of Clark's control that day; however, no one has blamed such a superior driver as Clark, even as he also was closely in tune with the engineering and setup of his cars. Likewise, no driver would want to pin such a severe outcome on any one mechanic, working alone under tight time constraints and with few facilities. If there had been a guardrail, Clark may have made it.

What can be recalled is what Clark said years earlier in his career—about never wanting to drive a Lotus Formula Two car again.

The loss of such a noted and gifted driver was felt around the world and left the motor sport community stunned. "Mere words are inadequate to express our feelings," wrote the editors of *Motor Sport* magazine under a photo of a smiling, in-car Clark.[20] Fellow racer Chris Amon's comment echoed for decades through the history of the sport: "If it could happen to him, what hope could the rest of us have?"[21]

LEGACY

Derek Bell pointed out that Clark may have been one of the first racers whom Jackie Stewart was close to who died on the track. If his fellow Scot was indeed the first, or one of the first, of his friends to die on a racetrack, the influence of Clark's death on Stewart's safety crusade could hardly be overestimated.

Stewart himself commented on this. "I had been trying for several years to get better safety within motor sport—and 68 was the turning point."[22] Other drivers before Clark had died, and more would die after him, but Clark's tragedy somehow drew a line in the sand.

"I don't believe that anyone thought Jimmy could be killed," Stewart said. "He was bulletproof in everybody's mind." More drivers perished in fairly quick succession in this period, and their fellow drivers were frequently first on the scene. Stewart described what it was like to come up on the scene of a fellow driver's accident: "If he was dead it was a very bad experience. It's deep and emotional and soul-destroying. We were not at war. We were competing in a sport—almost a leisure-time sport, for public enjoyment."[23]

After Jim Clark's death, Jackie Stewart intensified his campaign for improved safety in Formula One motor racing. Looked down on by track officials who did not want to spend the money, other drivers who questioned his courage, and still others who had their own agendas to protect, Stewart kept up his efforts. If Clark had one legacy that went beyond his own influence as a role model to other drivers, it would have to be the effect his death had on the sport in terms of the realization of how dire the present conditions were at that time in terms of safety.

As a driver and a star sportsman, Clark influenced many drivers who came after him, whether or not they raced against him. Indy star and fellow Scot Dario Franchitti, who was not yet born when Clark was alive, has spoken of his admiration for Clark. Franchitti not only collects Clark memorabilia but also has had the opportunity to demonstrate some of Clark's cars in action at historic racing events at tracks like Goodwood and Indianapolis. Perhaps it is impossible to quantify the influence a superstar like Clark has on other drivers, and through them, on the sport, and through the sport, on the world at large.

In his description of the man's talent, his kindness to fans and others, and his humility and quiet nature, Derek Bell, like so many other drivers and fans from that time, had nothing but good things to say. "He was the epitome of the perfect racing driver," Bell said, "both on and off the track."

A tree can represent many things: shade, comfort, protection. It is the material from which a Louisville Slugger is made that takes a baseball player to legend and glory; it can support a child's play swing, grow fruit, be cut into lumber for houses, and provide fuel for warmth and paper for writing. Sadly, it can also kill a driver who runs into it too fast. How many of us have seen signs and flowers and other tributes along roads and highways where such sad events have happened to drivers unknown to us.

A Scottish sheep farmer makes a name for himself driving a racing machine better than almost anyone else in his time. As skilled as he was, Clark was killed when his car ran away with him into the forest. A farmer dying in the woods. Tragic, indeed, but somehow it can sound almost natural.

——⟨ɷɷɷ⟩——

Racer: Jim Clark (UK), age thirty-two; b. March 4, 1936, in Kilmany, Fifeshire, Scotland; d. April 7, 1968, at Hockenheim Circuit, Germany.

Other Occupations: Farmer, shepherd.

Career Highlights: Formula One world champion, 1963, 1965; first British Indy 500 winner, 1965.

Among His Legacies: Widely regarded as one of the best drivers in the sport of his or any time; contributed to the development of Colin Chapman's Lotus race cars, which were a generational change in the technology of the sport; direct and indirect influence on contemporary and later drivers such as Sir Jackie Stewart and Dario Franchitti; the death of a driver of his superior skills gave more legitimacy to the safety concerns raised in his era by drivers; the sport entered a more professional, commercialized era after his death.

5

ACHIEVER

Bruce McLaren

"To do something well is so worthwhile that to die trying to do it better cannot be foolhardy. It would be a waste of life to do nothing with one's ability, for I feel that life is measured in achievement, not in years alone." —Bruce McLaren[1]

New Zealander Bruce Leslie McLaren wrote the words above as a tribute to a friend who had died in a motor racing accident, but they have come to be widely known and quoted in motor sport as a fitting epitaph for McLaren himself. Living just thirty-two years, McLaren became one of the highest achievers in the history of motor sport. He not only overcame great odds to drive and win races at the peak level of the sport but was also successful in designing and engineering race cars and starting and running his own racing team. Eventually, his legacy took to the normal streets as well, when the McLaren Automotive Company produced its first sports and luxury road vehicles. Given hardships he endured early on in his life, Bruce McLaren might be considered an unexpected success. His is a story that inspires people around the globe, not only those who enjoy the thrill of cars driving fast but also anyone who appreciates someone who has overcome enormous obstacles in life and gone on to thrive and make a lasting contribution to others.

McLaren was born on August 30, 1937, the middle child between two sisters. The family lived in Remuera, New Zealand, a few miles southeast of Auckland. McLaren's father, Les, and his three uncles all took part in motorcycle races in the area. In fact, motorized vehicles were part of the McLaren family business—before World War I, McLaren's grandfather had established a truck and bus transport company; Bruce's father owned and operated a service garage and gas station. Consequently, Bruce grew up with cars, talk of cars, and access to cars as part of his daily life. At ages nine and ten, he was drawing them all the time, a natural inclination that would soon develop to a sophisticated level.

About the same age, at nine and a half, he enjoyed playing football (European) and had aspirations of competing in rugby one day. Unfortunately, those dreams were short-lived. One day after a fall, the boy felt a sharp pain in his left hip and developed a slight limp. With polio a dreaded disease at the time, the family feared the worst, and tests were conducted. In fact, the diagnosis was not polio but another debilitating illness called Perthes disease, also known as Legg-Calve-Perthes disease. The condition, affecting a growing child, is characterized by a disruption in the blood supply to the ball joint of the hip. Bone cells die as a result, and the bone at the head of the femur begins to break apart. Over a period of years, circulation gradually returns, and the bone can heal.[2] If untreated, however, a child may not walk again. The prognosis after eighteen to twenty-four months these days is good. In the 1940s, treatment meant keeping a young body off its feet for this length of time or longer.

For treatment, Bruce McLaren's family admitted him to the Wilson Home, then called the Wilson Home for Crippled Children, in Auckland. The main treatment for the boy was to lie on a Bradshaw frame—a flat structure that would keep his weight off his hips. In his autobiography, *From the Cockpit*, McLaren writes that he was tied to a Bradshaw frame, and then his legs were encased in "thick elastic plaster with weights dangling from the end."[3] At times, these frames were affixed to a "bath-chair," a device with wheels that allowed the children to be wheeled around from one place to another. McLaren writes of several bath-chair "races" that he took part in with a few other boys who were likewise afflicted in the home. In one such adventure, the boys tied three or four of the devices together, train style, and rolled themselves out of the hospital, down the ramps, and out onto the grounds. Naturally, a great shunt took place, in this case pitching Bruce off the wheeled portion of the contraption into a flower bed. The boys somehow managed not only to get Bruce's frame back on its wheels and to fluff up the flower garden but also to get themselves back inside without being caught. Soon it became obvious, however, that Bruce's chair had taken damage, inhibiting its performance in future races. He was given a new device on smaller wheels when his nurses could not maneuver the old one any longer.

Bruce spent not only his tenth birthday at the Wilson Home but also his eleventh. Confined as he was for two years of his youth, he took to reading and studying. He also looked at car catalogs and magazines that his father brought to him. At one time, not long before he left the home, his father dropped by a brochure for a Jaguar XK120 sports car that he was trying to decide if he could find a way to buy. Les eventually did not purchase the car, but Bruce kept the brochure and studied it, particularly its cutaway drawing of a 3.4-liter engine. At the time, the car was advertised as the fastest production car ever made, and this caught McLaren's attention as it did that of other car enthusiasts around the world. McLaren studied the engine drawing so intently that he says he gradually figured out how the various parts of the machine worked. He marked this as a turning point for him in what would become his passion in life.

When the boy was finally allowed to stand again, it was an important moment for his doctors, his family, and himself. At first, his legs were completely straight, and the doctor, looking somber, turned to have a discussion with the nurses. Soon, Bruce realized that he needed to bend his knees slightly while standing, and this relieved everyone's worry. It was found, however, that his left leg was a little shorter than the right, meaning that he would have a permanent limp. However, the boy could walk again, and he went from crutches for a while, to sticks, and soon to walking on his own. Bruce never forgot the saving treatment that he received from the Wilson Home. On his first visit home to New Zealand after going to Europe to race, he brought a race car to the home and drove the children "all over the place" in it.[4]

One can only imagine what the effect of being immobilized for three years of one's youth can do to a person who is then given the gift of walking again; however, with Bruce McLaren, one need not imagine these effects. Not able to move on his own for so long, Bruce rarely stopped moving after that, but he also took his studious nature into his resumption of life on two feet. His older sister, Pat, described him as thoughtful, as one who understood suffering and brought a sense of compassion and an ability to get along with and help other people.[5] It makes sense that a person who has been so dependent on others for so long at such an impressionable, early age might develop a certain facility with charm that could serve him well in leadership roles as he got older.

What happened more obviously, however, at the time was that Bruce and Les became nearly inseparable in Les's garage, often working on Les's Ulster Austin Seven. Since he was too young to get his driver's license, Bruce set up a figure-eight "track" around the fruit trees of their suburban backyard. Their patient neighbors put up with his frequent drives around that little course, testing out changes to the car. Bruce could now get his hands on engines and car parts and see aspects of the drawings he studied come to life in metal that he could touch and watch spin and hear roar to life. McLaren never lost this habit of studying drawings and applying what he imagined from them to metal—in fact, as he participated in hill climbs and other local race events with his father, and then with just the backing of his father, he also studied engineering at Seddon Technical Memorial College and Auckland University.[6]

Driver's license finally in hand, McLaren moved up in club, local, and regional racing. He was a quick driver with efficient moves on the track. Most of all, he knew his car. If he did not like how it was behaving in one competition, he took it back to the garage, and he and his father worked on it to make improvements. In his autobiography, he describes how resourceful New Zealanders are, partly, he believes, due to their geographic isolation. If it took weeks for race information from Europe to reach the Southern Hemisphere island, as he says it did back in those days, one can only imagine how long it took for spare parts to arrive for an automobile. This left the Kiwi mechanics needing to know how to weld and so forth in order to make impromptu fixes, sometimes reconfiguring one car part to work as another.

Another New Zealander who knew a little bit about working on cars and racing them was in a position to help Bruce in his now growing desire to become a racing driver in the highest-level competitions in Europe and the United States. Jack Brabham was on track to become the Formula One (F1) world champion in 1959 as well as to build and drive his own cars in the series. When he spotted the talents of fellow

Kiwi McLaren at the wheel, he influenced the selection of the young man, about ten years his junior, as the first recipient of the "Driver to Europe" scheme set up to bring promising racing drivers from New Zealand to Europe to try out their skills in the best race cars in the world. On March 15, 1958, McLaren left his New Zealand home on this program for a trip to England, where his professional racing career took off. He had never been out of the country before, much less taken that big a trip by boat accompanying the shipment of race cars. He was twenty years old. He got seasick along the way.[7]

McLaren's star as a racer rose ever higher after that. In 1959, at age twenty-two, he was the youngest driver to date to win a Formula One grand prix, taking victory at the first United States Grand Prix, in Sebring, Florida. Race wins in Formula One besides the U.S. Grand Prix included the Monaco Grand Prix in 1962 and the Belgian Grand Prix in 1968. His placements in the World Drivers' Championship in Formula One included third in 1962, driving for Cooper, and again third in 1969, driving for a team closer to home. His other racing accomplishments over a few quick years included a win with partner Chris Amon at the 24 Hours of Le Mans in 1966; a win with co-driver Mario Andretti of the 12 Hours of Sebring in 1967; and the Can-Am (Canadian-American) Championship, which his team dominated, in 1967 and 1969. McLaren also took part in the Tasman series, a racing competition in Australia and New Zealand that took advantage of the off-season of Formula One in Europe and the United States in the early part of the calendar year. He won the Tasman Championship in 1964 and placed second in 1965.

McLaren is one of only two drivers to win a Formula One grand prix in a car with his name painted on the side twice—once as the driver and again as the constructor of the car. This was his 1968 win of the Belgian Grand Prix. Taking a cue from that New Zealander resourcefulness he had seen demonstrated by his father as well as the man he called his "godfather," Jack Brabham, McLaren started not only building his own F1 cars but also established the Bruce McLaren Formula One racing team. In Can-Am as well, he branched out to North America, building space-age-looking wide sports cars that dominated the competition.

Whether it was his personal story of overcoming Perthes disease to not only walk again but fly around a circuit in a race car, or his personal charisma, work ethic, racing talent, and engineering know-how, or

Bruce McLaren prepares for more action in his McLaren-Ford during the 1968 United States Grand Prix weekend at Watkins Glen International. *International Motor Racing Research Center/F1 Collection.*

something else, Bruce McLaren inspired his crew at the McLaren Motor Racing Team, and they became fiercely loyal to him. Perhaps his years laid up in his youth and the thought that he had a lot of time in life to make up spurred him to work harder and achieve more than the average race car driver. To help overcome his limp, he wore one shoe with a raised heel. When he was in his soft racing shoes, however, his limp became noticeable when he walked down through the pits. Still, his spirit of invention and innovation was his focus, not his past troubles. Early on in his career, when he made visits back home, McLaren also utilized his charm to meet and court a New Zealand woman named Patty Broad. They married in 1961, and their daughter, Amanda, was born in 1965.

Maybe the experience of lying nearly flat on his back for years as a boy caused him to relish life and appreciate the help of the people around him in a way that those more fortunate did not. One factor in his team's loyalty was certainly that he did not act arrogantly around them; he worked alongside them, late nights in the garage, trying this or that to improve the performance of the cars, listening to his crew's suggestions. McLaren knew the mechanics' language—he was one himself, after all. This loyalty would prove crucial to the continuation of his vision just a few years later.

Once, in the Can-Am series in North America, McLaren's business partner noticed a rival car that was painted orange. The partner liked it and suggested they paint their Can-Am car a similar color to help it stand out from the rest of the field. Their choice of "papaya orange" coincided with a surge in wins for the team, and that particular shade soon became a signature look on McLaren race cars. Even the Formula One cars were painted in this scheme. The winning cars stayed this color until sponsors started expecting their advertising to occupy the sides of race cars in the late 1960s and early 1970s. That's when McLaren shifted to a white background with sponsor colors. McLaren fans, though, know the history and miss seeing the papaya orange of the team's earliest successes. They take delight in seeing the color scheme come back in any form on McLaren cars, such as when splashes of it appeared for the 2017 Formula One season. Another distinctive and recognizable feature of the outside appearance of the McLaren cars is the logo. At one time a decal of a small black kiwi bird representing New Zealand was added to the side of the car. Over time, the logo changed into a stylized kiwi bird known as the "speedy kiwi," then to a "swoosh" or curved design simulating shapes from the cars' wings and side-pods.

Though fans frequently come to identify a race team by the aesthetics of its cars, the design and engineering of the cars, of course, are most important to car buffs in the racing world. One story shows how Bruce McLaren's mind worked in a practical sense. The story goes that he observed a gas cover on the top of a race car. The hinge faced the front of the car, so the expectation was that the airflow over the top of the car when it was driving would push the cover downward and help keep it closed. When McLaren drove the car, he noticed this cover bumping around. At first, he thought someone had not closed it properly. Sloppy garage work was not appreciated in his shop. Instead, when he studied it, he noticed that air pressure was building up underneath the cover and pushing it up. In a move that became famous around motor racing paddocks afterward, McLaren reportedly got out of the car and cut two "nostrils" in the body work toward the front nose to allow for airflow and to keep air pressure from building up underneath. This is one of the famed innovations in race car design that did indeed help the McLaren cars go faster and win races.

Besides building Formula One and Can-Am race cars, McLaren also had a dream of starting up a road car company, constructing automobiles that could be driven by the average person on the highway. In 1969, he designed, built, and drove one such road car, the McLaren M6 GT. It is the only one in existence. Unfortunately, it would be several years before the McLaren Automotive Company took off. One day in early June 1970 stalled that endeavor indefinitely; however, that day also marked a different kind of decision within the McLaren team.

WHAT HAPPENED

Another New Zealander, a successful driver named Denny Hulme, drove for McLaren at this time. Hulme had gotten burned in practice for the 1970 Indianapolis 500. The burns affected his hands, which were both bandaged heavily. Hulme was scheduled to do a test run of the McLaren Can-Am car, the M8D, in early June. His injury precipitated a change in plans, and Bruce McLaren himself drove the car out of the pits at the Goodwood Circuit in West Sussex, United Kingdom, on the pleasant summer day of June 2.

Goodwood had closed to professional racing series in 1966 when the track was deemed unsuitable for racing competition among the more powerful cars being built in that era. The track was, however, still used for testing and other purposes. McLaren had the track to himself on that testing day. The orange M8D, with its sweeping back body piece, had been nicknamed "the Batmobile" due to its size and shape. McLaren brought the car back to the pits several times, he and the crew made adjustments here and there, and he went back out again to run another series of laps. Testing went on like this throughout the morning. At a little after 12 p.m., McLaren said he would go out and run a few more laps, and they would stop for lunch. He was due to have lunch with another New Zealander friend, Bill Bryce, who was flying to the track grounds on his way to do some work nearby.

McLaren drove out of the pits. While driving down the Lavant Straight at Goodwood, just before the Woodcote corner, a pin holding bodywork went missing, and the rear bodywork came loose from the car and flew off. The resulting loss of downforce sent the car careening out of control until it slammed into the concrete wall of a steward's station at the side of the track. McLaren died instantly. Orange-colored parts were strewn for several yards at the spot.

Years later, after decades of silence, Bryce described the events of that day from his perspective. It just happened that he was the first person on the scene after the crash. He could see the McLaren Can-Am car doing laps out on the track when he was coming in, circling the airfield to land. After landing, he then started walking toward the pits to meet up with Bruce when he came in from his last test run. Bryce and a companion heard the car out on the track, then heard nothing, then heard a loud "whoompph" when the car hit the steward's station. Since he was not that far away, he ran to the site. He described a debris field about the size of a football field and the bloody scene he saw when he arrived. He said the car had exploded when it hit the marshal's stand.

> The gearbox was on fire on the circuit and Bruce was very close to it so we pulled him away from the burning magnesium. One thing that stuck in my mind was that his driving boots had come off in the crash. I was trying to get his helmet off, but I was shaking like a leaf. I was trying like hell but I couldn't undo the buckle. His chest was thumping up and down and when the other guys arrived I shouted at them to give me some bolt-cutters so that I could cut the helmet strap, but they pushed me aside. I said, "But he's still moving . . . he's OK." I don't remember who it was, but someone shook his head sorrowfully and said, "No . . . he's dead."[8]

AFTERMATH

The shock to a racing family can only be imagined, despite their knowledge, especially in those days, that the prospect of death in an accident rides with these drivers every time they steer their cars out of the pits. Bruce McLaren's young widow, Patty McLaren, whose daughter was only four years old at her husband's death, helped keep the team together. "My boys," she called them and urged them not only to hold together as a team in tribute to Bruce but to succeed.

She already had their support. When the team heard about the accident, they were given the next day off to digest what had happened. Instead, every member of the staff, around sixty members, arrived at work the very next morning, ready to carry out the tasks at hand to keep the McLaren Racing Team moving forward. Tyler Alexander, one of the founding members of the team, describes that day in his book, *A Life and Times with McLaren*. Teddy Mayer was another key, early member of the team:

> It was then that Teddy stood up in front of everyone at the factory and said, with no fuss or preamble, but in standard Mayer-speak, "We all realize that something not very pleasant has happened, but we have a company called Bruce McLaren Motor Racing, and it has a Can-Am race in two weeks—so we best get on with it!" And, by Christ, we did. I think just about everyone came in to work the following day. Those who had learned a great many things from Bruce were now the ones who knew it was up to them to get their shit together and to keep BMMR going. [9]

A press release from a sponsor soon followed in North America, announcing that the team would go on competing in Can-Am:

> A three-year tradition will end here Sunday (June 14) when the Canadian-American Challenge Cup begins a new season without its reigning champion.
>
> The man missing from the starting grid in the Labatt's Blue Can-Am race at the Mosport Park circuit here will be Bruce McLaren, who was killed June 2 in England while testing one of his team's new McLaren Mark 8D Can-Am cars.
>
> The team has announced that a single car will be entered in this first race of the 1970 series. It is scheduled to be driven by McLaren's long-time partner, friend, and fellow New Zealander, Denny Hulme.
>
> In the event that Hulme, whose hands were severely burned last month in an accident in practice for the Indianapolis 500 race, is not able to drive the car, it will be turned over to British driver Peter Gethin, team officials revealed in London.

It was further revealed that Dan Gurney of Santa Ana, Calif. will join Hulme on the McLaren team for the second race of the Can-Am season, at St. Jovite, Quebec, on June 28.

Team McLaren's decision to proceed with its plans to compete in the 1970 series is based on a desire to carry on the team's activities, "as Bruce would have wished," said team manager Teddy Mayer.

Stirling Moss, director of racing for Can-Am sponsor Johnson Wax, termed the team's decision "the best way the McLaren name could be perpetuated as a symbol of excellence in a sport which demands so much of men."

Moss added that it is sad that McLaren, "who played so much a part in making the Can-Am what it is today, should miss the start of what should be the series' finest season."

More than 30 cars have been entered for this first race of the 1970 Can-Am and Moss noted that at least half of them will be of McLaren manufacture. [10]

LEGACIES

Among the many legacies of Bruce McLaren, in addition to the way his personal story continues to inspire people to this day, is that his racing team is still competing nearly fifty years after his passing. Something about this man struck a deep chord in his team and the people who came after them. The stewardship of a dedicated team principal, Ron Dennis, who served in that role from 1981 to 2009, also helped. Only the Ferrari racing team, established years before McLaren, still remains on the starting grid in Formula One from the days in the 1960s when Bruce founded his team.

To date, the McLaren team has won eight Constructors' Championships in the Formula One series—in 1974, 1984, 1985, 1988, 1989, 1990, 1991, and 1998. It has also seen its many now famous drivers win twelve Drivers' Championships—Emerson Fittipaldi (Brazil) in 1974; James Hunt (U.K.) in 1976; Niki Lauda (Austria) in 1984; Alain Prost (France) in 1985; Alain Prost in 1986; Ayrton Senna (Brazil) in 1988; Alain Prost in 1989; Ayrton Senna in 1990; Ayrton Senna in 1991; Mika Häkkinen (Finland) in 1998; Mika Häkkinen in 1999; and Lewis Hamilton (U.K.) in 2008. The Can-Am sports car racing series in North America ran from 1966 to 1987, and McLaren was a star team in that series as well, dominating the 1960s period with five championship season wins in a row—by McLaren himself in 1967 and 1969; Denny Hulme in 1968 and 1970; and Peter Revson (U.S.) in 1971. Make no mistake—the British racing team has made its mark on the sport.

A pride and joy of the McLaren group nowadays (spearheaded by Ron Dennis, who recently left the team) is its state-of-the-art headquarters, the McLaren Technology Centre in Woking, Surrey, England. An example of modern architecture, the building is an artistic vision in white and glass, low to the landscape and curving around one of several human-made lakes on the property. Inside, at first the main building does not give the impression that the business here is designing and building cars—one would typically expect dirty floors, tools hanging on the walls, and so forth. Instead, here, the floors are spotlessly white—the building looks like something out of a science fiction film—pristine and bright; some of the company's historic racing cars are on display along the front windows, appearing to look out at the water. There are no pegboards along the walls with tools hanging from them. Secret, proprietary work takes place in sealed-off rooms where the few select visitors must step on a sticky mat to remove dirt from their shoes before entering. The place gives off an aura of precision in engineering and design, an impression the company, of course, has earned with its racing successes and wishes to keep.

What about Bruce's dream of establishing a road car company? Amanda McLaren, Bruce's daughter, now serves as the brand ambassador for McLaren Automotive, a newer venture that sets out to do just that—live out Bruce's road car dream. Recently, at a tribute to her father at the Goodwood Revival, on the same track where he died, Amanda drove demonstration laps in her father's M6 GT, a one-of-a-kind road car that he designed, built, and drove in 1969. In a recent interview, she described the experience, which was fairly comical for her. As she was shorter than her father was, she said, the clutch was a foot away from her, and the seat was not adjustable. Aids placed three pillows behind her to try to get her closer to the pedals, but by then she was only about six inches from the windshield, with the steering wheel nearly under her chin. She was to lead a group of McLaren cars of various racing types around the track. They were not racing, but she still needed to drive at a good pace; there were several powerful cars with her father's name on each of them roaring around behind her.

"Everyone's watching Bruce McLaren's daughter in Bruce McLaren's car—no pressure," she said. There was no power steering. "I understood why the drivers during the 60s and early 70s had such big shoulders and big necks because getting this car around the corners . . . I did three laps, and I was exhausted." Even so, the meaning of the moment to her, her family, and all present to watch at Goodwood was not lost on her. "What an absolute honor to be asked to drive that car," she said, "to be given the privilege to do that."[11]

One of the new company's first newer road models, the McLaren F1 luxury road car, utilized the light, carbon fiber chassis that the company developed for its Formula One racing cars. Interestingly, just like the Jaguar Bruce had admired and studied in the cutaway engine diagram his father brought to him at Wilson Home, the McLaren F1 was the fastest road car built to that date, its prototype clocking in at over 240 mph. More cars are coming in the future in the sports and luxury categories from the company. When asked about her father's legacy as it stands now, Amanda had this to say: "To have my father's name still out there on the race cars and, of course, now on the McLaren Automotive road cars is a fabulous tribute to his legacy, and I'm very, very proud of it, and I know my father would be very proud, too."[12]

As McLaren himself said, one need not measure a life in years. If it is assessed in terms of achievement instead, then his own success and legacies certainly outmeasure his own count of thirty-two.

——————

Racer: Bruce Leslie McLaren (New Zealand), age thirty-two; b. August 30, 1937, in Auckland, New Zealand; d. June 2, 1970, at Goodwood Circuit, West Sussex, England.

Career Highlights and Awards: Winner, 1959 U.S. Grand Prix—youngest driver to win a Formula One grand prix at the time at age twenty-two, a record that stood for over forty years; winner, 1962 Monaco Grand Prix; winner, 1968 Belgian Grand Prix driving his own car; started Bruce McLaren Motor Racing Team in 1963; second place, Formula One Drivers' Championship, 1960; third place, Formula One Driver's Championship, 1962; third place, F1 Drivers' Championship driving his own car, 1969.

Among His Legacies: Established F1 McLaren racing team in 1963, which still exists and competes in the series; McLaren F1 team, to date, has won eight Formula One Constructors' Championships and twelve Drivers' Championships; conceived of and worked toward establishment of McLaren Automotive Company to produce sports and luxury road cars, which was eventually realized after his death; created first carbon fiber chassis in Formula One and road cars; subject of 2016 documentary film *McLaren*.

6

ROMANTIC

François Cevert

In 1798, at twenty-seven years old, Ludwig van Beethoven composed a sonata of three movements that later became popularly known as the "Sonata Pathétique." Officially titled Piano Sonata No. 8 in C minor, op. 8, the *cantabile* from the second movement of the piece became known in the United States as the theme music for the popular classical music program *Adventures in Good Music*. In 1984 American popular musician Billy Joel adapted the *cantabile* in the chorus of his song "This Night," which appeared on his album *Innocent Man*.

Beethoven's "Sonata Pathétique" was the favorite piece of French Formula One racer François Cevert. That would be an interesting fact to note about an athlete's personality, but perhaps more fascinating is that Cevert was especially known not for his enjoyment of listening to this sonata but for playing it. According to Formula One triple world champion Sir Jackie Stewart and many others who knew the racer or were around him, Cevert would frequently sit down at a piano he discovered anywhere along his travels as a world-class racing driver and begin to play. In fact, again according to Stewart, Cevert performed the piece several times in the days before he and Stewart headed off for a vacation on what would be a fateful last race weekend of the season, the 1973 Formula One United States Grand Prix at Watkins Glen, New York.

Residents of the small town in upstate New York recall him playing at the local hangout for racing folks, the Seneca Lodge. Rick Hughey, now a local motor sport journalist who, in those days, occasionally helped out the Formula One racing crews who came to town, remembers there only being the piano bench left to sit on when Cevert arrived at the tavern late one evening. Someone jokingly told the Frenchman he should play something, and when he turned and played, the racer surprised everyone there with his classical training and ability.[1]

If Hollywood were ever to make a film about François Cevert, its most difficult task might be to find an actor who is nearly as attractive and charming as Cevert himself. With dark curly hair framing a handsome face, a broad, bright smile comprised of full lips and dimples, and, most of all, a set of mesmerizing, sparkling blue eyes issuing a piercing glance from underneath thick, dark brows, Cevert looked every bit a movie star, model, or anyone else whose startling physical beauty tends to stop people, quite literally, in their tracks. If Prince Charming were to have a "look," it could be well argued that François Cevert had that look. Not every existing photograph of Cevert is magazine cover worthy, but such a striking number of them are that it proves the point so many of his contemporaries, men and women alike, recall about his appearance. Perhaps more notable, however, is the fact that his colleagues in the racing world say his personality was just as pleasant and charming as his looks.

Born in Paris in 1944, Albert François Cevert Goldenberg was the son of a successful jeweler, Charles Goldenberg, and Huguette Cevert. Goldenberg was an émigré from Russia, brought to France by his family to escape tsarist persecution of Jews. His grandfather had money back in Russia. When the grandfather sent his family far away for their protection, he sent them a steady stream of funding as well so that none of them had to work for some time.[2] When he died, the money stopped, and Goldenberg found a trade in the jewelry business. Goldenberg and Huguette Cevert had four children, whom they gave their mother's surname, Cevert, to protect them from the Nazis in World War II. Even after the occupation, however, the Cevert name stuck.

François was born on February 25, 1944, the second of the four children. His younger sister, Jacqueline, remembers that his first words were an attempt to say *une auto* ("a car"), but her mother reported that the boy sounded out "toto, toto."[3] By ages twelve and thirteen, he was

François Cevert at the 1972 United States Grand Prix, Watkins Glen, New York.
International Motor Racing Research Center/F1 Collection.

already taking drives in the family car. In an interview, Cevert said that his "first passion was music." In fact, he practiced classical music for fifteen years, learning pieces and recording himself. He also loved riding motorbikes. "Unfortunately, I just didn't have enough time anymore," he said about not pursuing his music further. Presumably, his new interest in going fast took over as he got older. As far as racing goes, Cevert noted, "it came very progressively. I didn't decide one day that my ambition was to become a racing driver."[4]

During his required military service, while based in Ravensburg, Cevert took to driving tanks, which he found he could accelerate up to 80 mph, going either forward or backward. If he took off the gun turrets, he discovered the tanks handled better, and he entertained his comrades with races around the barracks.[5] After his military service, his father wanted him to work in the family jewelry business. Cevert suggested that he would do that if he could have weekends off to go racing. This plan did not go down well with a man who did not see how racing could be profitable, and soon Cevert was out on his own. He took to doing odd jobs, selling records or women's clothing. He signed up for the Volant Shell racing competition at the Magny-Cours-based Winfield racing school. Winning the 1966 contest, Cevert was awarded a Formula Three car. Unfortunately, the Alpine-Renault did not run well for him. The car retired in sixteen out of twenty-two races with mechanical problems; still, Cevert was noticed for his assertive driving style.

More time in Formula Three and then Formula Two racing followed. The Frenchman showed promise, but he had not yet raced very long, and it would take the notice and guidance of a mentor and a supporter to move him along much from there. Thankfully, for Cevert, that support came in the form of Jackie Stewart and Ken Tyrrell in Formula One. Over the years, the two men described a bit differently from one another how it happened. Tyrrell said that Stewart pointed out Cevert to him and recommended they give the talented young driver a chance. Cevert had said that he and Stewart eyed each other when they were side by side in a race in Reims and that he thought Stewart remembered him from that competition. Years later, Stewart said,

> No, no, it wasn't that. No one would ever have used Reims as an indicator of driver talent. We knew it was a matter of, "Who's the

best French driver available?" and Ken asked me to keep an eye on François. He seemed sufficiently good for me to say, "Well, he looks OK to me . . ." although I can't claim that at that stage I knew he was going to be special—it wasn't like seeing Ayrton Senna in the rain at Monte Carlo, for example. Of the options available, I thought François was the best.[6]

The reason Ken Tyrrell was on the lookout for a new driver was that he lost Stewart's teammate in 1970 after the Monaco Grand Prix. When Johnny Servoz-Gavin had an accident in practice for that race, he lost his confidence. He went to Tyrrell and told him that he no longer wanted to continue racing. One person's misfortune is another's gain, and Cevert immediately joined the team. Speculation ran at the time that Cevert brought Elf, a French fuel company, sponsorship money with him, but the team said that was not the reason he was brought on board. Elf approved of the French driver, of course, but according to the team the company did not base its support on whether François Cevert filled the vacant seat.

Asked in a documentary film about where his education in racing came from with so few years in the sport by the time he joined Formula One, Cevert responded, "I think it's very simple. Jackie did all my education. Jackie Stewart." He described how, before he reached Formula One, he had raced for two years in Formula Three, which he described as "nothing" in terms of an education for a driver, and one year in Formula Two. He described himself then as a "mad driver, driving like hell. I was not thinking about what I was doing,"[7] but Stewart set him straight.

After Cevert joined Stewart at the Tyrrell racing team in Formula One in 1970 and during his subsequent years with the team, the Scottish driver, who appreciated this young Frenchman, taught him to analyze the car, to think. Jackie was the "maestro" to him, Cevert said, because he was the only driver he knew who could race for two hours without making a mistake. He described Stewart's technique of setting up the car so that it was the easiest one on the track to drive. He did not have to fight the car in the corners. By studying Stewart's technique and having the luck to drive a fast car, especially when he moved from the March 701 he first drove for the Tyrrell organization to the Tyrell 002, Cevert got faster but also smarter. He was a quick learner.

In 1971, only his second year in Formula One, Cevert came in second in his home French Grand Prix and second and third, respectively, in the German and Italian grands prix; he saw his first victory in a Formula One race at the United States Grand Prix in Watkins Glen. Overall, Cevert's record that year gave him third place in the World Driving Championship, with first going to Stewart and second to Ronnie Peterson of STP March. With his promise being realized, Cevert was now a full-fledged protégé of Stewart's, a driver the Scotsman envisioned taking over for him as lead driver for the team should Stewart ever decide he had had enough of racing. At times, both men knew how quickly Cevert was catching up to Stewart in speed and technique. Stories circulated that Cevert could have passed Stewart at times but did not, out of respect.

One time, for example, Stewart had a problem with his car when he was running first and almost at the finish line. Cevert could have easily taken advantage of his teammate's situation, passed him, and snatched the win for himself. However, he later said that he would not have wanted to win that way. It is also clear that he had respect for his

François Cevert exits pit road during the 1972 United States Grand Prix, Watkins Glen, New York. *International Motor Racing Research Center/F1 Collection.*

teacher. He was happy to bide his time, knowing as he did that he was catching up to him more and more consistently. In one interview, Cevert admitted that he thought he was as good as Stewart for one lap but needed more experience and concentration to drive as many perfect laps in a race as he thought his master did with exceptional consistency.[8]

Several times, they stood in victory lane together adorned with wreaths and trophies and champagne after both cars of their team had dominated a race. The sight of a respectful and modest secondary driver not trying to usurp the glory of the number one driver on the team is rare in Formula One today, even when that number one driver is a defending world champion. Teammates are their own chief rivals since, theoretically, each has the same car to race. While the quickness of cars varies from team to team, the engineering and design of cars within a team are virtually the same. Sending two drivers out in two cars from the same team is like having each driver run out and have a go in as much the same car as possible in a race. If one places high and one retires due to mechanical problems, the team holds together, but not without questions being asked and answered of the mechanics and crew. If there are no mechanical failures but one driver simply out races the other, then the shadow of doubt begins to fall on the driver and the decisions made in race craft on the track.

Fans of Formula One in 2016, for example, saw a very different pairing between Mercedes teammates Nico Rosberg (Germany) and Lewis Hamilton (UK) than on the collegial, 1970s-era Stewart-Cevert Tyrrell team. Hamilton was the defending world champion who had won the last two consecutive years with the team and an earlier year with another team, McLaren. Rosberg, a childhood friend of Hamilton's from their karting days, had not yet won a championship. The Mercedes teammates had a fierce rivalry on the track. When Rosberg took the world championship away from Hamilton at the end of the 2016 season, the German promptly retired. He had reached his goal of obtaining a world championship and wanted to have more time with his wife and young daughter as well as to explore other pursuits. Hamilton, still single and with the desire to race, would come back to fight again in 2017 and try to win back his championship against not only the full field of other racers and teams but also a new rival teammate, Finnish driver Valtteri Bottas, filling in the seat that Rosberg left.

Unlike that of Hamilton and Rosberg, Stewart and Cevert's relationship, according to many, was like father and son, though the two were only a little over four years apart, with Stewart the elder of the two. Perhaps it was more like older and younger brothers, where the Frenchman was keen to learn from a mature, multiple world champion. For his part, Cevert knew his place, was modest, and felt confident that his day would eventually arrive. The affection Stewart and his wife, Helen, had for the single and charming Cevert extended beyond their time at the track. Not only is there video footage of Stewart bending down beside a Formula One racing car with Cevert in the driving seat, advising him on what gears he might use at certain points on the track and so forth, but Stewart has also said that Cevert joined the Stewarts on vacations. When he talks about Cevert to this day, Stewart admits that he considered him family.

WHAT HAPPENED

On October 6, 1973, Cevert was back in a place that he enjoyed—Watkins Glen, New York. He had happy memories there, of course, because it was the track where he had won his first and only grand prix race to date, just two years before. Back then, "the Glen," as it is commonly called, was the last race of the Formula One season, so the drivers and crews had a more relaxed feeling once they got there; soon they would be off the road, both the traveling kind and the racing kind, for the holidays.

As many of the racers did in those days, Cevert checked in to the Glen Motor Inn on a hill overlooking Seneca Lake, one of the Finger Lakes in the center of the state. His was Room 7; many of the returning drivers stayed in their same room of choice each season. Stewart and his wife were staying at the motel, too. The Glen Motor Inn was a small, family-run establishment that also had a restaurant attached where the public could come and eat. So different were the times back then that frequently, over race weekends, motor sport enthusiasts could have a meal in the restaurant and catch a glimpse of a Formula One racer or team members eating at the next table.

The Saturday morning of the 1973 United States Grand Prix, practice and qualifying day in fact, local motor sport enthusiast Steve Bieler and his wife, Marilyn, were doing just that, having breakfast at the inn. Bieler describes what he saw on that fateful day:

> At breakfast at the Glen Motor Inn, [Cevert] was sitting alone at a table near us, and he said something to the waitress to hurry her up. "Oh, you're one of those," she said, playfully. "Yes," he said, "I'm one of those who can't spend 45 minutes on breakfast." Cevert didn't seem playful; didn't seem hurried or agitated; he seemed like he was just giving a straight reply, not harsh but direct—yes, I am that way; that's how I live my life. The server seemed charmed, maybe was being flirtatious. I know she wasn't a senior but can't remember if she was in her twenties or thirties. I don't remember if there were any other racers there, but there often were at the Motor Inn. I just remember it was rather busy, active, and he was sitting at a small table alone. Oh, and his big, blue eyes were very noticeable.[9]

Up at the track that same day, Cevert was intent on qualifying well, gaining pole position, if possible. He seemed confident as he spoke to mechanic Jo Ramirez. Ramirez remembered that the driver noticed all the number sixes that were around; their consistency seemed like a lucky sign to the Frenchman. It was October 6; he was driving the Tyrrell 006 designed car; his car number was six; and he was sitting in front of a DFV number 066 engine. Racers will tell you that their favorite tracks are ones on which they do well. With a victory at the Glen once before, Cevert had the knowledge that he had done well at the scenic American track; there was no reason to think he could not be successful there again.[10]

Two weeks had gone by since the last race, the Canadian Grand Prix at Mosport, where Cevert had gotten into a controversial incident with Jody Scheckter (South Africa), who was then driving for McLaren. There was an accident, and Cevert was not too keen on Scheckter afterward. In fact, the Frenchman left for a trip with the Stewarts to Niagara Falls and then Bermuda with bruised and sore ankles and a limp. Another Watkins Glen motor sport enthusiast, Kevin Hughey, saw the crash in Canada—it happened right in front of him. Knowing how racers remember incidents like that, he could not help but wonder later, back at Watkins Glen, if the crash and Scheckter might still be weighing on Cevert's mind the weekend of the United States Grand Prix.[11]

Whether he was feeling confident about the run or had the incident with Scheckter on his mind with something to prove, no one will ever know for sure. What is known is that Cevert got in his blue Tyrrell No. 6 race car and went out on track to take his final practice runs before qualifying. He was running fourth in the session and had just driven his two fastest laps when he lost control of the car going up the esses, a fast, uphill portion of the track that curves in both directions like the letter *s*. The car bounced against one set of blue Armco guardrails and shot across the track, where it hit the rails there, sending Cevert over the side.

Ironically, it was Jody Scheckter in his McLaren who drove up on the scene first. He describes going over to the crash site and seeing sparks flying from the car's battery. He said years later that he does not know what he saw, but it was enough to tell him that a rescue of the driver was not needed. Jackie Stewart also went to the scene. He also saw that François had not survived, and instead of staying to help in any way, he immediately left his dear friend there, something that bothered

François Cevert looks intent as he prepares for action on the track. *International Motor Racing Research Center/Michael Keyser.*

him for years afterward. When asked in a telephone interview years later why he thinks he left, he replied,

> I was angry. In the way that the sport could be so brutal, that it could be so cruel, that it could take the life of somebody as good as he was, as nice as he was, as deep a friend as he was. Having the accident that he did have was such a big one, and the shock of it, and the loss, I suppose. I knew I was going to be retiring at the end of that week anyway, that weekend. Just the conglomeration of all of these elements and emotions. There was nothing I could do. I mean, there was nothing that I could do for François. That was clearly obvious. The brutality of the accident was enormous.

Thinking back on the scene, Stewart reflected more on the nature of motor sport, the sport so many people love and to which he has dedicated much of his life as a driver and an advocate:

> I suppose I was shocked and angered that the sport could be this destructive, and yet we all love it; we all loved it, and I still love it. . . . That was another side of the sport that you just had to get used to, or you'd have left, and not many of these people left. So, therefore, we were exposed to many funerals, many memorial services, many families—fathers and mothers losing a son, or the sisters and brothers, or the wives and the children. It was a huge kaleidoscope of emotion and feelings as well as fulfillment and excitement . . . and pleasure. But, you know, death is an ugly thing, and it's something that was part of our sport at that time that everyone just had to deal with. [12]

AFTERMATH

In fact, Stewart did go back up to the esses to help indirectly. The mechanics, especially Jo Ramirez, were worried that the accident might have been caused by a mechanical failure on the car. Stewart assured them that he thought he understood what had happened, but to ease their emotional burden, he got back in his car that afternoon and took a drive over the same spot where Cevert had just gone off. He described the experience later in his autobiography:

So I climbed into my car and headed out and, approaching the narrow Bridge complex at a speed of 130 mph, I noticed a small hump in the road. It was just past the apex and close to the exit of the left-hand corner and the disruption was enough to make the short-wheel-base Tyrrell feel pointy and nervous. Suddenly driving the car felt like riding a highly-strung horse; it ran perfectly if you held it in a straight line, but if it was disturbed in any way, it could be unpredictable and react negatively. It was usual at Watkins Glen for the track to become cleaner and quicker as the weekend progressed, and my preference was to take this section in fifth gear, using the low end of the engine's rev range. This meant the car was more docile and able to cushion the nervousness of the car going over the hump. I was almost certain that François had chosen to approach the Bridge in fourth gear, at the top end of his engine's rev range, which might have made his car faster through the combination of corners but which also would have made the car's reaction to the hump even more nervous, twitchy and unpredictable.

It seemed to me that, on that fateful lap, his high-spirited thoroughbred car had hit the hump and responded in an overly nervous fashion, whipping on him as he came off the throttle at almost maximum revs, which would have made the car even more reactive. In those few milliseconds, he would have been unable to catch it and regain control. The car would have pointed itself towards the right side of the track, crashing heavily into the Armco barrier and then ricocheting at high speed across the track and colliding violently into the barrier on the left side, turning upside down in the process. Just to make absolutely sure, I decided to do another lap and to approach the Bridge in fourth gear as François had done, and the vehicle's reaction confirmed my view. Even though I was taking care and was prepared, it was not easy to keep control. [13]

When Stewart went back to the pits and explained to the mechanics that his theory tested out, he said, they looked visibly relieved.

Tyrrell pulled out of the United States Grand Prix out of respect for the tragic loss of its young driver. That meant that Jackie Stewart would not be on the grid for his hundredth and final time in a Formula One car. Though he had already decided to retire after the season ended with the United States Grand Prix of 1973, he had not let many people know about it, not even his wife. The tragedy of François Cevert, as close as he was, was not the reason for Stewart's prompt retirement after that event, as many fans and colleagues thought at the time. While many in the sport believed, and still think, that Stewart had more in him as a racer—he was thirty-four and a three-time world champion—the "flying Scot" was ready to go. He had seen so much death around him in his career, lost so many friends; so many times Helen and his sons had had to wonder whether he would come back from a race weekend or a test or a practice. He said he had not told Helen to avoid the inevitable "counting down" of races left to go, knowing how much more difficult it would be for her had he not come back and she had known that in only one or two races he would have been out of that dangerous line of work.

After Cevert's crash at the esses at the Glen, Stewart and Helen went back to their room at the Glen Motor Inn, overlooking Seneca Lake. That is where the three-time world champion informed his wife that he was retiring from racing, that he had planned on retiring that weekend, whatever happened. It was a decision Stewart seems to have been happy with ever afterward. Unlike many world champion athletes, he has not come back to see if he can do it again. Though he has stayed involved with the sport in terms of safety and promotion, one does not hear interviews in which Jackie Stewart ever pines about having made the wrong decision.

Of course, in the immediate aftermath of any death, there are details to be handled. With a French citizen passing away in the United States, these details included resolving the technical matter of getting François's body back to France. Journalist Jabby Crombac, a personal friend of Cevert's, was given that task by Ken Tyrrell. First, he and Jean-Pierre Beltoise, another racing driver who was married to Cevert's sister, Jacqueline, needed to inform the family. Jacqueline was normally at the races to watch her husband and brother compete, but she was expecting her second baby, had not felt well, and decided not to travel.

The next task for Crombac was to go with Ken Tyrrell's wife, Norah, and retrieve Cevert's belongings from his room at the Glen Motor Inn. He described it as "one of the saddest things you can do" to pack a dead man's suitcase for such a trip home. He also had to choose a casket for the fallen racer and then make arrangements for the flight. A lot of red tape and delay could have been involved, but Crombac called François Guiter, who worked with Elf at that time but had worked with the secret service previously. The next morning, a French secret service agent appeared who was able to get the required approvals to move the process forward so that young François could go home.[14]

Samy C. G. Beau-Marquet, a friend of Jacqueline's who also knew François and the family and was their neighbor in Neuilly, west of Paris, remembers François as "a gifted human being." He said he helped the family at the time of the funeral and stayed close, much later having lunch with the racer's mother, Huguette, to keep her company and drive her the three hours to visit her son's grave in Vaudelay.[15] The racer was just twenty-nine when he died.

LEGACY

When an admired and high-profile athlete dies, one who was so close to fulfilling his promise and talent, his fans mourn; his colleagues and rivals mourn; his entire sport and the world of sport in general mourns; and his country mourns. François Cevert was not a world champion, though many thought, including his friend, Jackie Stewart, the eventual holder of the championship the year Cevert died, that he might have succeeded in reaching that goal in 1974. Others have said that France would have had its first Formula One world champion ten or more years before Alain Prost in 1985, had Cevert lived.

He was not yet a champion; nor was Cevert a husband or a father. At twenty-nine, he was still enjoying the single life of an international racing driver, the glamor, the challenge, the travel, and the lifestyle as it was in the 1970s. Some said he was becoming more serious with his current girlfriend. He was, however, a beloved son, brother, uncle, and so forth, who left a legacy in the form of a tragic loss in the Cevert family. Fans still remember him to this day, over forty years later, and mark the anniversaries of his birth and death via social media on the Internet as though he were alive to see their tributes. The Stewarts have not forgotten; Jackie attended a fortieth anniversary gathering in France in 2013 where Jacqueline Cevert-Beltoise was in attendance. Stewart spoke of his fond memories of his protégé.

Strange coincidences have emerged in Cevert lore. The story has been told since his passing that years before he once visited a clairvoyant on a lark with his then girlfriend, who urged him to come along. The sage predicted that he would have a successful career and see much happiness. Then the fortune-teller went silent, seemingly seeing a vision. She then said he would not see his thirtieth year. Other inexplicable occurrences took place as well. Right after the crash, the parts of the car were retrieved and analyzed. When the engine was being taken apart, the mechanics reported that somehow it dropped from the bench down to the floor. None of the men there at the time could explain how it happened. When I went to lay flowers at the track at Watkins Glen on the fortieth anniversary of Cevert's passing, an amateur racing event was happening at the time. At the exact moment I was investigating the outside of the track at the spot where Cevert went off, a loose tire flew up into the catch fencing right at that spot. Jackie Stewart has said that, for those who believe, Cevert's spirit has definitely been around and made itself noticed.

It is hard to measure a legacy of spirit. How can one define the impact a soul has on the earth in big and small ways or how long that impact may last? Those affected by the life of François Cevert—by remembering him as the person they knew and may have listened to as he played piano, or as a racer they watched, or as a racer they have read about or watched in videos and become enamored with—carry the romance of the man and his story with them for as long as they feel it is warranted. It seems a performer of Beethoven's "Sonata Pathétique," who knew the risks he was taking with his life in motor sport and who knew he had made his choice and was at peace with it, might not expect his legacy to the world to be anything else than the hope that he might be remembered. Remembered, he is.

—⟨∾∿∾⟩—

Racer: Albert François Cevert Goldenberg (France), age twenty-nine; b. February 25, 1944, in Paris, France; d. October 6, 1973, in Watkins Glen, New York.

Career Highlights and Honors: Winner, 1971 United States Formula One Grand Prix; second place, 1972 24 Hours of Le Mans; protégé of three-time Formula One world champion Jackie Stewart at Tyrrell racing team.

Among His Legacies: French nationalistic pride; influence and effect on Jackie Stewart's work on safety in the sport; enduring remembrance and affection in France and around the world; safety improvements to Watkins Glen racetrack; film appearances in documentaries *One by One* (1973) and *O Fabuloso Fittipaldi* (1974).

—∾—

7

DRIVEN

Gilles Villeneuve

Legends are made in moments. A physically active World War II navy veteran living in a small town gets his motorcycle license for the first time at age eighty. On his eightieth birthday, he takes a deep breath, with all gathered there watching, and extinguishes all eighty candles spread out before him on a large cake in one, powerful, extraordinary blow. In his family and among his friends and the people of that town who see him riding around on his motorcycle every day, driving accurately and safely with a ready wave and a smile, an American flag flapping in the breeze from his bike behind him, the man becomes a local legend. A hero rescues a boy who has fallen down on a set of subway tracks, or a pilot named Sully lands dozens of passengers and crew members safely on the Hudson River when the plane's engines cut out from a bird strike. These moments are memorable; the stories are told over and over, and in the retelling they gather power until the legends grow and become part of family, local, national, or even international lore.

In sport, on the national or international stage, some of these moments might be championship victories, or incredible comebacks, or Olympic gold medal wins, perhaps a game particularly well played with excellence and skill against tough odds. In motor racing, where the stakes can be as high as life itself, legends tend to inspire the respect and memories of fellow competitors, crews, series officials, the media, and certainly the fans. One racer may be a legend despite never having won a world championship. The way he raced and the manner in which he conducted himself on and off the track may inspire those who have watched his career over time—or he may just make a remarkable and memorable story. Another driver may be a big winner, which is certainly what most racers strive to be and work to achieve, but he may still lack that certain something that turns him from a widely successful driver into a legend whose story dwells in the hearts of others and gets passed down.

In the case of Gilles Villeneuve, a French Canadian Formula One (F1) race car driver, it could be argued that a combination of fabulous drives, especially in the rain, raw speed, fearlessness, and a sense of fairness, both on and off the track, contribute to the frequent mention of his name on lists of "Who is the greatest driver ever" even decades after his passing. Perhaps the best way to describe both the man and the racer is to say that he was driven.

Born in 1950 and raised in Quebec, Villeneuve was a small, quiet boy who did well in school and always seemed to challenge himself with his studies or music lessons. He played with small cars and trucks but wanted to make sure they had all their basic parts first; he took the machines his uncles used in their construction business as comparisons for his playthings to make sure they looked right. He learned to play piano; then his interest turned to the trumpet, which he practiced five or six hours a day, at one time having ambitions to become a professional musician. Soon, the trumpet went the way of the piano, and he was on to other interests entirely.

Villeneuve often rode in a car with his father, who liked to drive fast. His father was not a racing driver, so Gilles did not inherit a predisposition to compete in professional motor sport through his family, as some drivers did back then and still do today. Still, it might be said that a thirst for speed may have come naturally to him. His father, Seville, was a piano tuner who was on the road a lot at first, then later worked with Gilles's mother, Georgette, a seamstress, in a women's clothing shop they set up in Berthierville, a town about forty miles northeast of Montreal. Seville was still on the road, since he often had to drive to the nearby city to pick up material for the business. Gilles's fondest childhood memory was when he was about nine or ten years old, and his father let him drive their new Volkswagen on a country road. "What a thrill," Gilles said, remembering. Gilles also had a younger brother, Jacques, a name that would reappear in the family later when the racer had a son who would likewise turn to the trade of driving a car fast for a living.

Though he would later be praised as genuine and honest, a fair racer as well as a fast one, if not overly determined at times, when Villeneuve was young, his sense of honesty was still developing. According to his biographer, Gerald Donaldson, although Seville had given his teenaged son a run-down, red 1958 MGA two-seater to fix up and drive, which he did, young Villeneuve took more of an interest in the new family car—a 1966 Pontiac Grand Parisienne. His father let him drive it on a back road behind the house whenever the teen washed it. With a speedometer that went to 120 mph, Gilles could not resist giving that car more of a workout. One night, he and a friend left a party and went back to Gilles's house, where they rolled the Pontiac some distance away so as not to wake his parents. Gilles started it up with a set of spare keys he had made earlier. All was fine as he drove it up to 108 mph on, importantly, a rainy road, until the straight road became a curve and Gilles lost control. He hit a telephone pole and wrecked the car. Given the damage, it was remarkable that neither Gilles nor his companion was badly hurt. Sneaking back to the house, Gilles might have had until morning to come up with an explanation to give his parents if it were not for the police call to the house in the middle of the night. Having traced the plates, the police notified the Villeneuves that their car had been stolen and was found crashed on the side of the road five miles away. Of course, Gilles had no way out now and had to tell the truth. When the police arrived at the house and filed their report that a nonlicensed driver was involved, that meant that Seville's insurance would not cover the damage. Seville lost both the car and the $4,000 he'd borrowed to buy it. Gilles's parents did not punish him severely for the episode. They took the mercy route instead, believing that the boy had learned his lesson from the experience.

Apparently, he had not. When he was sixteen and now had his driver's license, Gilles had another wreck driving a car too fast, this time in his own car, a black MGA that was in a little better shape than his previous red vehicle. On his way to his girlfriend's house in Joliette, he came up on a country road behind a racy Dodge Roadrunner and decided that it made a fine challenge to pass this large American car in his nimble little British sports car. Again, all was fine with this plan until he went to make his move and the Dodge had to slow unexpectedly for a herd of sheep crossing the road. This time, Gilles did not escape injury—when his parents were notified, they learned that their son was in the hospital in Joliette with eighty stitches crisscrossing his scalp.[1]

Things went on like this. There were more crashes. He was stopped for speeding so many times that the local police knew him by name. In those days, the only penalty was monetary, a $10 fee, which Villeneuve gladly paid time after time for the privilege. There was no points system or risk of suspension or revocation of license back then, which may have been more of a deterrent to the determined driver. When asked about the frequency of his speeding tickets, the future racer was always polite and explained once to an officer, "The urge to drive fast is stronger than I am." Later, he once described that summer in his teens of driving friends to parties and speeding all the way as the most enjoyable time of his life, a time when he felt "completely free." These comments, during and about that time in his life, say a lot about how the life of the French Canadian would unfold.

From there came years of racing, a bit of drag racing along the way and, arguably, a type of racing with a more Canadian flair—snowmobile racing. Despite getting thrown many times, Villeneuve said he never got injured racing the snow machines. He got cold. He could not see, he said. He learned to "build quick reactions" and "hang on." Was it his years of racing on snow, landing in drift after snowbank, getting thrown onto sheets of ice—on vehicles that offer not much more protection than a motorcycle on skis—that made him feel so impervious to injury later in his racing career? Did the experience enhance his ability to drive on slippery, wet surfaces? About the cold and rocky challenges of snowmobile racing on machines that he said were more like race cars than people give them credit for, Villeneuve added, "It helps, you know, to build a big heart."

As expected, with his zest for speed and his inner drive, Villeneuve did well in the sport. Race cars, however, like he studied in his *Road and Track* magazine, were calling his name. In fairly quick succession, he went to racing school, passed overwhelmingly and got his license, then raced Formula Fords and had a ride racing in Formula Atlantic, then the highest level of single-seaters in Canada. At one time, he raced in the summers with some money from the snowmobile company Skiroule, which sponsored his efforts in trade for his racing snowmobiles for them in the winter. The money, though, was never enough. It was especially in short supply because Joann, the girlfriend he was on his way to visit when he had the crash in his family's Pontiac, was now his wife, and they had two small children, Jacques and Melanie.

The problem with living with a driven person is that he or she can appear to have no other thoughts than his or her obsession. Again, according to Donaldson, this was the case with Villeneuve, especially in the early days when his family was young and struggling financially. Before Melanie was born, he would leave Joann with young Jacques in a mobile home. The pipes froze, and Joann needed to crawl underneath the mobile home to take care of that while fretting over where their young child might be while she did so. Though she was resourceful, perhaps to her own detriment since Gilles often acted as though she were handling everything at home without any help, money was scarce, and life was difficult. Gilles was either gone racing or home working on cars or plans for racing. He would use their last $20 to buy a fuel pump. He creatively "borrowed" mechanics' tools after hours to help maintain a car he wanted to race but could not afford to keep up. There was the constant pressure that racers starting out not flush with cash almost all seem to have—finding sponsorship to fuel their habit. Living conditions were tight as they went from one housing situation to another and lived partially with relatives and at times on benefits from the government. Joann had no car. Anyone in a First World country who has been home full-time raising two young children without a vehicle for running errands or to just get out of the house once in a while can relate to how isolating that can be. Another time, Gilles came home, and as Joann said, her husband announced, "I've sold the house to buy a car." Yet another time he came up with the idea of the family going with him on the road. They became a family of nomads, wandering around Canada from racetrack to racetrack. In fact, the Villeneuves became quite close as a family as a result, and Gilles developed a reputation later on as a family man. At this point, though, times were tough.

Once, he broke his leg in two places from an accident in a Formula Atlantic car at Mosport. Strangely, Gilles did not believe the doctor— because believing the doctor would mean that he could not race until his leg was healed. At this point Joann began to wonder if the man's obsession with speed had affected his grip on reality. Finally, the racer was fitted with a cast from his hip to his toe, which was not a situation that made him happy. He was less happy still when he learned that he had lost his seat racing for the Ecurie Canada team. He picked at the cast and tried to get Joann to help him take it off. She would not do so, but she did consult other doctors with him, and they found one who removed the full-leg cast and replaced it with a smaller one that allowed him to bend his knee and ankle. This was enough to encourage Ville-neuve to go driving again, despite everyone else involved saying he was not ready. He tried to prepare his leg for racing by driving his family's Mustang to a race in Newfoundland. He would be allowed to compete there if he could get out of the race car without help in sixty seconds or less, the stipulation at that time in case of fire. Villeneuve failed the test. Six weeks after his accident, however, he was back in a race car and out on the track trying to win. Throughout his and his family's struggles, Villeneuve continued to improve and do well in his racing, drawing the attention of key observers in the sport.

By the later part of 1977, when he was in his late twenties, Ville-neuve had climbed his way to the world's highest level of motor sport—Formula One. His willingness to race with such confidence, with seem-ing disregard for his own safety, soon garnered him the attention of Enzo Ferrari. Ferrari, team namesake and patriarch—a stout, suited character almost always seen in public wearing sunglasses—liked his racers to be this way: quite rare and willing to put their blood on the line for a win in a racing car. And not just any racing car but a Ferrari. The two men were a match—Villeneuve with his unquenchable thirst for speed and Ferrari with his zeal for having racers win for the team with a desire to bring home that win at all costs. Ferrari became fond of the French Canadian; many believed that he even viewed him like a son.

Ferrari's signing of Villeneuve was not misplaced, though in his first full season in 1978, there were three accidents, three DNFs, and a drop back to seventh place from second in the high-profile Italian Grand Prix at Monza. The penalty was for jumping the start. The Canadian came in no lower than twelfth in races and finished ninth overall in the world championship that year. The greatest victory for Villeneuve, however, other than making it to Formula One and Ferrari in the first place, was winning his home Canadian Grand Prix at Île Notre-Dame in October. To this date, he remains the only Canadian to win his home grand prix.

In 1979, Villeneuve finished second in the world championship to his teammate at Ferrari, Jody Scheckter (Germany), with several wins that season, including a victory across the border from his homeland at the United States Grand Prix at Watkins Glen, New York. He followed up his first-place win in 1978 with second place at the Canadian Grand Prix in 1979. If Canadians had been waiting for decades for a native son to root for in the Olympics-like international racing series of Formula One, they found him in Gilles Villeneuve. His record in the Canadian Grand Prix remained promising, if not as strong, in the years that followed. Competition in car design and teams from one year to the next can affect a driver's individual standings and performance compared with others. In 1980, he finished fifth in the Canadian Grand Prix, and he was third in 1981. Unfortunately, he never raced another grand prix at home again.

One of many of Villeneuve's famous drives stands out as particularly remembered today. Arguably, some of the best moments in motor racing happen when two cars are in a close battle on the track, shifting positions back and forth. Which one will be in front at the finish line? Which one will dominate? Can a pass be made safely? Surely, this car is going to win, but wait—how did that driver get around? Will they collide, driving so close to one another? And back and forth, again and again.

If you ask longtime Formula One fans who won the 1979 French Grand Prix at Dijon, they may remember it was Frenchman Jean-Pierre Jabouille, driving for Renault, a French team. In fact, the race was a shining moment all around for France. A French driver, competing for a French team, on French Michelin tires, propelled by Elf French fuel won the French Grand Prix. That is memorable enough. However, what the enthusiast will most likely immediately talk about is the battle not for first but for second place between the other Renault driver, René Arnoux of France, and Gilles Villeneuve, the French Canadian, driving for Ferrari. Back and forth these two went, first one ahead of the other, then the other way around. Neither driver was giving up. Also impressive was how fairly this battle was fought—no pushing or shoving, banging or scraping paint; both drivers just watched for a gap on one side of the driver ahead and capitalized on it. Each time a pass was made, the other driver gave just enough fair room. There was no closing off or moving in that would lead to an accident and take both drivers out. There was brief, wheel-to-wheel contact from the fierce competition, which the drivers were later warned about in terms of safety in those especially dangerous times, but for their part, the two men were nearly giddy after the race, which in the end found Villeneuve taking second and Arnoux finishing third. In the interviews afterward, Arnoux said he did not mind taking third in such a contest, that he enjoyed it very much. The racing had exhilarated both men, who found each other afterward and walked arm in arm, laughing, through the paddock. From that day on, they were fast (so to speak!) friends. Other drivers said they were both crazy, that either one of them or both could have been killed by one false move, but the drivers responded that their lack of fear with each other had produced that fantastic drive from both of them. Villeneuve said about the famous on-track battle, even two years later,

> That is my best memory of Grand Prix racing. Those few laps were just fantastic to me—out-braking each other and trying to race for the line, touching each other but without wanting to put the other car out. It was just two guys battling for second place without trying to be dirty but having to touch because of wanting to be first. It was just fantastic! I loved that moment.

This incredible car control, even when he seemed to take reckless chances, was a hallmark of Villeneuve's driving style. What other driving gifts brought so much attention to him and kept him a favorite among fans, even today looking back? Another of his skills was his ability to drive in the rain. When drivers in better cars adjusted their driving styles to suit the more slippery track conditions, Villeneuve seized on what he saw as a situation that equalized the cars and put the emphasis more on the driver. He always claimed that he could not be hurt, but he could hurt the car. Driving for Ferrari, he was ever cognizant of that. Was it the cushioning of snow from his snowmobile racing days that made him believe this? He frequently admitted how much the experience helped him in cars. Villeneuve simply liked to drive and kept driving even in some seemingly irrational situations. Once, an entire back tire was peeling off the car, but because it kept moving; he kept driving it—in the wet—rather than stop and have a recovery vehicle come pick it up.

Another time, a large body piece of the car flew up and blocked his view, but still the car ran, so Villeneuve kept driving it. In a downpour that kept several drivers off the track due to the poor track surface conditions for practice, Villeneuve went out anyway; no matter what, he kept driving. Three-time Formula One world champion Niki Lauda once said Villeneuve was the craziest kind of devil he had ever seen in the series; yet when he was away from the track, the Canadian was a sensitive and lovable sort of person, which made him unique.

Off track with his colleagues, the quiet and small-statured French Canadian was known for playing it straight—he would tell it like he saw it. He kept his musician's sensitivity and attention to detail about him, and he had a good sense of humor. Fellow drivers said he was a man confident in his own skin. They admired his courage; even as they themselves were risk takers, they warned him about the chances he kept taking in an already highly risky business. The races went up and down in success, as they tend to do when cars and drivers change; results change, requiring adaptation and improvement. Villeneuve had not yet won a world championship, but many observers thought it was only a matter of time. Ferrari remained behind him, keeping him in their cars. By the 1982 Belgian Grand Prix, he had won six grands prix at the highest level of motor sport. He was thirty-two.

While, overall, the relationship with Ferrari was sound on paper, discontent was brewing for Villeneuve in the name of his new team-mate, Didier Pironi (France). What might seem like a small disagreement inside teams to outsiders can matter a lot to a racing driver. It is a bad day at work, for example, if your teammate is given your spare car to qualify in, and you find that you need it due to an issue with your first car. Timing is important, and so is team loyalty and team decisions made regarding two or more drivers. Any whiff of preference between drivers on a team always causes tension on one side of the garage or the other. When a series of perceived slights is experienced, a driver can sometimes begin to take out his ill feelings on the track. His emotions begin to weigh on his performance and his choices. The best drivers will tell you that emotion is something you want to drive with as little as possible—clear thinking and split-second decision making on the track keep the driver concentrating on the task at hand and keep the car on the road; they prevent accidents and mistakes that cost places in the race.

Two weeks before the Belgian Grand Prix, at the San Marino Grand Prix in Imola, Italy, Villeneuve got into an argument with Pironi. Ville-

Gilles Villeneuve. *International Motor Racing Research Center/The Randy Barnett Collection.*

neuve was obeying what he thought were "team orders" from Ferrari—
a "slow" sign had been put out, a signal that Villeneuve took to mean, as

he always did, that the team wanted the drivers to back off a bit to save fuel or tires in the race. He and Pironi had been running first and second in the race, respectively, after the stronger team that year, Renault, had both cars retire. The two drivers were battling in their red Ferraris in front of an enthusiastic Italian crowd.

"Team orders" are often controversial in motor sport: basically, the team interferes with a racer's ability to pass or win for him- or herself in preference for the team to win overall. For example, if the crew and engineers in the pits calculate that a car may run out of fuel if the racer drives it too hard to the finish line, they risk losing the race, so they give out "team orders" for the driver to manage the car's fuel, even if that means giving up a place or two in the race. Cars that do not finish do not get any points for either the driver or the constructor (team). In Formula One, there is not only a Drivers' Championship but also a Constructors' Championship, so sometimes these two competitions are in tension with one another. Finishing the race and picking up constructor points can sometimes be a better strategy than going all-out for the driver to gain the most points for himself. Usually, a team wants a driver to place as high as possible, since that benefits both championship runs, but they have more than one driver on the track as well, so sometimes that plays a role, and the team strategizes between the drivers to its benefit.

Team orders can also come between two drivers on the same team. If one driver is higher in championship points for the season, for example, sometimes the team will order his teammate, who may be ahead in the race at the time, to allow the championship contender by and thereby sacrifice a potential win. The whole matter of team orders puts drivers in a bind. Do they stay loyal to what their teams want them to do for the benefit of the team overall, or do they drive only for themselves, ignoring their bosses and the role their team has played in giving them a good car and support to get them toward the front in the first place.

Villeneuve claimed to be a team player for Ferrari. When he saw the slow sign from the pits, he obeyed. Pironi, however, did not and got by Villeneuve. Laps went by, along with diminishing chances for Villeneuve to pass Pironi, but still he did not, keeping to team orders, while Pironi stayed out in front. The resulting one-two place on the podium showed a jubilant Pironi at the win but a visibly angry Villeneuve in second place. The French Canadian, normally respected for not blaming others or the car for any mistake he may have made, would not speak with his teammate. Pironi claimed there were engine problems with both cars and there were no team orders. Villeneuve said there were indeed team orders, which meant that they should hold their position and not pass. Villeneuve's anger is evident in what he said in an interview:

> People seem to think we had the battle of our lives! Jesus Christ! I'd been ahead of him most of the race, qualified a second and a half ahead of him. Where was my problem? I was coasting those last 15 laps. He was racing. I think I've proved that, in equal cars, if I want someone to stay behind me . . . well, I think he stays behind.
>
> I guess it looked like I was mad at finishing second. Okay, I'd have been mad at myself for not going quick enough if I'd been plain beaten. Second is one thing, but second because he steals it, that's something else.

Of course, drivers are also known to be confident in their own abilities—if they are not, they do not get a car to drive in professional

Gilles Villeneuve flies in the rain in the 1979 United States Grand Prix, Watkins Glen, New York. *International Motor Racing Research Center/F1 Collection.*

racing series. Too many other drivers who believe they can win are waiting for the chance. This is how a racer gets a reputation for being honest or a blowhard, though—depending on whether or not evidence backs his claims about his own abilities or about being cheated out of a win.

No lesser person in the team organization than Enzo Ferrari himself took Villeneuve's side about the Imola 1982 incident. Uncharacteristically, the team's namesake made a public statement on the matter saying that Pironi had misinterpreted the signal given. Ferrari said he understood why Villeneuve was upset. Nonetheless, the race placements stayed, and it was time to prepare for the next contest in two weeks.

WHAT HAPPENED

Unfortunately, some people, even in the motor sport community, thought all along that Villeneuve enjoyed speed too much for his own good. Reportedly, he would speed anything he drove, even just driving to the racetrack. Finally, what many had feared for some time might happen to him back in those more dangerous days did come to pass.

Gilles felt deeply betrayed by his teammate, Pironi, whom he had trusted as a friend. He was still not over it when he arrived in Belgium for the next grand prix. Speaking with him by telephone, a journalist thought Gilles's simmering anger to be frightening. Everyone knows that a racetrack is not a good place to carry out a vendetta, but everyone who watches motor sport over time knows that this is exactly what can happen in the heat of competition, when a driver feels wronged, when a team's or personal wins are down and the pressure is on, and especially when one driver seems to have treated another unfairly.

At the very least, teams know that a driver who is highly emotional while in the car risks not only his or her own safety and performance but the safety and performance of others out on the track as well. On that day in Belgium, one of the factors believed by some to have played a part in what happened was Villeneuve's continuing anger over Imola, even though Pironi was not immediately involved in what was about to happen. There is no way to know for sure, of course, how much emotion played a role that day, if any.

Prior to Saturday's qualifying, Villeneuve complained about not having enough grip with the hard Goodyear tires and about the slower cars out on the track being a hazard to the faster ones. He had had to slam on his brakes coming up behind one such slower car, a March driven by Jochen Mass (Germany). In an interview with *Le Soir*, Villeneuve commented that he knew about the risks involved in motor racing and accepted them. He also admitted, however, that there are times on the track when there is not much a driver can do. "If at Zolder my car skids, all I can do is call mama and cross myself," he said.

At Circuit Zolder in Belgium on May 8, 1982, driving his qualifying run for the Belgian Grand Prix for Ferrari (some sources say it was during final practice), Villeneuve came up behind driver Jochen Mass of the March racing team. In qualifying in Formula One, racers are not racing against one another; they are racing against the clock. In the sense that they are trying to lay down their fastest time to determine their starting position on the grid in the race, the drivers are competing, of course, but passing on the track is not the important thing. Still, one driver does not want to get in the way of another doing a "flying" qualifying lap. Mass was on his way back to the pits. Both drivers took a left-hand corner. Mass was in the middle of the track and moved to the right to allow Villeneuve to pass on the left. Instead, Villeneuve also went right. At that moment, Villeneuve caught the back of Mass's car, his left front tire rolling up on Mass's back right. Villeneuve's car sailed up into the air, flipped, came down, and crashed and spun as it continued to rush down the track in flying bits and pieces at 140 mph.

In the process, the exploded Ferrari ejected Gilles from the cockpit; even his helmet was knocked off. In a horrible irony, the man once known as the "flying driver" flew across the track airborne, defenseless, without either a car or a helmet for protection. His body, head first, crashed into the low catch fencing along the opposite side of the track. Gilles's motionless body lay on the ground, his brown hair visible against the fence, while marshals and medical crews rushed to his aid. Dr. Sid Watkins, the Formula One doctor at that time, said later, "It was obvious immediately that there was nothing that I could do for him."[2] Eleven minutes after the accident, a helicopter transported the Canadian to the University of St. Raphael Hospital in Louvain. Doctors reported that his injuries included a severed spinal cord, fractured cervical vertebrae, and severe injuries to his brainstem and neck. The driver was on life support until he died at 9:12 p.m. that evening.

AFTERMATH

Joann was not at the track that weekend, though it was one of very few races in her husband's career that she did not attend. Instead, when she got the call, she was at their home in Monaco, baking cookies for their daughter's First Communion weekend. Retired racer Jody Scheckter (South Africa), Gilles's former teammate and good friend at Ferrari as well as the 1979 world champion, immediately went to help the family.

The Canadian government diverted a military jet to bring Gilles's body home to Canada from Belgium. His racing helmet and gloves were set inside the casket with him for the wake. When the casket was carried in and out of L'Église Sainte-Geneviève-de-Berthier in Quebec for the Requiem Mass, it was draped with a black-and-white checkered flag. Thousands of people waited outside the church, standing on bridges and along the road to watch the procession, while nine hundred guests attended inside. Canadian dignitaries such as Prime Minister Pierre Trudeau and the Quebec premier René Lévesque attended the funeral, as did many officials and people from the racing community. On Joann's solid black dress was pinned a diamond broach in the shape of the Ferrari prancing horse, given to her by Enzo Ferrari. Gilles's and Joann's children were still young—just eleven and eight.

Scheckter delivered memorable remarks in a simple eulogy that has stayed in the minds of those present and those who read about Gilles Villeneuve to this day: "I will miss Gilles for two reasons," he said. "First, he was the fastest driver in the history of motor racing. Second, he was the most genuine man I have ever known. But he has not gone. The memory of what he has done, what he has achieved, will always be there."[3]

LEGACIES

Soon after the funeral, the Montreal government renamed the race-track on Île Notre-Dame after the fallen hero. The words "Salut Gilles" remain freshly maintained at the start/finish line. His hometown named a park after him and erected a statue and plaque in his honor. Corners or grid spots at tracks, particularly in Italy, are named for him. While these honors are noteworthy and express the fans' and the public's affection for the lost driver, Villeneuve's living legacies, of course, are his children. One of his children has stayed in the public eye. Jacques went into the racing business himself against the wishes of his mother. He managed to outdo his father in terms of the written record. Jacques won not only the 1997 Formula One World Championship but also the 1995 IndyCar series championship and the 1995 Indianapolis 500. To date, Jacques is the only Canadian to have won the F1 championship and the only Canadian to win the Indy 500. He has raced in NASCAR and came in second in the 24 Hours of Le Mans of 2008; most recently, he has competed in the electric car series, Formula E.

Scheckter once said that driving for Ferrari, unlike for any other team, is like driving for the team's country, Italy. The enthusiasm of the *tifosi* ("fans" in Italian) is widely evident at any grand prix but especially at the Italian Grand Prix, where thousands turn up, waving Italian and Ferrari "prancing horse" flags with great pageantry, chants, and cheers. Their devotion to Ferrari exceeds that of any other team's fans. Ferrari, the team that, to date, has won more Constructors' Championships in Formula One than any other in the series' history, is like a family. Its teams and drivers are treated that way, even to this day. The loss of a Ferrari driver would get a lot of attention within the sport even if he were not a top driver or champion, simply because he drove for Ferrari, the dream team of so many racers. Villeneuve's legacy endures partly because he drove for that team. His story was cemented in Ferrari lore, if not for his talent then for how much the founder thought of him. Enzo Ferrari said about Gilles, "In my eyes he was one of my family. I loved him."[4]

Likewise, up to that time, Canada never had a racing champion in Formula One or a driver who came as close to achieving that goal as Gilles Villeneuve. The French, as well, originators of the grand prix historically, felt a connection with the French Canadian who spoke their language. The loss of Gilles Villeneuve, a spirited driver admired by many for his sheer speed, his determination never to give up, and his fearlessness and sense of fair play, was deeply felt throughout the sport around the world.

In Canada, among those who remember him or have heard about him, affection for this native son runs deep, and the emotion over his loss, deeper still. As retired executive and historic Formula One racer/owner Bud Moeller shares, when he races his 1980 Ferrari 312 T5 race car in Canada these days, a car driven in eight grands prix in the 1980 season, fans approach the car with emotion even now, decades after Villeneuve's passing.

> The car is an amazing piece of F1 history having been driven by both Gilles Villeneuve and Jody Scheckter. When we take the car to Canada to race at both the Canadian Grand Prix and Mont Tremblant it's always one of the fan favorites. Gilles died in a racing accident in 1982 and many Canadian fans still mourn him. There have been several instances of people who, upon seeing the car, come over and are in reverence of this historical connection with Gilles. Some weep, some kneel down to kiss the car, and others just stare in amazement as memories of Gilles flood through their heads. I'm honored to be a caretaker of this wonderful machine.[5]

Years later, after his memorable remarks at Villeneuve's funeral, Jody Scheckter still had high praise for his friend. Thirty years later he said, "More than anyone I've known, Gilles was in love with motor racing."[6]

At the time of Villeneuve's death, even the fans began to wonder about safety in the sport. A reader of *On Track* wrote this to the editor; the letter was published in the June 3, 1982, issue:

> "Seeking a Commitment"
>
> As all race drivers, Gilles Villeneuve was too young to die. I was among the thousands who loved to watch Gilles make the corner-workers' jaws drop as he attacked the circuit with his Prancing Horse. How many other "entertainers" can you name who put their life literally on the line every time they practice their talent?
>
> In the wake of his death, I would like now to see an immediate commitment by all the organizations in F1 to put safety ahead of spectacle. I realize that Gilles' death may not have been the result of the sheer speed he was traveling, but in all the crashes I have witnessed as a race fan, I have *never* seen a driver literally blown out of his harness.
>
> What is ahead for us in the way of horrible accidents when most of the F1 teams will have carbon fiber turbocharged ground-effect

rockets that would be more at home in Bonneville [salt flats, where world land-speed records are set] than the world's road courses and street circuits.

Please understand, M. Balestre [head of F1 at the time], and all of your cohorts, that we do not want to lose any more of our young heroes . . . we only want to see them in close competition and in cars that will not cross over the limits of survivability. Gilles' life has already been far too much to pay!

The editor's reply to this letter is most telling about how the organizers and fans of the era saw the relationship between danger and motor sport:

From what we can tell, the initial impact with the ground at the end of the first flip generated forces on the order of 9Gs, more than enough to stretch and snap a driver's neck, and obviously sufficient to rip the belts from their attachments on the monocoque [chassis]. We all share in the grief of his death, but regardless of the cause or the fault, every driver knows he is putting his life in peril every time he belts himself into the car. We do not feel that death need be an essential part of the sport, but without the risk the achievement is lessened.[7]

Adrenaline fuels the racing driver as it does athletes in other sports, of course. Some have accused racing drivers of being addicted to the stuff, as though the rush itself that courses through their bodies makes them want to repeat the experience of driving fast at high risk, of taking their cars to the limit, over and over again. Some drivers admit it. Others say that, at the professional level, there has to be something more than the thrill and body rush alone that keeps them at it, and certainly much more than that is required to make them successful.

Drivers who manage to make a career out of chasing speed are sometimes asked what else they may have done for an occupation in life if they did not become professional race car drivers. Some really do not know; this is all they've ever known. Some say probably something still to do with cars—mechanics or engineering, perhaps. Others may have had other interests before racing that are quite removed from it, like music with Villeneuve and François Cevert. Still others go on to other careers in business, farming, or other pursuits once they retire from their racing careers.

It is hard to envision what kind of future Gilles Villeneuve would have had if he had lived. Many say he would have certainly been Canada's first Formula One world champion racing driver, a feat achieved fifteen years after his death by his son. It is difficult to envision him going into a completely different line of work, as Jody Scheckter did—organic farming in his home country of South Africa.

For a man as driven and in love with racing as Gilles Villeneuve, one cannot help but wonder, in the end, if he was truly in the driver's seat all along or, instead, if speed was really driving him. Either way, Gilles Villeneuve has become a Canadian legend.

Racer: Joseph Gilles Henri Villeneuve (Canada), age thirty-two; b. January 18, 1950, in Saint-John-sur-Richelieu, Quebec, Canada; d. May 8, 1982, in Leuven, Belgium.

Career Highlights and Honors: Placed second in 1979 Formula One World Championship; winner, 1978 Canadian Grand Prix; winner, 1979 South African Grand Prix, United States Grand Prix West, United States Grand Prix; winner, 1981 Monaco Grand Prix and Spanish Grand Prix; inducted into Canada's Sports Hall of Fame, 1983; inducted into Canadian Motor Sports Hall of Fame, 1993; image on a Canadian postage stamp, 1997.

Among His Legacies: Beloved in Canada; Formula One grand prix track in Montreal renamed Circuit Gilles Villeneuve; several areas of racetracks named after him or feature painted Canadian flags or some other commemorative symbol—for example, corner and starting grid spot at Autodromo Enzo e Dino Ferrari (San Marino Grand Prix) in Italy, bronze statue at entrance to Ferrari test track at Fiorano, Italy; son, Jacques Villeneuve, raced and won 1995 Indy 500 and IndyCar (CART) championship and became 1997 Formula One world champion.

8

MYSTIC

Ayrton Senna

When people seek inspiration, they may take a walk in the woods or a stroll along the beach. They may engage in a craft or art to express a bit of their creative side and, in doing so, find new aspects of themselves in the process. Maybe they play music, or go out for a good dinner and lively conversation with friends, or snuggle up in their favorite armchair at home and read a great book. Church, prayer, or meditation work for some; others may find that spark they are looking for through an intense physical workout, playing their favorite sport, attending a conference, or doing volunteer work, serving as an inspiration for others. Some may visit museums or hike or camp in national parks. Others may get inspired by lying on the grass on a summer night, looking up at the wonder of the sparkling stars set against an ink-black sky.

If one were looking for inspiration on any given day, a racetrack full of roaring automobiles might not be the first place that would come to mind. After all, it is a noisy place, usually crowded, and the smells of burning fuel and rubber do not appeal to everyone. The place, in fact, can be a major turn-off for people who have no interest in motor racing whatsoever. However, hearing that one of the drivers racing that day is among the best and fastest in a generation, maybe ever, might change a person's mind about staying around. The suggestion that spectators might witness a drive that will send chills down their spines or give them goosebumps might change the desire to leave. Perhaps if a group of people new to racing were told they would likely see something that day that they have never seen before—an artist at the wheel, a man who was doing something more than driving, who transformed the experience into something more than a human being piloting a machine built by other human beings—that might pique more than a bit of interest. Before these people climbed into their cars to escape the racetrack where they may not want to be, if they caught a glimpse of this man at work—a human being doing his thing in life, which just happened to involve an automobile—well, who would not want to watch such a person, someone truly inspired in his work, whatever that work may be?

The Brazilian three-time Formula One world champion Ayrton Senna da Silva drove a race car like a man possessed—not by the devil, though sometimes an aggressive move here or there may have led his opponents to wonder about that, but by a mission. Senna, who kept his mother's name for his racing, since da Silva was such a common last name in Brazil, could do things with a car that most drivers do not even dream about. Not only did he have great talent, speed, and excellent control, but it was as though he was finding new territory together with the machine—not fighting the car to get it to go where he wanted it to go but rather discovering with the car and himself inside it where they both could go for the best possible result around this corner, down that straight, leaning into this turn, or wrangling that maneuver or pass. He grew up enjoying sports and competitiveness, certainly; however, race car driving was more than a sport to Ayrton Senna—it was a pathway to somewhere higher, somewhere divine.

Born into a wealthy family that could afford to support his interests in a country ravaged by poverty, Senna left Brazil in the early 1980s for the heart of international open-wheel racing in Europe. He was not new to the continent—he had started racing karts in Brazil at the age of thirteen and had competed in karting championships there. Cars, however, were a new challenge, but he said that he was ready. In Europe, though he was noticed for his speed, he also often faced criticism. A devout Catholic, Senna sometimes spoke about God or his faith in interviews, which prompted the press and other racers to claim that he felt protected by God in his racing, that he thought he was infallible. He certainly drove that way, fearlessly, even in his early years in Formula Three on his way up to Formula One. By 1994, at the age of twenty-four, he was offered a seat in Formula One, though for a less competitive team called Toleman. Smaller teams tend to have fewer funds to work with and slower cars as a result. They tend to give their drivers experience racing behind the leaders of the pack, from the back.

Driving in his rookie year for Toleman at the Monaco Grand Prix of 1984, Senna gave the spectators on site and television viewers around the world a sampling of what he could do, even in a noncompetitive car. Rain, it is said in motor sport, equalizes the faster and slower cars and puts more emphasis on the skills of the drivers to keep the cars not only on the road but racing, despite the loss of grip. All teams in Formula One run with rain tires, "wets" as they are called, when the conditions call for them. These tires have deep treads that literally push the water on the road away from the cars—the rooster-tail spray, the sheer quantity of water, thrown back and away behind a Formula One car on a terribly rainy day is a sight to behold in person. On this day, a few unlucky results for other drivers worked in Senna's favor.

Monaco is the shining jewel every year on the Formula One racing calendar. Drivers like it for its challenge—it was, and remains, entirely a street circuit running through the glamorous city of Monte Carlo and along its harbor on the Mediterranean Sea. The streets are narrow, with none of the runoff areas or room for error now built into the newer Formula One racing circuits around the world. Qualifying at Monaco is thought to be even more important than at other races, since overtaking on the narrow, twisty roads between high walls and buildings and even through a tunnel is nearly impossible. Certainly, success at passing more than one car along the way becomes highly doubtful. Add to these challenges the factor of cars losing grip on the road in rainy conditions, and a stellar drive there becomes all the more spectacular.

In the 1984 race, with the rainy conditions being so bad, several cars retired, leaving a field of only eight that would eventually complete the race. Alain Prost (France) was leading as he had from his pole position. In his inferior car, Ayrton Senna had started in thirteenth place on the grid. Some of Senna's race came to him through the attrition of retiring cars; however, the young driver still made passes by apparently being more confident in the rain than some of those still on the track. Once he had some road room ahead of him, he started gaining on Prost's time by the measure of three or four seconds per lap. It is widely believed that at the rate he was going, he would have caught up to the leader and quite possibly passed him and won the race.

Alas, that was not to happen. Prost put his hand up with a few laps to go. This was an indication that he thought the conditions were so poor that the driving was unsafe and that he was asking that officials stop the race. The television commentators and other people watching could see how Senna was gaining on Prost, so while they agreed that the conditions were bad, an argument was made that as the water does not tend to collect on the streets of Monaco, there might be reason to keep going. In the end, Prost got his wish: a (notably) French official in charge—head of the governing body, the Federation Internationale de l'Automobile (FIA), Jean-Marie Balestre—put an end to the race.

Senna had been steadily gaining on Prost's McLaren in his Toleman car. When the red flag went out, stopping the race, Prost slowed down in his approach to the finish line, then stopped right there. Thinking he might still have a chance, Senna crossed the line at speed, throwing his arm up in the air in victory as though he had won the race. It was determined that Prost's car had indeed crossed the line before Senna's; however, Senna had announced his arrival in Formula One as a likely future champion and certainly as a racer to be reckoned with in the future. The incident also set in motion what would become an intense rivalry between these two drivers. Sometime later, Senna told Jacky Ickx (Belgium), a retired Formula One racer who had served as clerk of the course that day, that he agreed that the right call of the race due to weather was made in Monaco that day.[1]

Senna made his move to the Lotus team in 1985, but it was not until he moved from Lotus to become Prost's teammate on the British team of McLaren in 1988 that their famed rivalry really heated up. So dramatic was the competition between the Frenchman and the Brazilian that it is said to have driven up television ratings and other signs of interest in Formula One motor racing at the time. Years later, the famous rivalry became a major part of an award-winning documentary feature film about Senna's life, *Senna*, released in 2012. Senna won the Formula One World Championship in 1988, 1990, and 1991, all racing for McLaren. Prost won it in 1985, 1986, and 1989 for McLaren and again in 1993 for Williams.

There were several differences between the two drivers. Senna was newer on the scene; he was Brazilian, somewhat of an outsider in the European-based international racing scene. He was just five years younger than Prost, but even that many years can make a sizeable

Ayrton Senna. *International Motor Racing Research Center/National Speed Sport News Collection.*

difference in background, training, and so forth, at the highest level of any international sport. Another factor was the influence Senna had from rising up through the various racing levels to Formula One, starting in karting as a teenager. Karting is safer, of course, than automobile racing. Young drivers slide their karts, which are low to the ground, through corners. They make contact with each other fairly regularly; it is part of the game. They make their way around the course trying to beat everyone else through skill, speed, and strategy. Senna was one of the first Formula One racers to bring this karting technique of going head-to-head, as it were, of allowing the cars to touch one another, to grand prix races.

By the time Senna came on the scene in the world's premier racing series, Alain Prost had already been there for four years. He raced for McLaren starting in 1980, switched to the French team, Renault, for the 1981 to 1983 seasons, then moved back to McLaren in 1984. Each season, he was continually improving toward a world championship in overall points. In 1980, for example, he finished the season in sixteenth place; in 1981 he was fifth; in 1982, fourth; and in both 1983 and 1984, second. This made the rivalry with an upstart on the scene all the more compelling for both competitors and fans alike. Prost must have certainly believed that he had by now paid his dues and was deserving of a championship. Also, Prost was just enough older than Senna and of a European upbringing rather than Brazilian that he was arguably more influenced by the older fashion of race car driving, which was distinctly different from karting at that time. Though Prost also competed in karting and won championships as a teen, he was perhaps more attuned to the expectations of grand prix racing, coming in fact, as the grand prix did, from France. He was also well connected and more politically oriented than Senna. Known as "The Professor," Prost was quick, but he was also thought to be calculating, planning moves and points to win a championship. Senna just went flat-out to win each race.

Senna's pushing in a race, not only of himself and the car but also sometimes of his opponent, as done in karting, was a newer strategy in the sport at that time. Formula One had gone through such a dangerous period in the 1950s, 1960s, and 1970s that contact between two cars was certainly thought of by most drivers, and the rules, as something to be avoided. One touch, and both cars could not only spin out of the race but also out of control of the drivers; it was also highly likely that there would be serious harm done to both human and machine. Part of the challenge for drivers with that way of thinking was to see just how close they could get to opponents without touching. The best drivers kept control to within inches, or even fractions of inches at some points.

Fans' feelings about some of the key races between these two drivers in their intense rivalry tended to side one way or the other. The Prost followers, for example, found Senna arrogant and an unfair player who tried to shove Prost out of his way when he did not have the right to do so. Instead of biding his time in the series, racing hard but paying respect to the older, more seasoned racers, Senna, in their view, was out to beat Prost as his targeted rival as soon and as badly as he possibly could. It was a matter not only of winning to Senna, so went the argument against him among Prost fans, but also of destroying his opposition to prove a point.

The more passionate Senna fans liked that Senna gave his all in every race. He did not sit back and calculate how many points he would need in this race or that to stay in contention for the championship. Points would be awarded, for example, not just for wins but also for second, third, and fourth place finishes, and so on. In other words, one need not win the race to earn points toward the championship. Some drivers, rather than take a chance on a difficult or dangerous pass that might result in an accident putting them out of the race entirely, would calculate that they would be better off finishing the race in a position somewhere behind first and taking the points. Instead of doing the math and driving for points, Senna went out each and every time to win the race outright. He drove with passion and determination, accordingly. If contact came as a result of that, well, to Senna that was simply part of racing. A driver like Senna tends to be, of course, more exciting to watch because he is taking risks that may take him out of the race, leaving him with no points at all. Fans of the sport tend to enjoy the all-or-nothing approach most. Still, fans vary in their opinions on strategy.

Senna raced just as passionately, however, even when he was out front in a race with little competition coming up behind him. In the 1988 Monaco Grand Prix, for example, Senna drove a shattering performance on the tricky circuit. He drove so fast, so precisely, and so consistently that even watching the drive on television at the time or on video since, it is almost impossible to believe. He said later that he reached a nirvana-like state of concentration in that performance. Unfortunately, his concentration was broken by McLaren actually asking him to slow down. He was so far in front of his teammate Prost in second place, nearly a full minute, that he had no need to drive that hard to win the race. With just a few laps left in the race, which he was going to win, the break in concentration caused him to lose control of the car. He hit the guardrail along the Mediterranean side of the circuit and was out of the race entirely as a result.

Senna said later that he learned an important lesson that day. Furious with himself, rather than going back to the paddock, he walked to his apartment in Monaco and thought things over for a couple of hours. He said that he had experienced a race that was so close to perfection that he had allowed himself to relax, leading to a mistake. He then needed some time to work on and regain his confidence, but once it returned, he was stronger as a result. He went on to win six of the next eight races that season. He also said in the press that the experience had brought him closer to God, which, he shared, was very important to him as a man.

Finally, at the 1988 Japanese Grand Prix, Senna won his first world championship in Formula One. He made several passes from back in the pack to work his way toward the front, when it began to rain, a feature that always worked in his favor. Eventually, he made a clean, fair pass of Prost and took over the lead, winning the race and the title. The Brazilians back home cheered as he raised the Brazilian flag in honor of his country. He said that on the last lap he felt the presence of God, that he "saw God." These were the kinds of comments that left some fans puzzled or cynical; others felt wonder, amazement. What was he talking about?

In the 1989 season, Senna and Prost were running close in points to each other in the championship. At the Japanese Grand Prix at Suzuka yet again, the championship could be decided. In the points, if Senna did not finish the race, Prost would win. Prost took an early lead, with Senna close behind. Senna went to make a pass, and Prost appeared to cut him off at the corner—Prost fans said that Senna caused an accident by trying to pass where there was not enough room. Both cars edged over to the slip road alongside the track and stopped. Prost got out of his car, thinking both McLaren cars were now retired and that he had won the title. Instead, Senna got his car going again and raced it to the

Ayrton Senna drives a McLaren. *International Motor Racing Research Center/National Speed Sport News Collection.*

pits. There he got the car tended to and rejoined the race, this time now behind another car. Eventually, he passed the leader and won the race.

Of course, this did not go down well with Alain Prost, whose championship was jeopardized by his retirement due to the mix-up with Senna. The Frenchman immediately walked to the control tower and filed a complaint. A strange regulation stipulated that if a car goes down the slip road (a short runoff area where a car in trouble can exit the track and get back on), it must turn around in the reverse direction and exit it to rejoin the race. The Senna camp argued that this policy was unsafe. The debate wore on, but it did not, in the end, change the outcome. Prost won the title in 1989, and Senna received a hefty fine, levied by FIA head Jean-Marie Balestre, for causing an accident. Senna held on to a deep feeling that, once again, he had been treated unfairly by Prost and people he saw as Prost's French cronies. One small advantage came his way, however, at the end of that season. Prost moved on from the McLaren team to Ferrari.

An incident in the 1990 season foreshadowed what would happen later in Senna's career. At the Spanish Grand Prix in Jerez, a driver from Northern Ireland, Martin Donnelly, driving for Lotus, suffered a serious accident during qualifying. The event shook Senna up; he felt it necessary to go to the scene of the crash and see what had happened. This is not normally allowed, but Senna showed up at the scene, not out of a sick desire to look at trouble but because he knew that accidents were a part of racing and he wanted to learn as much as he could about this darker side of the sport. He had never been involved in a race where an accident had been so damaging, and he wanted to face for himself what could happen, to look into the abyss, as it were. The accident was a bad one indeed—so bad, in fact, that it took Donnelly out of Formula One with injuries to his brain and lung and damage so bad to his leg that it almost required amputation. The driver lived, however, and much later competed for a year in the British Touring Car series. In his quest to learn, Senna asked the medical staff later on what they had done in working with Donnelly and why, and how a driver coming up on a crash scene could be of any help in a similar situation. The incident also contributed to Senna's increasing interest in driver safety, a campaign he found important and on which he wished to continue working.

The famous rivalry then driving much of the popularity of Formula One the world over raged on between Senna and Prost, despite their now driving for different teams. It was time for the 1990 Japanese Grand Prix, and the two were yet again close in the championship points from races each had won or placed high in all season. If Prost did not finish the race this time, Senna would win the title. The idea about how unsafe it was to reverse a car that goes down the slip road came up in the drivers' meeting. The drivers agreed that it was an unsafe rule, and it was changed. Senna got up and left the meeting, incredulous that this was happening after all he had gone through the year before, when the rules worked against him. Another problem that weekend was that he had gotten pole position on the grid. This was normally a plus, of course, but a decision was made, purportedly with Balestre's assistance, to move the pole position to the "dirty" side of the track, which would give Prost the advantage at the start by giving his tires better grip on the pavement. Senna had had enough of what he saw as politics and favoritism for Prost. He was not going to put up with it again.

This time, when the race started, Prost got the early lead, with Senna close behind. At the first turn, Senna again tried to pass on the inside, and a collision between him and Prost ensued, driving them both off the track yet again. Senna won his second championship, but his methods were definitely questioned. Notable among the doubters was three-time world champion Jackie Stewart, then working as a racing commentator. He interviewed Senna and mentioned that the Brazilian had had more contact with opponents than all the previous champions combined. By this time, of course, Stewart had retired from racing, but he was still highly concerned with safety in the sport. Senna challenged him back, saying, "If you no longer go for a gap that exists, you are no longer a racing driver because we are competing; we are competing to win."[2] Senna had his second world championship to Prost's three, but it was one that the Brazilian could not enjoy with a totally clear conscience.

All this time, over many races in Formula One, one prize remained elusive for Ayrton Senna: he had yet to win the Brazilian Grand Prix; he had yet to win at home. A regime in his country was driving the poor into more and more desperate circumstances. Millions of Brazilians followed Senna's racing career because he was a proud Brazilian on the world stage rather than an embarrassed one who hid his nationality, and his success and national pride gave them hope at a time when little else did. News of his philanthropic work with children during the off-season spread as well, though at this time Senna was helping on a more sporadic basis, when people asked for it, rather than in the organized fashion that would develop later.

"There is a great desire in me of improving," Senna said, "getting better. That makes me happy." He continued,

> Every time that I feel I am slowing down my learning process, my learning curve is getting flat, or whatever, then it doesn't make me very happy. That applies not only as a professional, as a racing driver but as a man. Of course, I shall have a lot more to learn as a man than as a racing driver because my career could last . . . not many years. My life, hopefully, will go still for a long time. Maybe I am only at half of my life right now. There is a lot to go, a lot to learn, a lot to do still in life. Happiness will come when I feel complete as a whole, which definitely I don't feel today, but I have plenty of time to fulfill that, too.

In 1991, Senna was on pole for his nation's grand prix in São Paulo, his hometown. He got out to an early lead, and it looked like it was going to be an easy win for him, finally, in this race of all races for him at home.

Ayrton Senna, suited up for McLaren, 1992. *International Motor Racing Research Center/National Speed Sport News Collection.*

With a few laps to go, however, Senna's gearbox in the McLaren jammed, leaving him with only sixth gear to drive the rest of the race. People thought it would be impossible. With much physical exertion, Senna kept driving the car as fast as possible. When he crossed the finish line, he stayed in the car, in obvious discomfort. He was suffering severe pain from muscle spasms in his neck and shoulders.

With great effort, he finally made it up to the podium. He knew how important and symbolic this win was for his country. He tried once to lift the trophy for the viewing benefit of his countrymen, but visible pain brought his partially raised arms down again. Finally, putting the trophy in one hand, he hoisted it high above his head with one arm. The crowd cheered and got their time to finally celebrate their racing hero's win at home. Later that year, again at the Japanese Grand Prix, but without Prost racing because Ferrari had released him for criticizing the car, Senna also won the 1991 world championship. The same year that he won his home grand prix, Senna also took home his third world title. Now he and Prost were equals, with three world championships each.

WHAT HAPPENED

One of the key strategies for a racing driver is to have a good sense of which team is building the fastest car in any given year. While a strong driver can often get more out of an inferior car than an inferior driver can, he or she cannot work miracles with it. This is how dynasties form in Formula One, where a single team and driver or drivers will dominate the series for years—the best drivers are always seeking out the teams with the best cars, and vice versa. For the 1994 season, Senna determined that a move to Williams was a good idea. After the Brazilian's title win in 1991, Williams had gone on to take the Constructors' Championship in 1992 and 1993, with its team drivers Nigel Mansell (UK) and Alain Prost, respectively, winning the Drivers' Championships. Prost had gone one up again on Senna; the Frenchman now had four world titles to Senna's three. Prost did it in a Williams car. What made the move to Williams even more enticing to Senna was that Alain Prost retired from racing that year. Prost's contract with Williams was up, and he learned that Senna might be joining the team. Pushing forty,

Prost was not up for another round of close rivalry with Senna as a teammate.

Electronics were making a game-changing shift in the abilities of the cars. Williams was ahead of the curve on using them, especially in electronic suspensions, hence the team's advantage over the last two years. Senna believed that a driver facing what he called "the electronic war" was "stuck." He said it didn't matter who was put in the car; the electronics did all the work, anyway. Still, it was the way things were going, and the way things work was that the best driver on the grid would seek out the team with the fastest car, and vice versa. Unfortunately, the year Senna left his beloved McLaren team on good terms and went with Williams, the rules were changed for the racing series, as frequently happens even today, and electronics in certain parts of the cars were banned by the governing body of the sport. This left Williams scrambling to work out several problems in their car for the 1994 season. Instead of finding himself in the fastest car, as he had thought, Senna now found himself working as a development driver, helping the team figure out the problems the car was having under the sport's new regulations.

Along with the generational shift in car technology, a new racer had appeared on the scene as well—a quick German by the name of Michael Schumacher. Driving for a team called Benetton, Schumacher won both of the first two races in 1994, in Senna's beloved Brazil and in Japan. In fact, not only had Senna not won either of the first two races of the 1994 season, but he had yet to even score a point, something that was highly unusual and certainly worrying for the three-time world champion in his first season with a new team. Not only that, but Senna had watched Schumacher in the Benetton and was convinced that the Benetton team was breaking the rules, that the car had traction control that eliminated wheel spin, which was enabling the already talented Schumacher to go far and away ahead of the rest of the field. Senna asked the Williams team to issue a protest against Benetton, but the team did not.

When the traveling circus of Formula One moved on to Imola, Italy, for the San Marino Grand Prix, the problems with the Williams car were still not resolved. Senna reported back to engineering that the car was not balanced; it changed its behavior in the middle of a corner—one of the worst things a car can do in the hands of any driver. Understeer and oversteer within the same corner gave the driver the signal that the car did not have integrity; that is, it could not be trusted because the driver could not predict what it would do. Fast or slow, a car needs to respond to the driver's handling of it, or he or she loses faith in it. A driver who does not like the car cannot and will not feel safe in it and will lose concentration. Rather than use it as a tool to go fast, to strategize in the race and stay focused on winning, the driver is fighting with the car and cannot understand what is happening because it is not responding to the driver's commands. It is not trustworthy. Behaving unpredictably, the car seems to have a "mind" of its own.

The weekend of April 30 and May 1, 1994, saw several accidents at Imola. It was almost as though Senna's God were trying to tell him, and everybody else, that something was dreadfully wrong. Senna was already acting worried and concerned about the car. He was under a lot of pressure to gain championship points that weekend, or the season might very well get away from him completely. He had to face the prospect of racing a car that he did not trust against a competitor he thought was cheating. It was already not going to be a good weekend for the champion.

The first incident happened when rookie Rubens Barrichello, a young Brazilian who looked up to Senna, had a bad crash in practice in his Jordan team car. Senna watched the replay on a television screen in the garage and looked visibly concerned. With the help of Formula One doctor Sid Watkins, a fatherly figure with white hair and glasses and a close friend of Senna's, Barrichello came out all right from the crash. It looked much worse than it turned out to be in terms of physical harm to the driver. Again, as he had done with Martin Donnelly years before, Senna went to the medical center himself to see the young Brazilian. At first he was not allowed in, but he got in anyway. He wanted to see for himself how his fellow countryman was; then he reassured the fearful Brazilians waiting for word that Barrichello was all right. The next incident of the weekend, unfortunately, did not turn out as lucky.

The next day, during qualifying, Roland Ratzenberger (Austria), driving for the Simtek team with a large MTV logo on the side of his car, also had a horrible crash. Again, watching on a television screen back in the garage, Senna took off his helmet and balaclava and grimaced at the sight of Ratzenberger's head bobbing loosely side to side as the car finally came to a stop. Dr. Sid Watkins and his team worked on the Austrian, and when Senna saw the frightening image of CPR, the pumping of the Ratzenberger's chest to try to revive him, he knew how bad it was and turned away, visibly shaken. This time, he was not allowed into the medical center when he went to check on the hurt driver. Unfortunately, Ratzenberger passed away from his injuries.

Sid Watkins talked with Senna. When he told him what had happened, Senna got upset and cried. Unlike so many of his ancestor champions in Formula One, Senna had won three world championships without experiencing a single fatality of a racing colleague. Unlike competitors in decades earlier, when death was almost another regular, ghostly opponent to race against on the track, no one of his generation had lived with that so far. Ratzenberger's death hit Senna hard. When Watkins saw how emotional he was, he asked his friend to not race the next day. Watkins described his conversation with his friend later. When not at the racetrack, both men liked to fish:

> It hit him very, very hard. That's when I said to him, "Ayrton, I don't think you should race," I said, "what's more, I've got a better idea. You've been the World Champion three times; everybody knows you are the fastest guy on wheels; you're a very rich man. Why don't you give it up? If you do that, I'll give it up and we'll both go fishing."[3]

Watkins said he knew better than to push Senna for an immediate response. He waited. Finally, after giving it some thought, Senna said, "No, Sid; I can't stop; I have to go on." The next morning, race morning, at the drivers' meeting, there was a moment of silence out of respect for Ratzenberger, and Watkins noticed Senna getting visibly upset again. He knew in his heart that his friend should not get in a race car that day.

Also on race morning, in an ironic twist of fate, Senna met with his old teammate and now retired rival Alain Prost. Senna wanted to pursue driver safety, especially in light of the tragedy the day before and also in view of the increasing instability of the cars and so many crashes overall that weekend. The two were considering bringing back the Grand Prix Drivers' Association set up decades earlier to address these and other concerns.

Car problems and all, Senna had managed to fight and win his battle with the Williams car enough to qualify it on pole for the May 1, 1994, San Marino Grand Prix. Footage of Senna in his Williams car awaiting the start of the race on the grid shows him looking particularly reflective and concerned, even worried. His sister, Viviane, would say later that he had read his Bible that morning, praying for guidance, and what he read was "God would give him the greatest of all gifts, which was God himself."

At the start of the race that bright, sunny day, yet another accident took place. This time, a driver by the name of J. J. Lehto (Finland) stalled his Benetton on the grid, but another driver, Pedro Lamy (Portugal), driving for Lotus, had his view of the stalled car obstructed by other cars and momentarily ran into the stationary driver at starting speed. Both drivers were all right, but debris flew around the track. The track needed to be cleaned up, and the race restarted. It was the third accident of the weekend. Still, it might be said, those who needed to listen to this cosmic message were choosing to race anyway.

Finally, the race started again. Senna was in front, with Michael Schumacher chasing him in second in the Benetton. On lap six of the fifty-eight-lap race, Senna steered left to take Tamburello Corner at Imola. The corner was known for being a dangerous one where others had crashed before. In fact, in his efforts at racing safety, Senna had looked at the geographic layout of the corner with others to determine if it could be made safer but was shown that there was a river behind it and nowhere to build a runoff. Senna suffered a mechanical failure in the car. It did not make the turn but instead drove straight off the track into the wall.

Dr. Sid Watkins and his crew arrived quickly on the scene. Watkins said that, after immediately examining his condition and making an airway, even though the driver had no bruises or broken bones, he knew this was going to be a fatal accident. In a few moments, he said, Senna emitted a deep sigh. Though he was not religious, Watkins said, he could not help but think this was Senna's spirit being released from his body.

As bad an accident as it was, it was later determined that the Brazilian might have survived had it not been for a freak angle of the suspension shaft penetrating his helmet. Had it struck inches away in one direction or another, Senna could have walked away from the accident. Of course, the search for a cause began immediately and continued for some time afterward. It was found that the steering shaft had been altered before the race; maybe that had malfunctioned, and Senna could not steer. Perhaps the temperature of the tires was to blame—

they had cooled during the time between the first start of the race and the second. Few if any blamed the driver. Something mechanical most certainly had gone wrong. The great Brazilian champion, some said the greatest racing driver of his generation if not of all time, was gone.

AFTERMATH

At that time, Brazil did not have a high international profile. Senna represented his country on the world stage. Rather than hide the fact that he came from Brazil when he went to Europe and became successful, he never forgot where he came from or how much so many of his people at home were suffering. He carried the Brazilian flag in victory. He went home and helped through charitable donations. In many ways, Senna became a saintlike figure to poor Brazilians. He gave them hope. If this seems like an overstatement, one only need consider the outpouring of love he was shown when his body arrived back in his country after the tragedy at Imola.

The Brazilian government proclaimed three days of national mourning at the death of the racing hero. At the airport, Senna's coffin was loaded onto a fire truck that then drove down a wide, multilane highway toward the city, with all lanes crowded with cars behind it. Reports said as many as three million people paid tribute along the road, on bridges over the road, and hanging out of building windows. They stood in silence or waved banners, signs, and flags. Many cried; others threw flowers as his coffin rode into the city.

Senna's casket, covered with the Brazilian flag with his racing helmet on top, lay in state at the São Paulo state assembly for twenty-four hours. People waited for seven and eight hours at a time for the chance to pay their respects. An estimated eight thousand people filed past the casket every hour. Some lay trinkets or memorials nearby. People of all ages cried, held one another, blessed themselves in prayer, and otherwise showed how much this man meant to them and their country.

Pallbearers made up of racers, including Jackie Stewart, Emerson Fittipaldi, Alain Prost, Rubens Barrichello, and others, carried Senna's body to his gravesite at Morumbi Cemetery in São Paulo. The head of the FIA at that time, Max Mosley, attended Ratzenberger's funeral instead, to compensate for the lack of attention, relatively, given his

death on the same weekend. After Senna's graveside service, the Brazilian air force flew overhead, creating a heart with a signature Senna *S*
over it in colored smoke in the sky. His gravestone includes an inscrip-
tion that reads, in Portuguese, *Nada pode me separar do amor de Deus*
("Nothing can separate me from the love of God").[4]

LEGACY

No doubt Senna's greatest legacy is that his work in helping disadvantaged children in Brazil continues in a formalized way to this day. The
Ayrton Senna Institute, the nonprofit organization that the driver set in
motion before he died, has now been running for over twenty years. To
date, the institute aids in the education of more than 1.9 million children annually. It also supports the emergence of seventy thousand education professionals per year. The Ayrton Senna Institute operates in
seventeen states and more than 660 municipalities. Funds to support
the program come from donations, licensing of the Senna logo and
other products, and partnerships with other private-sector groups. Children in Brazil today, just like their parents and grandparents who followed his racing, definitely know who Ayrton Senna is.[5]

Senna's legacy in motor racing, of course, can hardly be overstated.
After his death, safety at racetracks, in cars, in the rules, and in many
other ways was again reconsidered vigorously in the sport of Formula
One racing. Sid Watkins, in fact, was tasked with looking into this again
for the sport. When a world champion driver dies on a racetrack, and a
multiple world champion at that, it is usually, though not always, found
to be a mechanical error and not a driver mistake. Of course, the
Williams team underwent much improvement and testing of its cars.
The electronic age in motor racing continued and in fact only expanded.

Senna has also inspired fans, other drivers, organizers, and simply
those who hear about his life and career. Whether they continue to
admire him as fans, or driving schools teach studied tactics from his
driving style, or people in the paddock or the grandstands share their
personal stories or remembrances of him and his racing, he continues to
be a figure of lively interest in the sport. Some professional drivers, like
three-time Formula One world champion Lewis Hamilton (UK), admit
Senna is an active and lasting inspiration for what they do today.

Thousands of amateur racers, too, have been influenced by watching Ayrton Senna. Retired engineer and historic racer/owner Marc Giroux (U.S.) is just one of these. He saw Senna race in person against Prost at Hockenheim when Giroux was working in Germany. "At the time, I was mostly impressed by Senna's driving skill," Giroux said. He elaborated on how Senna's car appeared on the track:

> His car seemed to dance because he had it at the limit of physics so much of the time. There is a difference in how a car appears at the limit: it "hunts" ever so slightly. Well, sometimes it gets completely "out of shape" which means that the direction the car is moving and the direction it is pointing are pretty different. But typically, it just looks a little light on its feet and dances around a bit. [6]

A few years later, Giroux passed his racing test and bought a race car, then another. He is still out on the track competing today. Interestingly, he was able to purchase a custom-designed helmet for himself by Senna's own helmet designer, Sid Mosca. As much as Giroux admired Senna's driving style and skill, he admits that the mystique of Senna goes beyond the Brazilian's stellar ability with a car. "Another factor is no doubt his early death," Giroux said.

> It makes somebody stay seemingly frozen in time, so they don't have the inevitable decline in performance or ungraceful aging. In the subsequent years, I read his biography and was impressed by his involvement with Brazilian kids, but honestly that came after I was impressed with his driving. I guess that will be his most important legacy, aided by his racing notoriety.

Giroux sums up what many people involved or interested in motor racing say about Ayrton Senna, "I guess my admiration of him comes from a pretty simple basis: he was a hell of a driver!"

Senna continues to be an inspirational figure for Brazilians and for motor racing fans and participants all around the world. As a man of faith, perhaps he saw a higher calling through his motor racing, particularly as he became more and more successful with it and achieved some of his own personal goals. Racing, or celebrity and money from any global pursuit, could be a means through which someone like Senna could accomplish more in the world, such as helping the disadvantaged children of his country. Perhaps, if he did believe he had a calling, that may have led him to appear arrogant or entitled at times or to be aggressive on the racetrack in ways that not everyone thought was always fair. If he saw himself as having a mission, maybe he felt he had an extra incentive to win. In any case, no one will know what the man, just thirty-four years old when he died, might have accomplished in and for racing and for the people of Brazil, had he lived. In the end, all that is known for sure is that Senna's legacy is one of the few forces that outraced him.

Racer: Ayrton Senna da Silva (Brazil), age thirty-four; b. March 21, 1960, in São Paulo, Brazil; d. May 1, 1994, Bologna, Italy.

Career Highlights and Honors: Three-time Formula One world champion (1988, 1990, 1991).

Among His Legacies: Increased safety measures at tracks and in race cars; the Instituto Ayrton Senna (Ayrton Senna Institute) established as a philanthropic organization to aid disadvantaged children through education; award-winning 2012 documentary film *Senna* based on the racer's life and career; nationalistic pride in Brazil.

9

REBEL

Dale Earnhardt

Intimidation—it may or may not have a place in the world, depending on a person's worldview. One might say, for example, that a prosecutor, convinced of the guilt of a defendant accused of domestic terrorism, might do some good when she verbally intimidates an evasive witness for the defense in a courtroom. Perhaps there is a role for measured intimidation when a disrespectful teen needs to be reminded how to behave in the home or classroom, on the ballfield, or at his first workplace. Sometimes a perceived threat, not of violence or physical harm but of some kind of unpleasant outcome that the individual does not want to happen—a decrease in popularity or income or favor or progress of some kind—is enough to deter someone from doing harm to someone else, or from taking advantage of a situation, or from arriving late all the time, or from hogging all the dessert in the dining room. When competitors intimidate one another in the world of sport, those individuals are projecting a sense that they are superior in talent and ability, that they can beat their opponents, and most of all that they can win the trophies and all the prize money and take them home to polish and spend as they please. When those competitors are race car drivers, intimidating actions on the track might suggest that they will do anything they can to win, even if it means the other drivers lose their cars or their health. Aggressive drivers are perceived to be willing to take risks that others might not, to put their own and others' cars and personal safety on the line, to nearly wreck all who are in the way, if need be, in the process of crossing that finish line first.

Hank Jones, a NASCAR souvenir entrepreneur, claims to have come up with the now famed nickname "The Intimidator" for stock car driver Dale Earnhardt Sr. At first Jones tried putting "The Dominator" on T-shirts and other paraphernalia that he was offering for sale at racetracks, but since Earnhardt was not particularly dominant on the track in the period when Jones was doing this, the stuff did not sell. Jones said Earnhardt was pressing his competitors out on the racetrack, trying to make passes, even if he was not winning races, so Jones tried printing the new moniker "The Intimidator" on his Earnhardt products instead.

"Dale didn't like it," Jones said, "but it worked."[1] Given this history, in addition to his popularity, it is perhaps no accident that, these days, Earnhardt's son Dale Jr.'s section of the souvenir tent "mall" at NAS-CAR races is the largest display of souvenirs of any single driver. In any case, the nickname "The Intimidator" stuck with Earnhardt Sr. throughout the rest of his career. If it is true that the driver did not particularly like it, then perhaps that is one of many indications of the complexity of his character.

Earnhardt was one of those guys whose public persona tended to divide fans' opinions—he was often described as a driver people either loved or hated, "a man who was, in many ways, a series of impossible contradictions—both a hero and a villain."[2] He had a hard exterior that he rarely allowed anyone to penetrate. Those who knew Dale Earnhardt describe a different man from the tough sort of take-no-prisoners guy others saw on television.

NASCAR driver and television commentator Michael Waltrip (U.S.) described Earnhardt's story as the "American Dream": "You grow up. You admire your father and believe that, if you work hard, anything is possible. Dale proved that."[3] Ralph Dale Earnhardt was a child of the American South, the Southeast in particular, the motherland of stock car racing. He was born on April 29, 1951, in the mill town of Kannapolis, North Carolina, at that time the kind of place where either your parents worked at the mill, or your brother or sister, your aunt or uncle, or most of the people you knew did. Life in a company town revolves around the prosperity, or lack of it, of that business and factory since it is the basis of the livelihoods of most of the people who live there. Talk in diners turns to contracts and gossip about middle and upper manag-

Dale Earnhardt prepares himself for action on the track. *International Motor Racing Research Center/National Speed Sport News Collection.*

ers, about orders and whether production is up or down or sales are steady. Every nuance about the company, whether true or not, impacted life in Kannapolis in the 1950s, just as it still does in company towns all over America to this day.

Both Earnhardt's father and Earnhardt himself could have very likely worked all their lives, like so most of their townspeople did, as "linters"—factory workers at the local mill. Cannon Mills sheets and towels made in Kannapolis have touched the skin of sleepers, cooks, and bathers across the United States and around the world for decades. Founded by James William Cannon, the company spun its own cotton into yarn and instead of shipping it north, as most southern companies did in the nineteenth century, Cannon wove the yarn into its own material and called it Cannon Cloth. In 1890, the company made its first towels, a product that would make its name especially when the weave changed to the terry or Turkish variety. By the end of World War I, Cannon was the largest towel manufacturer in the United States.[4] Cannon's success led to growth through the acquisition of other mills, including Coleman Mills in Concord, North Carolina, which had been founded by a former slave. In 1906, the company purchased six hundred acres of land a few miles north of the first factory. There, Cannon constructed a company town, including a school and houses that workers could rent.

Dale Earnhardt's father quit the mill to go racing, so like many other drivers, the more famous Earnhardt was born into a racing family. His father, Ralph, after whom he was named, had also quit school to drive cars around dirt tracks in the area. Ralph had a style—since he owned and built and rebuilt his own family car for racing, he needed the machine to come home in one piece without severe damage. Rather than scramble for the front throughout the race and risk damage to the car, he held back for a little while. When the race neared its conclusion, he made a run for the finish line, passing cars in front of him right and left. When Ralph's method succeeded, he took prize money home to his family. When it didn't, at least he didn't have to tow home a wreck that he'd spend the rest of the week before the next race fixing up with money he did not have.

Ralph had figured out a trick in the shop that helped him win. A lot of the drivers were competing in Fords with a truck back that had a small axle key that kept breaking. Ralph figured out that if he configured a Craftsman screwdriver of a certain type and replaced the flimsy axle key with that, it did not break. This not only saved his car over and over again but also gave him a competitive advantage when other drivers continued to have problems. Once the other drivers figured out what Ralph Earnhardt was doing, they tried to buy the same screwdrivers to make the same fix. When they got to the store, however, they found that Ralph had already bought up all supplies of that size tool in the area.

Dale grew up standing on a truck, watching his father race. He also joined in as he got older, helping with the car in the garage, then at the track. When school got too boring compared to the excitement of the racetrack, he wanted to drop out, just like his daddy had. Ralph did not want his son to make the same mistake he had and urged him to stay in school. It was tough making ends meet on racing money; plus it took money to race in the first place. Ralph had dropped out in the sixth grade, then quit the mill to race full-time. He wasn't about to see his son do the same thing and struggle like he did.

Unfortunately, Dale was too much like his father in that respect. He was sixteen and in high school but just did not see any value in sitting behind a desk in a classroom, getting more education. Against his father's wishes, the adolescent dropped out. Later on, the future multi-champion and millionaire would say it was one of his deepest regrets in life.

"I disappointed my daddy," he said. "If I could do one thing over, I'd stay in school."[5]

Also like his father, Dale married and started a family young. He hopped from odd job to odd job to garage work and in and out. Unlike the young racers starting out today, Dale Earnhardt was already nineteen years old when he raced his first race, and that was in his brother-in-law's old car. It was a 1956 Ford Club Sedan that the family team decided needed a fresh coat of paint. The car had a purple roof, so the idea was to paint the body an avocado green, someone's idea of a complementing color. The enthusiasts set up to give the car the dyno treatment, but when the paint came out, it was not green but pink. Thus Dale Earnhardt, the future "Intimidator," drove a pink car for his first race.[6]

No one remembers whether Dale won that first race or not at the old Concord Speedway, and there are no records. They do remember that he did not come home with damage to the car, but there were no trophies for the trouble either. His former brother-in-law, who raced the family's other car in the same competition, recalled that he did not lap Dale, so he must have been quick enough. There was a memory that the young rookie seemed to drive like he knew what he was doing from observing his father Ralph all those years.

Give a guy who is already thirsty a drink of what he wants, and it is pretty likely he will do everything but beg, and maybe even a bit of that too, for more. That's pretty much the trail that Dale Earnhardt then set for himself. Racing was what mattered most. He worked to race; job, family, and everything else had to get along with that or be left by the wayside. Soon he was divorced from his first wife. The adoption of his son, Kerry, by his first wife's second husband went pretty smoothly, given that Dale had not been honoring his child support payments. It was a good thing for the Earnhardt family that some of this family hurt was mended later.

Another casualty of this period of Earnhardt's life was the early death of his father. His mother found Ralph on the kitchen floor, dead of a heart attack at the age of forty-five. Dale was twenty-two. "He was really the guiding force in my life," Dale said. "When he first died, I was mad for several years about it. I was upset and mad about it; I just didn't even think about it; I didn't even want to think about it."[7] Dale threw himself into his racing all the more.

He did have a favorite story he would tell of his father and him racing in the same race, which they only managed to do one time. Dale was put into service to drive a car in a Sportsman race at Metrolina Speedway near Charlotte. He had finished second in the semimodified race, and the top five finishers in that contest were recruited to fill open slots due to calendar conflicts for some of the regular drivers. In the race, Ralph was leading, and Dale was running fourth. He kept trying to pass the car in third, another driver from the semimodified class, and was having a tough time. Soon, he saw his father drive up behind him, ready to lap him. Dale moved over to let his father pass, but instead his father drove up to his bumper and gave him a push. Ralph finished first, with Dale third. The now fourth-place driver was not happy with the Earnhardts that day. The story shows a lot about their father-son relationship, of course, but it also foreshadows the Daytona 500 of 2001 in some respects, when Dale Jr. was racing ahead of his father. About the influence of his father, Dale Earnhardt Sr. said that he learned how to drive from watching him, but his father's influence went far beyond that. "Everything I've ever done was with the goal of making my Daddy proud," he said.[8]

It was a long, tough road with lots of races, not much money, and a long and faithful dedication to his trade, ambitions, and dreams that marked Earnhardt's journey into NASCAR and into the eventual levels of success that he reached in the sport. In NASCAR when he entered it, the drivers were accustomed to giving a bit of a show for the fans for the majority of the laps but not really getting into serious racing until toward the end. Earnhardt made aggressive moves all the way through the race. This technique did not sit well with his colleagues on the track, who wondered why he was in such a hurry. Earnhardt had to earn money through wins. A victory was not just for bragging rights; it was for money to feed his family. Earnhardt wasn't the only racer who raced for his supper and his family's livelihood, but somehow his style on the track bothered the other racers. "When you saw him coming, you braced yourself," said Richard "The King" Petty (U.S.).[9]

He raced and struggled until he got the financial break he needed in terms of a supporter, the kind of break that everyone with talent in almost any area needs if he or she is not born with means or early opportunities. By the time Earnhardt won his first championship in NASCAR, he was twenty-nine years old. By comparison, in a different era in the sport that came right after Dale's dominance, Jeff Gordon was twenty-four when he won his first championship, a record that remains today. Gordon had been racing quarter midget cars since the age of five with early and steady success and support. Their different backgrounds, with Earnhardt perceived to have worked his way up on his own and Gordon, coming from California and Indiana, not the Southeast, and thought by many Earnhardt fans to have been nurtured into his career, made Gordon unpopular in NASCAR for quite some time when he started. Earnhardt was a crowd favorite, the traditional NASCAR driver. With car and team owner Richard Childress and throughout his career, Earnhardt went on to win seven NASCAR premier series championships, tying Richard Petty's record at the time.

Earnhardt could be scrappy on the track, and that was his known style, where "The Intimidator" moniker came from and stuck. He was not afraid of pushing and budging when he felt the need. Some people in racing do not like this style and feel it is unfair, while others admire the persistence of it and the unwillingness to lose. Why was Dale Earnhardt such a favorite among his fans? Fans say it was because of this determination, the will to win. Others say it was because he was a self-made racer; he had to struggle and did not have advantages handed to him or an early hand up. There was something about the American spirit in him that way, people say, fighting his way out of the cotton mill company town to travel the country and find financial success and awards pursuing a passion he loved.

The successes—multiple NASCAR premier series championships and more—still did not come without personal sacrifices on the way up. Before the support he received, he was known for not paying his bills, and he was still struggling to move up a ladder that did not have clear rungs in those days. He suffered injuries from crashes and came back. Earnhardt married and divorced a second time, this time having two more children, a daughter, Kelley, in 1972 and a son, Dale Jr., in 1974.

A third marriage for Earnhardt, to a young bride, Teresa, remained intact the rest of his life, and their daughter, Taylor, was born in 1988. In 1994, Earnhardt lost his best friend to the sport they both loved—besides regularly hunting and fishing with Earnhardt, Neil Bonnett also loved to race stock cars; an accident on the track took his life.

After that accident, Earnhardt started putting something new in his race car before every race. Darrell Waltrip's wife, Stevie, used to hand her husband a card on which she'd handwritten scripture to tape to his dashboard for every race. After Bonnett's death, Earnhardt saw Stevie give Darrell a piece of paper and asked what it was. When Waltrip explained, Earnhardt asked where the scripture for him was. Stevie quickly provided him with one. Every race after that, Stevie Waltrip gave Dale Earnhardt scripture for him to have in his car.

As Dale Jr. joined him on the track, and Earnhardt mellowed into middle age, he was still a favorite among his fans. If Jeff Gordon expanded the appeal of NASCAR beyond the American Southeast, taking it to more of a national sport than a regional one, Dale Earnhardt may be said to be the last big champion of that southern era. In all, Earnhardt won the NASCAR premier series (cup) championship seven times—in 1980, 1986, 1987, 1990, 1991, 1993, and 1994—tying the record for the most career championship wins with Richard Petty. Jimmie Johnson, in 2016, is so far the only driver to equal these two men's achievement with that number of championships.

One prize eluded Dale Earnhardt for a frustrating length of time. In all his career, before 1998, he had never won the Daytona 500. Daytona, of course, is NASCAR country. Stock car racing started there after World War II, when the cars actually raced on the sandy beaches of Daytona Beach, Florida. Grandstands were set up along the dunes for spectators to watch. The first speedway was built inland and completed in 1958, with the first Daytona 500 held in February 1959. The famed high-banked curves were constructed of lime rock covered with asphalt. Machines at the top of the bank and at the bottom had to move in sync with one another during the bank creation and paving process. Driving the No. 42 Oldsmobile, Lee Petty, father of the future star Richard Petty, was the winner of the inaugural Daytona 500 in 1959. His son would go on to win it himself for the first time in 1964 and no fewer than six times afterward. [10]

Dale Earnhardt. *International Motor Racing Research Center/National Speed Sport News Collection.*

Even today, the famed five-hundred-mile race at Daytona Beach is the "Super Bowl" of NASCAR, but unlike the big game of the NFL, this biggest event of the season in stock car racing is the first contest on the calendar, not the last. Earnhardt came close to winning it many times. He would even lead the race for most of the laps at one point, only to get edged out and have the win stolen on the last lap. It seemed like a jinx or curse that he could not break.

On the Saturday before the Daytona 500 of 1998, Earnhardt met a young fan. The little girl, in a wheelchair, gave him a penny and told him it was lucky and that he was going to win the race. He glued the penny to his dashboard and said later that something about the small gesture made him feel like it was going to be his day. He did win the race—on his twentieth attempt—and even the spectators who were not Earnhardt fans applauded his tenacity. Crews from every team on the grid came out and stood in a line to greet him and his car as he came into victory lane. The scene of his high-fiving each one of these people from the driver's seat is an iconic one in NASCAR. If winning championships over and over again is one sign of success, certainly winning the respect of one's peers and competitors, even after beating them so many times, has to be a success on a different level.

WHAT HAPPENED

When Dale Earnhardt entered the 2001 Daytona 500 at age forty-nine, he was in a good place in his life. His family life had come together as he worked to make amends for past wrongs. He was involved in the business side of the sport, helping Dale Jr. and other racers get a chance earlier than he did. He still enjoyed the outdoors as he always had, hunting and fishing. He had enough money that his family did not need to worry, but he also never forgot his roots in North Carolina. His quiet but considerable charitable work stayed under the radar, as he liked it; he made donations here or an encouraging phone call to a sick fan there. Teresa was also involved in the business, which made the whole enterprise even stronger as a family effort.

On February 18, 2001, Dale Earnhardt kissed his wife, as he always did before a race, and readied for the start. His scripture from Stevie Waltrip that day was Proverbs 18:10—"The Lord was a strong tower.

The righteous will run to it and be safe."[11] He was starting that day seventh on the grid; Dale Jr. was in sixth position. If he was not winning quite as often as he did during the years of his championship streak, Dale Sr. and his black No. 3 car were still as beloved by his fans as ever. His name was synonymous with NASCAR, and vice versa. So big a megastar was he in his and NASCAR's home state of North Carolina that it was rumored North Carolina school children used to learn to count by saying, "One, two, Dale Earnhardt, four, five."[12]

One thing about having a rather rebellious, outlaw spirit—about needing to be resourceful for oneself for so long and through such hard times—is that one can reach a point where a substantial amount of stubbornness kicks in. If you've had to do it on your own for so long, you may not be amenable to someone else coming along and trying to tell you how to do things better. Who knows whether choosing to wear the full helmet that other racers were wearing that day would have helped. Some have said that the new HANS—head and neck safety—device that he also would not wear may have saved his life in the crash that day in Florida.

On the last lap of the race, Earnhardt was helping play defense for the two drivers who were running one and two in front of him—his own son in second place and Michael Waltrip in first, both racing for Earnhardt's own team. If he helped keep cars behind him from moving up on them, one of his guys was going to take the win; the best of all scenarios would be that the top three would be all Earnhardt cars. On the last lap, people were on their feet, cheering for this picture—a father helping his son and a teammate cross the finish line before him. Echoes of Ralph pushing Dale Sr. so many years ago show that this was an ultimate act of love on the part of the seasoned racer, not to mention his team, as his legacy was going to go to victory lane.

Suddenly, Earnhardt's car touched Sterling Marlin's No. 40 car, then turned a bit sideways, causing Ken Schrader's No. 36 car coming behind him to strike Earnhardt, who spun head-on into the retaining wall. On television, the crash did not look that horrific. People are used to the bumper-car style of racing that is NASCAR. Cars bump against one another all the time. Cars spin and hit the wall. No one wants anyone to get hurt, and remarkably most of the time the drivers climb out dejected but not seriously harmed.

At the same time as Dale hit the wall, at the front, Waltrip crossed the finish line, Dale Jr. followed right behind, and the cheering swelled anew. Michael Waltrip's older brother, Darrell, was commentating in the booth for FOX-TV. The camera focused on him as deep emotion at his brother's win rendered him nearly speechless. When he did speak, it was not long before Darrell asked about Dale Earnhardt, who was running third but had yet to cross the finish line. The attention on Michael Waltrip's long-awaited first win soon got divided as the camera focused on the No. 3 car and whether its driver was getting out on his own.

While Schrader escaped with minor injuries, Earnhardt had to be removed from his car and taken to the Halifax Medical Center for treatment. Health-care professionals were not able to revive him, and Dale Earnhardt was pronounced dead at 5:16 p.m. that day from blunt force trauma to the head and other injuries.

AFTERMATH

"We've lost Dale Earnhardt," came the public announcement that evening from NASCAR official Mike Helton. Television commentator Mike Joy expressed the emotion of many of the fans on hearing those words when he said, "The compass of this sport has lost its true North." Fans indeed were shaken and took the news personally. They had bonded with this man, even if they had never met him in person. They left flowers as impromptu memorials. They shed tears; they gave interviews about how much he had meant to them. He was a hero to them, someone who was on the world stage of sport but had come up through the ranks from a place like where they came from—they felt he was one of them. It was the kind of announcement that was broadcast on all the major television news and other media outlets in the country; it was not just a sports story but a news story.

Earnhardt's memorial service was held at Calvary Church in Charlotte, North Carolina, a church that held sixty-two hundred people. Millions more watched on television on FOX Sports Net.[13] In covering the event, Mike Joy told the audience that he did not know where his compass words had come from on the night of the 500, when everyone was in shock, and words had to come for those who reported the story on television. From the studio, Joy told the audience at home waiting for the service to begin that he and his crew had visited Dale Earnhardt Incorporated headquarters while preparing for the broadcast. He showed the audience at home a plaque of the logo of the company. In the center was a compass.

LEGACIES

NASCAR launched a full-scale investigation into the death of its star racer, Dale Earnhardt Sr., as well as into improving safety in its motor sport series. Other series of motor sport took notice too. Largely as a result of what happened to Earnhardt in NASCAR, a couple years later the international Formula One series required all of its drivers to wear HANS devices for protection. This rippled through other professional series of racing and even into the amateur ranks. This may be the single farthest-reaching effect of Earnhardt's legacy to other racers. As well, NASCAR instituted softer, specialized walls called "SAFER Barriers" around racetracks and worked on a new generation of race cars that also had more safety measures in place.

Dale Earnhardt's legacy went beyond the racetrack too. In addition to his gift to the sport of his son Dale Jr., voted each year by fans as the most popular driver until concussion injuries prompted his final full-time season in 2017, Earnhardt's charitable work took on a public profile through the Dale Earnhardt Foundation.

Of course, his legacy to his family is the most important, but a figure so public and in the sporting world for so long leaves memories for many other people too. In no small measure, his personal popularity increased the profile and reach of NASCAR as a sport in a way that set it up for others after him to capitalize on and spread even wider across the country. When fans like a driver, they will pay money to watch him race, and Earnhardt brought a lot of spectators to the racetracks around the country. So deep was his popularity that many of his fans have transferred their love for him to his son and his career.

Fans who loved Dale Earnhardt as the racer they watched at the track, or in public appearances, or on TV valued his brashness and self-made confidence. He came from very little means, kept aiming for his dream, and reached it. They liked that, and they will never forget him for showing them that it could be done.

———⦾⦾⦾———

Racer: Ralph Dale Earnhardt (U.S.), age forty-nine; b. April 29, 1951, in Kannapolis, North Carolina; d. February 18, 2001, Daytona Beach, Florida.

Career Highlights and Honors: Seven NASCAR premier (cup) series championships (1980, 1986, 1987, 1990, 1991, 1993, and 1994 (record tied only with Richard Petty and Jimmie Johnson); 1998 Daytona 500 winner; 1995 Brickyard 400 winner; inducted (posthumously) into Motorsports Hall of Fame of America (2002); inducted into the International Motor Sports Hall of Fame (2006); inducted into the inaugural class of NASCAR Hall of Fame (2010); 1998 season helmet part of collection at National Museum of American History, Smithsonian Institution, Washington, DC; named one of "NASCAR's 50 Greatest Drivers" in 1998.

Among His Legacies: HANS, or similar head and neck protection device, became required for most race car drivers; son, Dale Earnhardt Jr., races in NASCAR and is one of the series' most popular drivers; Dale Earnhardt Foundation offers an annual scholarship to an undergraduate interested in mechanical engineering, motor sport, or automotive engineering.

———⦾⦾⦾———

10

STILL HAPPENING

Bianchi, Wheldon, Wilson

Motor sport does not, of course, wait until a driver is lost before it looks into improving the safety of the sport; however, high-profile fatalities definitely have played a role over the last several years in increasing and intensifying that effort. One would think that after more than a century of activity, and with so many countries around the world involved, including many of the most technologically advanced nations, the sport would be about as safe in the early twenty-first century as it can get. Certainly, one could reasonably expect that lives would no longer be lost from jumping into a race car, driving around a track, and trying to go faster than anyone else, especially for the entertainment of the paying public. Lessons learned by racing teams, car manufacturers, track facilities, governing bodies, sponsors, drivers, and others involved in the sport must surely have worked to ensure that, though risk can never be entirely eradicated in such a daring sport in which human beings play with machines, death must no longer be accepted as a consequence. No matter how intense the competition, sport is not war. It is not natural disaster. Someone is dying at the expense of what—other people's entertainment? No one inside or outside motor sport thinks that death should be the consequence for a driver who wants to compete. It is important to note that the deaths in motor sport have decreased dramatically from the most dangerous era of the mid-twentieth century, when the technological advances in the cars outpaced the knowable and needed enhancements of the tracks. After all this time, the deaths, and high-profile ones at that, in the most professional and overseen racing series in the world still happen. Still.

So concerned was Sir Jackie Stewart about safety in Formula One even in the years after he retired from racing himself that if someone asked him what time it was, he would regularly respond with how many days, hours, and minutes it had been since the last fatality of a racer competing in a Formula One grand prix. His efforts with the Grand Prix Drivers' Association, racetracks, safety commissions, and others, in addition to raising awareness purely on his own at every opportunity, have made a significant contribution to motor sport safety. After Ayrton Senna and Roland Ratzenberger died on the same weekend at Imola, Italy, in 1994, the safety clock stopped and had to be restarted all over again. When the series crossed over into the new millennium and the decade after that went by without a grand prix–related fatality, Stewart must have thought that a good measure of safety had been finally achieved. The next death resulting from a racing incident in Formula One did not happen for over twenty years—the longest span in the series' history.

Stewart mentioned a frightening statistic looking back at his career: "If I were to take five years—from '68 to '73—there was only a one out of three chance I was going to live. There was a two out of three chance I was going to die."[1] Going to so many funerals, suffering the grief, and aiding the families, in addition to his own near-death experiences, motivated Stewart to take action in the first place.

"I lost most of my friends," Stewart said in an interview with the BBC. Looking back on it with his wife, he said, "Helen and I counted 57 people that had died that we knew well enough to call friends. What sport in the world do you know that could see that number of people being killed?"[2] Indeed, in what job in the world, short of the military or perhaps the police force, would numbers like that even be conceived of within the span of a typical career?

JULES BIANCHI

Unfortunately, the safety streak in Formula One was broken at the Japanese Grand Prix in Suzuka on October 5, 2014. It was a wet track; a typhoon had soaked the region. On the forty-third lap of the race, Jules

Bianchi, twenty-five, a French driver competing in his No. 17 car for the Marussia-Ferrari team, drove up quickly on the recovery scene of another car, the German Adrian Sutil's Sauber No. 99, which had spun off the track at the same spot where Bianchi now was. The French driver tried to slow down and stop, only to strike the emergency recovery vehicle that was trying to remove Sutil's car. The front end of Bianchi's car dove underneath the tractor crane, even lifting the heavy machine up in the process due to the car's momentum. Bianchi's head was severely injured when his roofless car drove underneath the crane. Sutil's car, hanging from the crane, swung and dropped to the ground. The race was stopped, and the leader at the time, Lewis Hamilton (UK), was declared the winner. On the podium, racers were not celebrating; they were clearly thinking only of Bianchi and wondering if he was all right.

Bianchi was quickly transported to the nearest hospital, nine miles away. While a helicopter must be on stand-by at racetracks for emergencies such as these nowadays in Formula One, it was determined that the nature of Bianchi's injuries required ground transport. After a few weeks in the hospital in Japan, Bianchi's condition had improved enough that the family had the young driver moved to their hometown of Nice, where he was treated for several months. In the end, Jules Bianchi succumbed to his injuries on July 17, 2015, a few weeks before his twenty-sixth birthday.

Bianchi was not a Formula One champion; he was only in his third season with the series when he had his accident at Suzuka. He had earned two championship points that year by finishing ninth in the Monaco Grand Prix in May. It is important to note that Bianchi's fellow drivers had never raced in Formula One when another driver had died. They knew the history of their sport, of course, and they knew that risks still existed. Some, like Hamilton, were young boys when Senna and Ratzenberger were killed, and they remembered that. However, they had not lived that history themselves and were racing in safer times. Several drivers went to Bianchi's funeral; some even served as pallbearers, as was the custom for drivers in the decades before. Bianchi's death brought home to his fellow drivers that their sport was still not that dissimilar from their predecessors'. They knew it was risky, but perhaps they did not feel that risk as strongly as earlier drivers in the sport who faced the loss of one or more of their colleagues every season. Even in

2015, a generation after the last fatality in a Formula One grand prix, death was still a very real and present danger in their chosen occupation.

Bianchi's accident and death, of course, caused another serious round of safety analyses in Formula One. Safety vehicles, the virtual safety car, start times for races facing darkness, and more measures were considered, changed, or adopted as a result. Several tributes took place, both during the period when Bianchi was fighting for his life in a hospital bed and after he passed. Instead of moving their reserve driver into Bianchi's seat, Marussia left his side of the garage empty at the next grand prix to mark that he was not there to compete. Drivers dedicated races and wins; they wore commemorative decals on their helmets and cars. Social media outlets gave fans channels through which to grieve together, to express their emotions over his accident and loss, a place to leave messages that he and his family remained in their thoughts and prayers.

Ferrari let it be known that Bianchi had been next in line to move up to their team had the crash not happened. Eventually, Bianchi's car number, seventeen, was retired in honor of his participation in the sport. As part of Bianchi's many legacies and tributes, his family set up a foundation, the Jules Bianchi Society, to help train young drivers in karting who had their sights set, like Jules did, on Formula One. People on the outside of motor sport might find the cause of the foundation ironic, given what happened to Jules; however, racing is what he loved doing, so his family sees the foundation as a way to honor the young Frenchman. They believe their mission of aiding young drivers like those they observed through Jules's progress, who may have the talent and ambition but lack much-needed financial support to move forward, is a good cause.[3]

Of course, Formula One, while universally regarded as the pinnacle of motor sport, is not the only world-class or high-profile professional racing series in existence. One might argue that, overall, it may be the most technologically advanced and innovative, thereby increasing the risks to its drivers in that respect, but other series, such as the highly progressive sports car World Endurance Championship and races like the 24 Hours of Le Mans and Daytona, have their own records of fatalities, as does NASCAR. The American open-wheel series of Indy-Car has certainly not been free from the loss of drivers on its tracks in the early twenty-first century. Two recent drivers lost in IndyCar are Justin Wilson (UK) and Dan Wheldon (UK).

———

Racer: Jules Lucien André Bianchi (France), age twenty-five; b. August 3, 1989, in Nice, France; d. July 17, 2015, in Nice, France.

Career Highlights and Honors: Earned two Formula One championship points in 2014 racing for Marussia; 2007 French Formula Renault 2.0 series champion; winner, 2009 Formula Three Euro Series.

Among His Legacies: Jules Bianchi Society helping young drivers.

———

JUSTIN WILSON

The racing world was just recuperating from the bad news of July 2015 that Jules Bianchi of Formula One had not survived his injuries from the previous season, when motor sport was rocked once again by a death in the family. This time, the branch of relatives was the IndyCar series in the United States, another open-wheel and, importantly, open-cockpit racing series. Justin Wilson, age thirty-seven, who had formerly raced in Formula One in 2003 and earned one championship point in that series, and who had had podium finishes in endurance racing at Le Mans and Daytona, died in an IndyCar crash at Pocono Raceway on August 23, 2015.

In this incident, the leader of the race, Sage Karem, suddenly lost control of his car. He swerved and crashed into the outside wall. When he did so, debris from his car went flying all over the track. Wilson, some cars back, was trying to avoid the accident and the debris like everyone else. In a freak chance of circumstance, the flying nose cone of Karem's car hit Wilson's helmet, and Wilson's car swerved and hit the inside wall. While Karem walked away from his crash, Wilson needed to be extricated from his car. He was airlifted to Lehigh Valley Hospital in Allentown, Pennsylvania, where he died the next day from blunt force trauma to the head.

Justin Wilson drives out of the Boot section of the track during the 2009 IndyCar (IRL) race at Watkins Glen International, Watkins Glen, New York. *International Motor Racing Research Center/Bill Bauman Collection.*

The motor sport community banded together once again, helping where possible as well as paying tribute to Wilson in events that followed. NASCAR star Tony Stewart gave use of his private plane to the Wilson family so they could make the trip to Pennsylvania. A fund was set up for donations for Wilson's children. A little later, IndyCar drivers such as Marco Andretti, Graham Rahal, James Hinchcliffe, and others were set to do a promotional drive across the Golden Gate Bridge to advertise the final race of the season at Sonoma, California. Instead, the drivers dedicated the drive to Wilson. Stefan Wilson did not let his brother's tragedy stop him from competing. As he had done in 2013, in the 2016 season, he raced in the IndyCar series.

Justin Wilson was dyslexic but had not drawn much public attention to his condition until he started his Internet social media account on Twitter. The words in his profile page give some clues to what he valued in life and to his personality. "Husband and father of 2," he wrote. "I love going fast and competing. Technology and adrenaline make me tick. Dyslexic in control, tweets might not make sense."[4]

Wilson's fatal accident was the first one IndyCar had suffered since Dan Wheldon's terrible crash of 2011—less than four years before.

Racer: Justin Boyd Wilson (UK), age thirty-seven; b. Sheffield, South Yorkshire, England; d. August 24, 2015, Allentown, Pennsylvania.

Career Highlights and Honors: Winner, 24 Hours of Daytona, 2012; third place in 24 Hours of Daytona, 2013; earned one championship point in Formula One in 2003 by placing eighth in the United States Grand Prix at Indianapolis Motor Speedway.

Among His Legacies: Influence on brother and racer Stefan Wilson; publicly announced organ donor to six people; dyslexia awareness.

DAN WHELDON

Daniel Clive Wheldon was born in Emberton, England, in the summer of 1978. His father, Clive, a kart racer himself, encouraged his son's interest in karting, an endeavor the younger Wheldon started at the age of four. Soon, Clive Wheldon decided he enjoyed funding and supporting Dan's karting ambitions more than his own. "You could see that focus once he dropped that helmet on; that's when Dan was at his best," the proud father said.[5]

Young Wheldon showed talent in the sport early on, something that seems a fairly common trait among future champions. He won races and karting championships in Britain and also won the Federation Internationale de l'Automobile Senna World Cup in karting in 1995. As is also the case with many future champions, the driver wanted to move on to the next level of competition—in this case, from karts to cars.

In cars, Dan drove in British Formula Vauxhall and Formula Ford. In 1998, he came in third in the championship of Formula Ford, behind the winner, a future champion himself, Jenson Button, who was on his way in a few years to a successful career in Formula One. About Wheldon, Button said later, "Dan was always the one who stood out because

Dan Wheldon waves to the crowd during the drivers' introductions at the 2008 IndyCar (IRL) race at Watkins Glen International, Watkins Glen, New York. *International Motor Racing Research Center/Bill Bauman Collection.*

he was such an intelligent driver as well. When you beat him you knew you'd done an exceptional job."[6]

When funding ran thin to keep competing in European racing, Wheldon moved to the United States to try out his racing chances there. In the United States, he raced in the F2000 series, winning that championship in 1999; in the Atlantic championship, taking second place in 2000; and in Indy Lights, taking second in 2001. Wheldon was an open-wheel, open-cockpit racer and was on track to drive in Indy-Car, the highest form of that kind of racing in North America. Starting in 2002, Wheldon raced in the IndyCar series for the rest of his career.

Wheldon's racing career seems to have had an unusual trajectory, ever upward: from karting to open-wheel racing in England, to open-wheel racing in the United States, to the premier open-wheel league there, to wins in premier races in that series and its championship. In 2003, he was voted the IndyCar series' Rookie of the Year. In 2005, he won his first Indianapolis 500 race, the first British winner of that race since Jim Clark won it exactly fifty years before. Wheldon also became the IndyCar series champion that year. In 2006, he got his only win at the 24 Hours of Daytona with teammates Scott Dixon and Casey Mears. Again, in 2011, he won the Indy 500, but this time he posed for the traditional photo on the "yard of bricks" (a section of the old "brick-yard" track that is a yard wide and stretches across the start/finish line) with his wife and two young children. Life was good.

Just a few months after his victorious May Indy 500 with his family by his side, that October, Wheldon and IndyCar went racing on a crowded, tight oval track in Las Vegas, Nevada. On lap eleven, a multi-car incident involving an incredible fifteen cars took place. They slid into and then over each other. Cars went airborne, and drivers going 220 mph in a fairly tight space heading into the melee ahead of them had no time to react; their cars slid and skidded and got airborne too. Cars caught on fire. While the walls of the track were cushioned with safety material designed to absorb impact forces, the catch fencing above the walls did not provide such protection for the drivers. Wheldon's car flew up into the catch fencing along the side of the track, cockpit first, and also hit a pole. When his car landed back on the track, amid the fourteen other cars involved, there was no movement. He needed to be extricated from the vehicle. Wheldon was airlifted to the University Medical Center of Southern Nevada, where he was pronounced dead on arrival. The cause was blunt force trauma to the head. The pole in the catch fencing had dealt the fatal blow. Dan Wheldon, IndyCar champion and two-time Indy 500 winner, father of two young children, was thirty-three.

After such a tragic and devastating incident involving so many cars, the race was abandoned and not restarted. Instead, the drivers with functioning cars decided to run a memorial five-lap salute around the track in honor of Dan Wheldon. Since it was the last race of the season that year, Dario Franchitti (UK) became the season champion; however, any celebration was postponed, and Franchitti has said that year will forever be a somber memory for him.

Even though they competed against each other and there were chilly periods off track due to incidents on track, Wheldon had established close friendships with some of his IndyCar teammates and competitors. Dario Franchitti was one of them. The next year at the Indy 500, the race Wheldon had won the previous year, memories of him were still fresh with his fellow racers and with the fans as well. Franchitti described sitting in his car ready for the race to begin and listening with tears in his eyes as Jim Nabors sang the traditional "Back Home in Indiana." He remembered having to shake off the emotion, telling himself he had to face five hundred miles of tough racing momentarily. He went on to win and remembered Wheldon in victory lane, raising the traditional bottle of milk skyward, looking up, and pointing.

Popular IndyCar driver Helio Castroneves (Brazil) has a fan-favorite habit of climbing the catch fencing along the side of the track whenever he wins a race. In St. Petersburg, Florida, local officials had named a street near the track and close to Wheldon's home "Dan Wheldon Way." Castroneves won the Grand Prix of St. Petersburg, the first race of the 2012 season, which also happened to be the next race after the big crash in Las Vegas. Having had the whole off-season to think about Wheldon's death and the horrible crash, the IndyCar community started the new season with fresh memories of how the previous season had ended so tragically.

When Castroneves had won St. Petersburg in seasons before, he climbed the fencing near Turn 1, where there was a big grandstand where people could share in and enjoy the stunt. For some reason, this time in 2012, he stopped near Turn 10 instead, where there is another big grandstand. As he ran to share his excitement at his victory, a safety worker was making sure he was clear of the cars that were still coming in on track after the end of the race. The safety worker also pointed above Castroneves, who had not seen the sign himself and had not stopped at this point on the track because of it. The large green and white sign read "Dan Wheldon Way." Castroneves climbed up the fencing and pointed at the sign in tribute. Television coverage picked it up. Castroneves said later, "It was a way to pay tribute and respect to someone we all loved. It was a way to recognize who Dan was. I didn't plan it or think it through. It was just spontaneous . . . a suitable representation for the way all the drivers felt that weekend. It was destiny that I stopped there and destiny that the safety worker pointed out the sign, but the tribute came from all of us."[7]

Fellow IndyCar driver Graham Rahal led an auction to help raise money for the young Wheldon family. The street was named after him, and special moments on the track continued for some time, including a brief memorial drive of his 2011 Indy 500–winning car before the Indy 500 the next year. One of Wheldon's most lasting legacies, other than his family, of course, and the charity work for Alzheimer's disease that his family has kept up after his passing, is his work in testing for a new, safer chassis due to be part of the cars the season after he died. The Dallara company named its new chassis for IndyCars the DW12 in honor of Wheldon. It has been suggested that Wheldon might have survived his crash had he been in the next year's car with the DW12 chassis that he helped develop.

Interestingly, one of the people who writes reminiscences in the book *Lionheart: Remembering Dan Wheldon* is Stefan Wilson, Justin Wilson's younger brother. Like Holly Wheldon, Dan's younger sister, who participated in the creation of the book, Stefan can relate to what it is like to lose an older brother you admire to the thief of life that racing can be.

Wheldon died a few years before Wilson, however, so Stefan first reacted as a driver in Indy Lights, the feeder series to IndyCar, which he raced in 2011. He said he should have reached out more to the Wheldon family after the tragedy, that Wheldon and his brother had shared a lot in common, both having been born in 1978 in the United Kingdom and coming up through karting together to race in the Indy-Car series in the United States. "I think we almost felt survivor's guilt that we lost Dan and Justin was still here," he said. In light of Justin's death, however, in 2015 Stefan added, "Now, though, we are sharing the same situation."[8]

—◦◦◦—

Racer: Daniel Clive Wheldon (UK), age thirty-three; b. June 22, 1978, in Emberton, Buckinghamshire, England; d. October 16, 2011, in Las Vegas, Nevada.

Career Highlights and Honors: 2005 IndyCar series champion; winner Indy 500, 2005, 2011; winner 24 Hours of Daytona, 2006.

Among His Legacies: Dallara chassis, modified with Wheldon's input to be safer and protect against the very kinds of crashes that ended up killing him, renamed the DW12 in his honor; street named "Dan Wheldon Way" in St. Petersburg, Florida; Dan Wheldon Foundation and continuation of his work for the Alzheimer's Association.

—◦◦◦—

IndyCar had not had the relief of the twenty-year gap that Formula One had between the death of Ayrton Senna in 1994 and Jules Bianchi's 2014 crash and 2015 passing. Before Dan Wheldon's fatal crash in 2011 and Justin Wilson's in 2015, American Paul Dana had died in an Indy-Car race at Homestead-Miami Speedway in 2006. That is four to five years on either side of Wheldon. To date, no one has died in a race in the NASCAR premier series since Dale Earnhardt passed away in 2001. Endurance racing suffered a loss at the 24 Hours of Le Mans in 2013 with Allan Simonsen.

Of course, these numbers in a few of the high-profile series of professional racing do not nearly reflect the total deaths overall in the sport worldwide when one takes into consideration the smaller professional series, trucks, modified cars, drag racing, and so forth, and add to all of those all the small amateur events that take place all around the United States, Europe, and the world. A racing-related death at a small-town dirt track or other amateur event might get mentioned in the local newspaper, and that's about it. Those families also ask why, when they are alone at night; they live with the loss of their loved ones just as the famous racers' families do. Their loved one enjoyed racing. The racers' families and friends repeat the well-known racer mantra over and over to themselves: "At least, he died doing what he loved." Statistics show there is a greater chance of getting killed on the highway driving to or from a race than there is of getting killed on a racetrack. Yet the contemplation of human beings and machines attempting to defy physics and nature at great risk, going around in ovals or irregular loops, prompts many people to ask why.

Some fans, racers, and others in the sport have the complete opposite view—they complain about the increasing number of new safety rules and regulations in motor racing, the increasing number of track runoff areas, and so forth, that take away some of the challenge and "character" of the various circuits. The newer tracks especially, goes the complaint, are "too safe," taking the excitement and required courage out of the contest. These folks contend that risk and danger are part of the sport, and an overzealous desire to protect the drivers is squashing an important element of it. The older tracks did not allow for as many mistakes; drivers had to be keen indeed, and highly skilled, not only to win there but to finish the race. If the sport were not dangerous, then anyone could do it, is the contention. The risk and danger are part of the deal when one becomes a racing driver, part of what makes the whole effort worthwhile—and worth watching.

Either way, whether one subscribes to the notion that safety has gone overboard in the last few years, taking away the essence of motor racing, or believes the sport can never be too safe, these more recent tragedies demonstrate that motor racing may be safer than it was in the 1950s, 1960s, and 1970s, but it is still dangerous. It can and does still kill.

11

GREAT ESCAPES

"Time and practice were molding me into a true professional. I had learned the trick of burying reason under layers of confidence and pretense." —Brian Redman[1]

In remembering and paying tribute to those auto racers who did not survive their sport, it is vital to acknowledge that motor racing would certainly not exist if these tragedies were more the norm than the exception. Even in its most dangerous era, auto racing never posted anywhere near the kinds of statistics that everyday drivers unfortunately rack up on highways, streets, and back roads all across the world every day. The World Health Organization (WHO) reported in its 2015 executive summary of road safety that traffic injuries are the ninth leading cause of death around the world and will likely rise to the seventh leading cause by 2030:

> More than 1.2 million people die each year on the world's roads, making road traffic injuries a leading cause of death globally. Most of these deaths are in low- and middle-income countries where rapid economic growth has been accompanied by increased motorization and road traffic injuries. As well as being a public health problem, road traffic injuries are a development issue: low- and middle-income countries lose approximately 3% of GDP as a result of road traffic crashes.[2]

The danger the world over is particularly great among young people. WHO reports that among the world's population fifteen to twenty-nine years of age, traffic injuries are in fact the leading cause of death. WHO points out that the problem is especially strong in developing nations that are becoming increasingly mobile, with more automobiles and trucks. In addition, the organization makes the point that traffic injuries and deaths not only impact global health but also affect nations' economies.

Motor racing accidents, like airplane crashes, get a lot of attention because they are highly visible; however, it is important to keep things in perspective and consider the history of the sport within the larger picture and to remember the math. Anyone who is a reluctant flyer can tell you about many times he or she has been told just how much safer it is, statistically speaking, to fly rather to go almost anywhere by car.

Auto racers who competed in those especially dangerous times in the twentieth century, when many did not survive, are now in their sixties, seventies, and eighties. Few to none of them got through his or her career entirely unscathed physically. As five-time Le Mans winner Derek Bell (UK) said recently by telephone about racing in Jim Clark's last race, many sat on the starting grid, eyeing a competitor in the rearview mirror, only to discover later that the very same driver they hoped to beat in the race did not in fact make it back alive. That kind of experience has got to have a lasting effect on a person.

Drivers from that period typically did not talk much about safety. Partly, it was a cultural matter. It just wasn't the thing to do, since a man could be accused of losing his nerve or not quite having the "right stuff" to hack the challenges of the job. It was then, as now, a highly competitive sport and a business—to let on that safety was a concern was like admitting weakness that a competitor could use to his or her advantage. There were the team and the sponsors to please as well. Like the famous fairy tale "The Emperor's New Clothes," in which no one wants to admit that the ruler is naked until one brave soul finally speaks up, safety was barely even considered when the sport began, but as the accidents and crashes kept happening and the on-track deaths increased with alarming frequency, it soon became too obvious a problem to ignore any longer. If the sport were to continue, someone had to speak up.

If a racing driver survived that period of particular danger, certainly he or she had many friends or colleagues in the sport who did not. Jackie Stewart claims to have had fifty-seven friends who died in his time in racing. Stewart reflected, "So many people died within a short time that the governing body of the sport at that time—who were trying to ignore the issue, the track owners—who were trying to avoid the issue, and a whole lot of the motoring writers—thought that drivers were gladiators, and were being paid for the risk rather than being paid for their skills as drivers."[3] Some team owners and engineers, in fact, were perceived as thinking of drivers as dispensable. Older, frequently more educated people with money took advantage of the desires, passions, and perhaps youthful recklessness of so many young people who wanted a chance to race in the fastest cars. Take a young man who did not finish school. He is working on his family farm or perhaps as a mechanic in a local garage. Take that driver with some talent, don't pay him much but give him a chance at quenching his thirst for speed in a super-fast car, a little glory to take home and boast about in the form of big trophies and bragging rights, and many of these guys will come running. If they die in the process of testing out new car components for a manufacturer or a race design for an engineer, that's too bad, but behind them there are lines of other young people just waiting to sign up for their chance in the seat. Anyone who spoke about concerns with the car's safety might as well just step aside; there were plenty more drivers to choose from who would jump into the car and go, no questions asked—which is how many of these owners and engineers liked it.

What made drivers more valuable to the powers that be, of course, was their winning records. Not every person in the driver's seat got results; performance was key. Wins not only bought time for the drivers by keeping their seats for the next season, but if the wins kept coming, their successes lengthened their careers overall. No one who was not producing results raced at the highest level of the various motor racing series for long. The same holds true today. Sure, there were many drivers who survived those especially dangerous years, but they may not have raced very long. To have won races and stayed at the top level for several years, even decades, and still managed to survive that era, when the odds against you increased the longer you raced, is truly a remarkable accomplishment. No matter how old they are, racers know their stats front to back, and they calculate the odds, the risks. Talk with any racer who was both highly successful and still alive after racing in that period, and you are truly chatting with an accomplished person who also knows how very lucky he or she is.

Successful or not, there were still close calls, some very close, and some crashes defy belief that the driver even survived, much less raced again. A few of these winning drivers who survived bad accidents included Sir Stirling Moss (UK), a Formula One and sports car racer from the 1940s into the 1960s; three-time Formula One world champion Sir Jackie Stewart (UK), who competed in the 1960s and 1970s; three-time Formula One world champion Niki Lauda (Austria), who drove in the 1970s and 1980s; multiple Formula 5000 champion and two-time Le Mans winner Brian Redman (UK), who raced in Formula One cars in the 1960s and 1970s; Mario Andretti (U.S.), the 1978 Formula One world champion and 1969 Indy 500 winner, as well as a winner in many different kinds of racing series in a career that spanned from the 1960s through the 1990s; and Bobby Rahal (U.S.), who competed in the 1980s and 1990s, becoming a three-time IndyCar series champion and 1986 Indianapolis 500 winner as a driver and 2004 Indy 500 winner as an owner, and who also drove in Formula One.

Since the problem of safety is not relegated to a bygone era, it is interesting to note some of the more recent drivers who survived bad crashes. Two of these include IndyCar drivers: four-time IndyCar champion and three-time Indy 500 winner Dario Franchitti (UK), whose career ended with a crash in 2013, and James Hinchcliffe (Canada), whose 2015 accident was so severe that it looked like he might not live, much less race again or, of all things, compete on a popular televised dancing competition.

Along with his remarkable five Le Mans wins, Derek Bell's accomplishments include two world championships in sports car racing, with three victories at the 24 Hours of Daytona. He also raced in Formula One for six years, competing against racers whose careers started earlier in their lives than his did; nevertheless, he scored one championship point in the series, at Watkins Glen in the 1970 United States Grand Prix, where he finished sixth. A few years later, he found his calling in endurance racing. The Brit also served as a professional driver in the production of the 1970 racing film *Le Mans*, starring Steve McQueen. During the film shoot, Bell suffered serious facial burns when he had to jump from the Ferrari 512 he was driving as it caught fire. It was his second escape from a burning race car—the first was in a thousand-kilometer (over 620-mile) endurance race at Spa driving a Ferrari 512M. In that race, he and his teammate still came in fourth.

Compared to so many others, however, including many whom he raced with as teammates or against as competitors, Bell knows how very lucky he was in a career that spanned fifty years, driving all over the world, racing in all kinds of conditions in a variety of series. "When you reflect, I was incredibly fortunate to survive," Bell said. Though he does not deny his own talent, he also attributes much of his success to the fact that he believes he raced for the best teams in the sport, driving the best cars in the world with the best teammates. "That really is it," he said. "I have had the most privileged career."[4]

At eighty-seven, Sir Stirling Moss is racing history incarnate. Thinking of the 24 Hours of Le Mans race of 1955? Moss was there racing for Mercedes as Juan Manuel Fangio's teammate when the team withdrew from the race out of respect for the fallen. He won his class at Le Mans in 1956. Thinking of the 1955 Mille Miglia? Moss was there, winning the thousand-mile endurance race around Italy in record time with a speed averaging 100 mph. That drive is often described as the best overall drive in motor racing history. The Monaco Grand Prix? Sure, he won that too. Since 1961, he has also become known for his series of near-perfect laps at that narrow street race, where he was driving a Lotus against the three shark-nosed Ferraris that everyone knew were more powerful. Moss is not just a motor sport hero in his homeland of Great Britain; he is a sporting legend there and regarded as a national treasure who was eventually knighted for his service to motor sport. He is frequently called the winningest driver to never win a world championship. He has come in second. In one of those runner-up positions, he would have won, were it not for an extraordinary gesture of honesty and sportsmanship on his part that kept a penalty from being wrongly applied to another driver, giving the other driver the championship that a less honest man would have claimed for himself. This kind of professionalism and character has kept Moss's fame and popularity in Great Britain alive.

In a recent conversation in his living room in London, Moss spoke about the contributions auto racing has made to the world. "Carbon fiber didn't exist," Moss said about developments since his time in racing. "You were driving with the best that was available at that time, but the best at that time wasn't good enough." Moss should know. "I drove 108 different kinds of cars," he said, in a highly active career in a period in the sport when a racer did not have to drive for one series exclusively but could fill every weekend with races all around the world with different makes, models, engines, designers, and tracks. For his part, Moss was involved in racing when the speed of automotive engineering was almost as quick as the cars on the track.

"Things are moving forward all the time," Moss reflected. "I think the period when I was involved was quite important. So much evolved—disc brakes, and so on." He added, "I can't say what the next developments will be, but I can't see them being as big as developments were happening in my career."[5]

Moss had two particularly bad accidents, the last one taking him out of the car for professional competition for good. In the first he suffered a broken back and legs in 1960 in the Belgian Grand Prix at Spa-Francorchamps when the wheels came off his Lotus-Climax race car. The second accident was also in a Lotus in 1962—at Goodwood Circuit in West Sussex, England. He was rendered unconscious and laid up for several months. When he tried to get back in a car the next year, he decided that he was not fit for racing. He has since said that he may not have waited long enough to get back in the car, that he probably retired too soon.

Moss is widely regarded as an elder statesman and superstar in the sport who had skill and bravery on the track in its rawest era. Moss drove when the drivers did not even wear seatbelts, much less have the safety provisions that are in place now. He also had a gentleman's approach to business and fan relations off the track. After his accident at Goodwood, Moss managed to craft a career in television commentating, real estate, and personal appearances that outlasted his actual racing years by decades. The influence of a racer so well known from the 1950s and 1960s era of the sport on future professionals and amateur racers alike all around the world is hard to measure. Some admire the way he presents himself, even today—his kindness with fans and his professionalism. Others are impressed with his bravery and driving skill at a time when the driver's abilities had to be fine-tuned in a different way with the car. Electronics that play so much a part of the driving experience today were not yet dreamed of as part of the equation.

The sport remains physically taxing, even now, with g-forces pushing the driver's body around at every turn. Still, many observers note how many more physical factors were involved in the days when drivers went to work without even having the benefit of seatbelts or full-face helmets and visors. Archival photographs of drivers such as Moss with black dust on their faces after a race, their eyes ringed from the shield of goggles only, show just how exposed to the elements, debris from the track, and other physical dangers these drivers were. Drivers had to be in good condition to be successful.

An executive in real estate development as well as an amateur racer/owner of historic cars in New York State, Larry Kessler said that Moss was his hero when he was young. Kessler dabbled in semiprofessional racing for a time. "I was impressed by his versatility racing sports cars and Formula 1," Kessler said, "his sportsmanship and clean racing, how he articulated the importance of physical fitness in the pursuit of victory, his athleticism. He was the first of the great drivers to make that connection."[6]

The argument that race car drivers are not athletes because they sit in a car and drive is an old one, long ago settled and substantiated by the evidence of professional racing decades ago. NASCAR drivers hurtling around ovals at over 200 mph for hours on end today will say the same thing: physical fitness is a requirement of the job.

Reflecting in his London home on his career in all its aspects, Moss said simply, "I always enjoyed my racing; I really did." Moss continues to participate regularly in historic racing events such as the Goodwood Revival in the United Kingdom, though in recent years he has abandoned competing in these events to drive demonstration runs, typically of the cars he made famous during his racing career.

Another man who was knighted for his work in motor sport, Sir Jackie Stewart (UK), also made incredible contributions to the sport and the world and was saved from a terrible accident that could have killed him. The easiest way to label Stewart's success in the sport is to simply say that he is a three-time world champion in Formula One. He was the British driver with the most championships in the series for over forty years—from his retirement in 1973 until Lewis Hamilton (UK) won his third world championship in 2015.

Stewart is widely appreciated now for his work in safety for the Formula One racing series in particular. He started his campaign after experiencing the ineptitude of help in his era firsthand at the 1966 Belgian Grand Prix at Spa-Francorchamps. He crashed during the race and got trapped underneath his upturned BRM car. Flammable liquid fuel leaked down on him, soaking his suit, and he could not extricate

Jackie Stewart talks with Colin Chapman (plaid hat, back to camera) at the 1969 United States Grand Prix, Watkins Glen, New York. *International Motor Racing Research Center/FI Collection.*

Jackie Stewart at the 1969 United States Grand Prix at Watkins Glen, New York. Stewart retired in the race but went on to win his first Drivers' Championship that year. His crash at Spa happened three years earlier. *International Motor Racing Research Center/F1 Collection.*

himself from the seat. Unlike today, when a safety crew would rush to a racer's aid, in those days help did not arrive for way too long. Finally, two other racers stopped and borrowed a wrench from a nearby spectator to get Stewart out of the car. From that day on, Stewart kept a wrench (called a "spanner" in the United Kingdom) taped to his steering wheel. The problem advanced the safety improvement of removable steering wheels on race cars in the future. When the trip to the hospital also took too long, Stewart also started bringing his own doctor to the track, and the BRM team began bringing a medical crew to races to help anyone who needed it.

When Stewart began losing friends left and right, fellow racers in contests he was also competing in, the desire for change rose up too strong for him to sit idly by. His status as a multiple champion gave him a platform to initiate change in safety in the sport and see it move forward. It was not an easy road. He had tracks, governing bodies, car manufacturers, and even fellow drivers against him, but he and others managed to bring about several important improvements.

In a recent telephone conversation, Stewart commented about the frequent deaths that prompted him to do something to help and how the sport could take a competitor's emotions both indescribably low and yet also so very high:

> That was another side of the sport that you just had to get used to, or you'd have left, and not many of these people left. We were exposed to many funerals, many memorial services, many families . . . fathers and mothers losing . . . a son, or sisters and brothers, or the wives and the children. It was a huge kaleidoscope of emotion and feelings as well as fulfillment and excitement . . . and pleasure. But death is an ugly thing; it's something that was part of our sport at that time, and everyone just had to deal with.[7]

Stewart's postracing career included television commentating, work for Ford, and a bout with team ownership. He remains a prominent spokesperson for and about the sport and continues to champion safety to this day.

Another three-time world champion Formula One driver, Niki Lauda, now works as a team executive for the AMG-Petronus Mercedes Formula One team. He has also worked as a manager of his own airline,

Jackie Stewart drives his Elf Matra. *International Motor Racing Research Center/Harr Collection.*

Lauda Air. His career-changing crash of 1976 was dramatized in the 2013 feature film *Rush*, directed by Ron Howard. Lauda's Ferrari crashed at the Nürburgring circuit and burst into flames. It was a race that Lauda, widely known as the fastest driver on that track, did not think should start, due to bad safety conditions at the track, but he was outvoted by his fellow drivers. Lauda suffered severe burns to his face, head, and body. The burns were so bad that he nearly lost one ear, lost the hair on half of his head, and had permanent scarring on his face. Today, Lauda wears a cap almost nonstop, in part to hide his scarring and in part, cleverly, to advertise for sponsors.

Remarkably Lauda was back in a car within six weeks of his fiery crash. At a press conference for the 1976 Italian Grand Prix at Monza, he arrived with his wounds still fresh and bandaged. Though he admitted later to being terrified to drive, he still placed fourth in the race. The film portrays the rivalry between Lauda and James Hunt. Hunt eventually won the championship that year when Lauda stopped racing in the Japanese Grand Prix due to bad weather conditions. He almost lost his life once when he knew better than to race that day in Germany;

going forward, he was no longer going to take risks that he thought were unreasonable.

Lauda is respected today not only for his multiple world championships but also in large part for his courage after his fiery crash, when he fought his way back to the highest level of racing in the world in just six weeks. A non–motor sports fan might question the sanity of an individual who would pull a helmet down over a painful, bandaged head and slip his body once again into a machine that had almost killed him a few weeks before. Others—particularly motor sport fans, of course, but others too—admire the kind of courage and determination it took to keep doing in life what he loved, no matter what.

Brian Redman (UK), a three-time Formula 5000 series champion, a former Formula One driver, and a two-time Le Mans winner in 1978 and 1980, is now a frequent speaker and driver on the historic racing

Niki Lauda answers journalist Chris Economacki's questions after winning the 1975 United States Grand Prix at Watkins Glen International, Watkins Glen, New York, October 5, 1975. *International Motor Racing Research Center/F1 Collection.*

circuit. Like others who do this work, especially in their advanced years, Redman tells good stories of his racing career for the entertainment of his listeners—about both his youthful antics on the international racing scene and the close calls that he managed to escape with his life when that prospect looked doubtful at the time.

Redman survived three particularly bad crashes. In the 1968 Formula One Belgian Grand Prix, a mishap resulting from a suspension failure left his arm trapped between a wall and the side of his Cooper race car. He suffered a compound fracture but returned to racing in sports cars later in the season. His second bad accident was in 1971, when he was driving a Porsche 908 in a Sicilian race called the Targa Florio. In this race, his steering broke. He could not stop his car in time to avoid hitting a concrete wall, which set his car ablaze. Burns to his face, neck, hands, and legs kept him out of competition for three months. His third and worst crash of all was in 1977 in practice for a Can-Am race at Mont-Tremblant in Canada. As he crested a hill at 170 mph, his Lola T332 lifted from air caught underneath it and flipped. All Redman could do was hold on while the car raked upside down along the track. It caught the edge of the track, which flipped it back upright again and allowed rescue workers to get Redman out. He was badly injured, even more so than in any previous crash. This time, he suffered a broken neck, shoulder, breastbone, and two ribs and partially lost his eyesight! If someone were trying to tell Brian Redman something—that he was in the wrong line of business, for instance—the driver certainly heard the message this time. As he recovered, he thought about going into another line of work, but when his bones healed and his eyesight came back, he knew he wanted to be nowhere other than back in a racing car.[8]

"I was extraordinarily lucky," Redman said in a recent telephone interview. "Most of my friends in that era, they had one accident, and they were dead." He continued, "In the grand prix . . . in the Cooper in 1968 . . . [in that race] only half the drivers wore seat belts." They wanted either to be able to jump out or to be thrown out in case the car caught on fire. "If I hadn't had seatbelts on," he said, "I would have been killed."[9]

About the 1971 incident and fire in the Porsche 908 at Targa Florio, Redman said, "How lucky can you be? The thing exploded. I was covered and soaked in fuel and burning. Nobody there. No attention for 45 minutes; they couldn't get to it. I was blind . . . but how lucky was that?" He also spoke about his worst accident:

> And then when the car took off in Canada, it came down upside down, and broke my neck, split my sternum. Broke my ribs, bruised my brain; my helmet went on the road. My heart stopped, but the car rolled back on its wheels just before it came to a halt. The track doctor was a heart specialist and got it going again, and then a half hour later the ambulance blew a tire on the way to the hospital.

How many times could one test fate this way? "Each time," Redman said, "I held that some unknown thing was trying to stop me." Conviction sounded in his voice, even at the memory of it. "I was determined not to be beaten by whatever this was," he said.

American superstar and racing patriarch Mario Andretti actually underwent one of the most spectacular incidents in racing, unbelievably, nine years after he retired. Mario is the father of Michael Andretti, another racer, who in 2003 was a team owner who needed to work out some details in the car that his driver, Tony Kanaan, would be driving in the Indy 500. Kanaan was recuperating from an injury, so Michael asked his dad, then sixty-three, if he wanted to take the car out for a spin. Mario agreed, took the car out, and at 220 mph came up on debris left by a minor crash some distance ahead of him. The debris launched his IndyCar up into the air; the car flipped, end for end, three to four times and landed on its wheels. Amazingly, Andretti suffered no injuries beyond a penny-sized cut to his chin.

In an interview after the practice run, Andretti said, "When you're doing your ride, you just hang on, you know, and hope that the man upstairs doesn't forget you. I'm very fortunate."[10]

Speaking recently by phone, Andretti talked about what he thought was his greatest accomplishment in racing. "Probably staying alive," he said, without hesitation. He elaborated:

> That's a fact, mainly because safety measures were not in place when I started and through the first few decades of my career, which was the 1960s and 1970s. Now, with the technology we have today, race teams have data from every incident. The cars are instrumented to give very valuable information back. Teams learn from that information and incredible changes have been made to the race cars. Manu-

Mario Andretti thinks over his next move in his Gold Leaf Lotus at the 1969 Grand Prix at Watkins Glen, New York. *International Motor Racing Research Center/F1 Collection.*

facturers do crash tests prior to finalizing the design for the chassis, with the purpose of improving crash-worthiness.[11]

Bobby Rahal, Dario Franchitti, and James Hinchcliffe all competed or are still competing in the IndyCar series. Rahal won the Indianapolis 500 in 1986 and the overall championship in the series three times—in 1986, 1987, and 1992. Franchitti was forced to retire after an accident in Houston in 2013. He is a four-time IndyCar series champion and a three-time Indy 500 winner. Hinchcliffe has yet to win an IndyCar championship or an Indy 500, but he is a popular driver in the series and uses his story of a remarkable comeback from a terrible crash in 2015 to inspire others.

Rahal is now a team owner in IndyCar, but before he retired from racing in 1998, he had a wreck that left him a bit shaken but not seriously injured. In a recent telephone interview, Rahal talked about

**Mario Andretti competes in his Lotus in the 1978 United States Grand Prix at
Watkins Glen, New York. Andretti won the Drivers' Championship that year.**
International Motor Racing Research Center/FI Collection.

what he thought was his greatest accomplishment in racing. He said it
was "determining when I retired rather than someone else determining
it." He elaborated, "Most drivers are retired by some other outside
force, whether they get hurt, or whether they lose sponsorship or
whether they are owners in the industry itself. Most drivers don't have
the freedom or luxury of saying when they've had enough." Rahal feels
fortunate that he could make that decision for himself, choosing his
timing based on how he felt about racing versus owning and managing a
team at the time.[12]

One IndyCar driver who had that decision made for him by an
outside force, unfortunately, was Dario Franchitti. Franchitti was still
racing, as many said, at the top of his game. He had hopes of adding not
only to his overall championship run but also increasing his Indy 500
wins. Unlike Rahal, who was ready in his mid-forties to move on to
another phase of his career in the sport, Franchitti had just turned forty
but still had a will to win behind the wheel. An accident in Houston on
October 6, 2013, changed his prospects if not his will to continue in the
sport.

On the final lap of the IndyCar 2013 Grand Prix of Houston, Franchitti's car made contact with Takuma Sato's, sending Franchitti airborne into the seemingly ever-problematic catch fencing. Parts of the car went flying and injured thirteen spectators. Franchitti's injuries included a concussion, spinal fracture, and broken right ankle. Recuperating from the dangerous injuries would require some time; however, Franchitti's doctor recommended, especially in consideration of his previous injuries over the years, that he not race again—the risk of paralysis was too great. Consequently, Franchitti retired from racing that year. On November 14, 2013, he issued a public statement that read in part,

> One month recovered from the crash, and based upon the expert advice of the doctors who have treated and assessed my head and spinal injuries post-accident, it is their best medical opinion that I must stop racing. They have made it very clear that the risks involved in further racing are too great and could be detrimental to my long-term well-being. Based on this medical advice, I have no choice but to stop. [13]

Franchitti is still highly visible within motor sport. He has worked with the Chip Ganassi racing team and done some television commentating, and he frequently appears at historic racing events such as the Goodwood Revival in England, where he talks about the difficulty of leaving the sport involuntarily. In talks and panel discussions at venues such as Goodwood, he brings the American professional open-wheel racing perspective, so fresh off the track, to European motor sport enthusiasts who are not as familiar with how the sport operates in the United States. At the 2015 Revival, for example, Franchitti was part of a panel that included other retired racers such as Sir Stirling Moss and Derek Bell, among others. He is also able to drive cars in noncompetitive settings, such as doing a demonstration run alongside Jackie Stewart of historic cars once raced by Jim Clark, a natural racing hero for both Scots. As a much younger man than many of these historic racing panelists, however, Franchitti still gives the impression that he is looking to settle into his new place in the world, post racing. Racers forced to retire due to injury or other causes can struggle to find their way outside the car in which they felt so alive and with which they associated so much of their identity.

Dario Franchitti drives out of the Boot section of the Watkins Glen International racetrack at the 2009 IndyCar (IRL) race at Watkins Glen, New York. *International Motor Racing Research Center/Bill Bauman Collection.*

James Hinchcliffe, or "Hinch," as he is called, is another popular driver in IndyCar who is still active in the sport, but it might not have turned out that way after a hard crash in practice for the 2015 Indy 500. Unlike Franchitti, whose injury forced his retirement from the sport, Hinchcliffe, more than ten years younger than the Scotsman, recovered to the point where he could race again. At the time of the accident, and later when he arrived at the hospital in Indianapolis, his injuries were thought to be life threatening. A piece of metal had pierced his left thigh like a dagger, and it was still there, causing heavy bleeding. Hinchcliffe underwent surgery to have the metal removed and stop the bleeding. A long road to recovery, to even walk again, which was not guaranteed at the time, lay ahead of the racer, and he was told he would not compete in IndyCar for the foreseeable future.

It turned out that the foreseeable future was not so far away. The Canadian was faithful to his treatment and therapy regime and was cleared to race for the 2016 season. In fact, one year after his life-threatening crash, he qualified on pole for the hundredth running of

James Hinchcliffe races into the Boot section of Watkins Glen International in the 2016 IndyCar race in Watkins Glen, New York. *International Motor Racing Research Center/Josh Ashby.*

the Indianapolis 500. In the off-season, he even joined the ranks of athletes like Helio Castroneves as an IndyCar driver who competed in a televised dance competition, *Dancing with the Stars.* Hinchcliffe placed second in the competition, behind Olympic Gold medal gymnast Laurie Hernandez. In several of the episodes, he described his accident and recovery and allowed his story to serve as the basis for his partner's choreography of their dances.

RACING IS LIFE

With so many racers gone from the earlier era, people these drivers knew—colleagues, teammates, friends—the natural question from those who do not race is why these drivers kept doing it. Why did they get back in the car when their comrades clearly showed them time after time how unsafe their sport was, especially in those days? It was not only their colleagues who had troubles, either, as these racers' own accidents and life-threatening crashes attest. With danger and peril reaching so closely into their lives, what made them keep racing? The answer usually takes several forms: it was their job, and they needed to put food on the table; they simply loved driving the car; their passion for driving was more than their fear of what could happen; they thought a fatal crash could not happen to them (or said that to themselves to help rationalize their other reasons); or they felt most alive when they were racing.

A famous scene from the movie *Le Mans* gets quoted a lot in motor sport circles. A racer's widow asks racer Michael Delaney, played by Steve McQueen, "When people risk their lives, shouldn't it be for something important?"

Delaney answers, "Well, it better be."

The widow responds, "But what is so important about driving faster than anyone else?"

Paraphrasing high-wire performer Karl Wallenda, Delaney says, "A lot of people go through life doing things badly. Racing is important to men who do it well. When you're racing, it's life. Anything that happens before or after is just waiting." [14]

Most races around the world happen normally and do not result in injury-inducing crashes or terrible fatalities. Someone wins, two other people come in second and third, and the rest finish the race in place numbers that rise from there. There may be a failure with the car, and a driver may have to pack it up and go home. The racers love the feeling of driving the car, of competing and pushing the car as close to its limit as they dare. Some dare more than others; some are more skilled or have better equipment or more experience. It all depends.

Racing is a passion. If you let it catch you, racers tell you, it will grab you by the heart.

CONCLUSION

Speed and Passion

If you never drive or are driven to where you want to go, then you might think you could completely justify not only an aversion to motor sport but a claim that it is too dangerous and not a benefit to you or anyone else in society. However, even if you avoid automobile travel as often as you can out of principle, the goods and services you enjoy every day do not. The fact is that our world is interconnected through automobiles and trucks, whether we care about the gases these vehicles spew out into our beautiful, clean, fresh air or not.

Years ago, noted Cornell astronomer Carl Sagan gave a talk at Keuka College in upstate New York. There he described how beings from another planet might view our own. Examining us from millions of miles away in space, he conjectured, they might notice that we tend to move forward more than backward. Through their viewing devices, they might see that we tend to be more orderly when we are clustered together, but we follow more winding and circuitous routes when we are farther apart. There are wide expanses on the planet that we do not inhabit at all, and these areas of the Earth appear to have a more intact atmosphere—we seem to be killing ourselves with our own breath. As these extraterrestrial beings' technology advances, Sagan suggested, they can see more clearly that our bodies come in many shapes, sizes, and colors. Some of us move slowly; others more quickly. Some live many years; others end up resting in the graveyard way too early. In daylight, these beings might observe, our bodies glisten in the sun. At night, our eyes gleam as though beams of light shine out from them to guide our way. Yes, on their planet, Sagan imagined, these beings may believe that Earth is inhabited not by human beings, which they cannot yet see, but by automobiles.

Like Sagan's imaginings suggest, from a broader view, in cultures where they are prevalent, these automobiles we have created say much about who we are as a species. We value mobility, for one thing, especially of the independent variety; we also value time and the saving of it. Once those basic needs for the automobile were met, we, and car manufacturers as well, found that humans also value comfort and style, design and power, performance and prestige. In the process of designing and manufacturing these contraptions, human beings soon also found that they valued speed.

In *The Speed Handbook*, critic Enda Duffy refers to novelist Aldous Huxley's claim that "speed provides the one genuinely modern pleasure."[1] He says Huxley was not just arguing that the twentieth century created machines for speed but "implicitly reckoning speed to be modernity's only newly invented experience." Duffy continues to argue that the invention of the automobile brought the "promise, through technology, of an experience lived at a new level of intensity." Unlike mass transportation such as trains, where people ride passively along the rails in compartments, the gas-powered automobile, first patented by Carl Benz in Germany in 1886, provided the opportunity for the individual to be in control over speed and the adrenaline rush it generates in the body.[2] Cars became the body's "prosthesis," and in that vein machines "took over some powers of locomotion of the body." In doing so, writes Duffy, the automobile then demanded of the body "new intensities of sensory perception"—that is, drivers needed to tune vision, hearing, and so forth, so as to gain the most advantage from the synchronicity between human and machine. At the first car crash, Duffy also points out, we realized that meeting our new thirst for speed came with a price to ourselves and others: we could now easily pilot our way to our own death or someone else's.

Some people find beauty in gaining some measure of control or order over chaos. Painting, for example, brings together color, shape, texture, and composition to gather some sort of meaning out of the world for the artist, and through the artist, the viewer. Passion fuels our search for the intensity Duffy writes about—what is life, after all, without any sense of heightened emotion, experience, excitement, clarity? If we could go to a new place in our consciousness on a regular basis in a healthy way and appreciate the experience fully, who would not try to do that? Runners know this. Artists do too. Those who have found a passion and are able to engage in that passion and break through to new places in the mind know that sense of transcendence where they feel most alive and present in the now of existence. Once these places are found, they know somewhere desirable to go and will go to great efforts to go there again and again. For a moment, however brief, these people have tamed the beastly side of life, while at the same time respecting its power to destroy as much as to create. Racers driving the perfect lap, going as fast as they can at the absolute limit of their car's and their own abilities, know the place where their minds go while driving—it is a place of wild and unpredictable beauty.

It is in our human nature to want more intensity. Once a child is tossed into the air and feels the thrill of falling into the safety of her father's arms for the first time, she may want her father to toss her skyward again and again. Once a driver becomes "one" with a car and feels the car become an extension of his body, it is in our nature for some of us to want to use this tool to go faster or with improved performance the next time and the next. It wasn't too many generations ago that grandparents went for casual "Sunday drives" in the country, simply for the pleasure of the ride itself and viewing a change of scenery before dinner. These people may have preferred reliability and comfort over speed in their vehicles; however, the compression of time and space that automobile technology provides means that on the engineering and design side of things, increasing speed while maintaining control became an ongoing quest. As soon as one speed was reached with some degree of reliability and safety, the "limit" inched out a bit further as a new goal for technology—and its manipulators—to reach.

Driving a car fast can be an adrenaline rush for some people that they want to experience, like a roller-coaster ride, again and again. Take that intense experience to a professional level, and you find one of the reasons why motor racing has been so popular from the turn of the twentieth century until now. People enjoy not only driving cars fast but watching others do the same. For those who find beauty more significant in nature, it might be difficult to imagine, but for those who love motor sport, there is a grace to the lines of a well-designed car once drawn first on paper by hand (more so on computers these days) and a peace to the smooth movement of a human-built machine humming along down a roadway or track or roaring to life in a garage or paddock. As a created extension of the body in the way Duffy suggests, the automobile takes on characteristics of the human body for enthusiasts. You will hear car fans talk about the curves and lines of a car's design, for example. Its movement too—the smooth way a good car takes a corner, for instance, or the way it accelerates with seemingly no effort at all.

Some environmentally minded sports fans do not like motor sport because they believe it intensifies, or at least glorifies, the harm to the atmosphere that the automobile causes. They certainly make a valid point; however, to single out a grand prix and ignore the thousands of cars parked outside a baseball stadium, for example, discounts how pervasive the problem is in our world. Formula E, a newer racing series that plays with electric-powered race cars, is one avenue such a concerned sports fan might investigate. In addition, some thinking ought to be paid to the hybrid technologies that Formula One racing, for example, is trying out. In so many ways and times, motor racing has served as a development ground for new technologies in transportation. If there is to be solution to the pollution problem caused by the automobile, continuing to encourage car manufacturers to test new technologies through sport might be at least one avenue toward facilitating change.

Few racers, even from the days when race cars regularly tried out new technologies, regard themselves first as test pilots. Even so, their feedback to engineers and designers has proven as invaluable to teams as their placement in a race. Sensitive drivers, typically those who also drive the best and often drive toward the front of the pack, pushing their cars to the limit, can tell their teams when something is not quite right in a car just by feel. Why not rely on the test drivers that auto manufacturers employ for this purpose to do the job? Automakers would have to answer this question, but it seems to an observer that testing cars at their limits against other manufacturers who wish to do the same may provide a different set of results and enhance the data for all involved. This is an opportunity that an international racing series like Formula One and the World Endurance Championship can provide.

A consideration of the danger involved in motor sport throughout its history up to today poses perhaps more questions than answers for society at large. Is it worth dying just to win a race? What is it about human nature that makes us look away from the danger we might face in any given situation in which we still want to engage? More people die on the highways every year than in motor racing by thousands of times over; yet the sport can be criticized for being too dangerous. Are people willing to give up their cars and trucks because it is even more dangerous to go out and drive those on the open road?

And what about passion in general? What fuels human beings to do what they do, most especially when the forces of nature are against them? Why do we want to go higher, faster, further, stronger, or for longer periods of time? In many ways, it seems the lost human being is the one without such a passion, a desire to pursue a dream, an inward drive and push to explore and accomplish, to learn, to grow. Of the more competitive among us, there is a passion to be the best, to achieve a level of excellence that is indisputably finer than anyone else has reached. Some of us simply want to do better than we did yesterday; the struggle is inside; we don't need outside validation or to prove ourselves against the value of others at a certain task.

What makes human beings face danger when they know it is in front of them, perhaps in the shape of an action they need not necessarily take? Facing the danger of a hurricane, a natural phenomenon that one can do nothing to prevent, is one thing. Driving in a race, where everyone else is going as fast as they dare and all are hoping to win, is something else again. Where should the line be drawn for sport?

As was mentioned early on in this book, it was the intent to explore a handful of racers and their stories and see what they may have to tell us about ourselves and our own passions. Perhaps we are left with more questions than answers, but maybe that is not such a bad thing, as long as we continue to keep thinking about the passions we are so intent on chasing.

APPENDIX A

Timeline of Selected Motor Sport, Automotive, World, and Cultural Events

Note: Events in *italics* are covered in this book.

1863—July 30: Henry Ford born in Greenfield Township, Michigan.

1865—April 15: Abraham Lincoln assassinated, Ford's Theatre, Washington, DC. **June 2:** American Civil War ends when last Confederate general, Edmund Kirby Smith, surrenders.

1869—May 10: First transcontinental railroad opens across North America.

1874—November 30: Winston Churchill born in Bleinham Palace, London.

1878—December 25: Louis-Joseph Chevrolet born in La Chaux-de-Fonds, Switzerland.

1886—January 29: Karl Benz files patent in Germany for first gasoline-powered automobile.

1894—July 18–22: Motoring exhibition "*La Petit Journal* Competition for Horseless Carriages" runs from Paris to Rouen.

1895—November 28: First U.S. automobile race, the *Chicago Times-Herald* race, runs from Chicago to Evanston, Illinois, and back.

1911—May 30: First Indianapolis 500, Speedway, Indiana.

1914—July 28: World War I begins.

1918—November 11: World War I ends.

1923—May 26–27: First 24 Hours of Le Mans (Grand Prix of Endurance) race, Le Mans, France.

1933—March 4: Franklin D. Roosevelt inaugurated as thirty-second U.S. president.

1940—July 10–October 31: Battle of Britain; Royal Air Force successfully defends England from German Luftwaffe.

1941—December 7: Japanese attack Pearl Harbor, Hawaii, igniting U.S. involvement in World War II.

1945—May 7: Germany surrenders (end of World War II).

1948—February 15: First NASCAR-sanctioned race, Daytona Beach, Florida. **October 2:** First postwar road race in the United States, Watkins Glen, New York.

1950—June 25: Korean War begins.

1953—January 20: Dwight D. Eisenhower inaugurated thirty-fourth U.S. president. **June 2:** Coronation of Queen Elizabeth II, United Kingdom. **June 13–14:** First time reliable disc brakes used at 24 Hours of Le Mans, in Jaguar C-type, which won, triggering addition to production vehicles.

1955—April 30–May 1: Stirling Moss (UK) and Denis Jenkinson (UK) win Mille Miglia, thousand-mile road race in Italy. **May 26:** *Alberto Ascari (Italy) dies at Monza, Italy.* **June 11:** *24 Hours of Le Mans disaster, Le Mans, France.* **September 30:** Actor and part-time racer James Dean (age twenty-four) dies in crash driving his Porsche 550 Spyder, Cholame, California. **October 29:** Film *Rebel Without a Cause*, starring James Dean, released.

1957—March 14: Eugenio Castellotti (Italy) dies in testing in Modeno, Italy.

1958—August 3: Peter Collins (UK) dies racing in the German Grand Prix, Nürburgring, Germany.

1959—January 22: Mike Hawthorn (UK), first British Formula One world champion and winner of 24 Hours of Le Mans, 1955, dies in road accident. **February 22:** First Daytona 500, Daytona Beach, Florida. **December 12:** Jack Brabham (Australia) becomes first Formula One world champion to drive a rear-engine race car, a Cooper-Climax, Sebring, Florida.

1960—June 19: Chris Bristow (UK) and Alan Stacey (UK) die racing in Belgian Grand Prix at Spa-Francorchamps, Liège, Belgium.

1961—January 20: John F. Kennedy inaugurated thirty-fifth U.S. president. **September 10:** Wolfgang von Trips (Germany) dies racing in the Italian Grand Prix, Monza, Italy. **September 10:** Phil Hill becomes first American-born racer to win the Formula One World Championship.

1962—April 24: *Stirling Moss (UK) crashes at Goodwood Circuit, UK, surviving but ending his professional racing career.* **November 1:** Ricardo Rodriquez (Mexico) dies in practice for the Mexican Grand Prix, Mexico City, Mexico.

1963—November 22: President John F. Kennedy assassinated in Dallas, Texas.

1964—April 17: Ford Mustang first introduced to public at New York World's Fair. **May 30:** *Eddie Sachs (U.S.) dies racing in Indy 500, Speedway, Indiana.* **May 30:** *Dave MacDonald (U.S.) dies racing in Indy 500, Speedway, Indiana.*

1966—December 21: Film *Grand Prix*, starring James Garner, released in the United States.

1968—April 7: *Jim Clark (Scotland) dies racing in Formula Two at Hockenheim, Germany.*

1969—May 11: Porsche 917 competition debut, the six-hour Spa-Francorchamps, Belgium. **July 20:** Neil Armstrong becomes the first human being to walk on the moon. **August 15–18:** Woodstock Music and Art Fair in Bethel, New York.

1970—June 2: *Bruce McLaren (New Zealand) dies in testing at Goodwood Circuit, UK.* **June 21:** Piers Courage (UK) dies racing in the Dutch Grand Prix, Zandvoort, Netherlands. **September 5:** Jochen Rindt (Austria/b. Germany) dies in practice for Italian Grand Prix, Monza, Italy.

1971—June 23: Film *Le Mans*, starring Steve McQueen, released in the United States. **October 24:** Jo Siffert (Switzerland) dies racing at Brands Hatch, Kent, UK.

1973—July 29: Roger Williamson (UK) dies racing in the Dutch Grand Prix, Zandvoort, Netherlands. **October 6:** *François Cevert (France) dies in practice for the United States Grand Prix,*

Watkins Glen, New York; Jackie Stewart (UK), three-time world champion, retires from racing.

1974—**March 22:** Peter Revson (U.S.) dies testing Shadow F1 car in Midrand, South Africa. **August 9:** President Richard Nixon resigns; Gerald Ford assumes office as thirty-eighth U.S. president. **October 6:** Helmuth Koinigg (Austria) dies racing in the United States Grand Prix, Watkins Glen, New York.

1975—**August 17:** Mark Donohue (U.S.) dies in practice for the Austrian Grand Prix, Graz, Austria.

1977—**March 5:** Tom Pryce (UK) dies in practice for the South African Grand Prix, Midrand, South Africa.

1978—**September 10:** Ronnie Peterson (Sweden) dies racing in the Italian Grand Prix, Monza, Italy, and Mario Andretti (U.S.) wins the Formula One World Championship.

1982—**May 8:** *Gilles Villeneuve (Canada) dies in qualifying for the Belgian Grand Prix at Zolder, Leuven, Belgium.*

1989—**November 9:** Berlin Wall starts coming down.

1994—**April 30:** *Roland Ratzenberger (Austria) dies in qualifying for the San Marino Grand Prix, Imola, Italy.* **May 1:** *Ayrton Senna (Brazil) dies racing in San Marino Grand Prix, Imola, Italy.*

2001—**February 18:** *Dale Earnhardt (U.S.) dies racing in the Daytona 500, Daytona Beach, Florida.* **September 11:** Terrorist attacks in New York City, Washington, DC, and Pennsylvania.

2009—**January 20:** Barack Obama inaugurated forty-fourth U.S. president.

2011—**October 16:** *Dan Wheldon (UK) dies racing in IndyCar race, Las Vegas, Nevada.*

2013—**September 20:** Film *Rush*, directed by Ron Howard, released in the United States. **December 29:** Seven-time Formula One world champion Michael Schumacher (Germany) suffers serious head injury from ski accident in Alps.

2015—**July 17:** *Julies Bianchi (France) dies in Nice, France months after his crash in the Japanese Grand Prix, on October 5, 2014, in Suzuka, Japan.* **August 24:** *Justin Wilson (UK) dies racing in IndyCar, Pocono Raceway, Pennsylvania.*

APPENDIX B

Timeline of Safety and Mechanical Changes in Formula One International Motor Racing

Widely considered the "pinnacle" of motor sport in the world, Formula One (F1) international motor racing, like all motor sports, will never be 100 percent safe. However, a look at this timeline shows that the sport has gone from virtually no safety concerns at its inception in the mid-twentieth century, to primitive measures, to gradual and refined improvements over its nearly seventy-year history thus far. [1]

Work on safety continues; though deaths in the sport are not as frequent as they once were, as of this book's publication, the last fatality resulting from racing in Formula One was as recent as that of Jules Bianchi (France) in 2015. Before that, the last fatalities in that series alone occurred over twenty years earlier—Roland Ratzenberger (Austria) and Ayrton Senna (Brazil), both killed in the same race weekend in 1994.

1950   Front engines and drum brakes make up the first race cars when the Formula One World Championship begins at the Silverstone racing circuit in England. Safety is not considered; drivers readily jump into cars that are basically fuel tanks attached to engines.

1955   Disc brakes are introduced, as is a relocation of the engine from the front to the middle of cars. Cooper is the first to introduce the change in engine in a Formula One race, with Australian racer Jack Brabham at the wheel.

1960   Formula One begins to adopt safety measures.

1961   Rollover bars are first introduced—these curved metal bars are designed to protect a driver's head should the car overturn.

1963   The sport's governing body, the Federation Internationale de l'Automobile (FIA), takes responsibility for ensuring safety at Formula One racetracks. Flag signals (which give drivers certain messages, such as "Caution," warning that there is a safety issue ahead on the track, such as a spun or stopped car) are first used. Issues of fire safety—a chief concern among drivers—are addressed by requiring drivers to wear fire-resistant suits. The cars have modified fuel tanks for the same reason. Additionally, the design of cockpits is reconfigured to allow easier exit by drivers in an emergency.

1968   Electronic systems now require interrupters. The rollover bar has an additional requirement that it be five centimeters (just under two inches) over the driver's head. A full-visor helmet is first worn in F1 by American driver Dan Gurney in practice for the British Grand Prix.

1969   A double system for extinguishing fires is introduced.

1970   FIA begins circuit inspections with required criteria relating to matters such as double crash barriers, a pit wall dividing the track and the pit lane, and a barrier of space equaling three meters (nearly ten feet) between fencing and spectators.

1971   Cars must be constructed so that a driver can be removed in five seconds or less if a rescue is necessary.

1972   FIA institutes a "code of conduct" for drivers. Safety requirements include the six-point seatbelt. Security foam is included with fuel tanks. Red back lights and headrests are introduced.

1973   Drivers must undergo medical tests. Fuel tanks are incorporated into fire-resistance and crash designs.

1974   Safety walls at racing circuits are required.

1975 FIA requires a medical center, training, and service for resuscitation. FIA also requires marshals and sets standards for fireproof racing suits.

1977 FIA sets standards for helmets as well as specs for gravel traps.

1978 FIA super license is required for drivers in F1 races. Front roll bars and sheet-pile wall behind drivers are first seen on cars.

1979 Larger cockpits are required. NASA's five-layer fireproof clothing is used by drivers Niki Lauda, Mario Andretti, and Carlos Reutemann.

1980 Medical centers at circuits must be permanent facilities.

1981 Drivers' feet must also be protected by the car safety cell.

1984 Fuel tank must be situated between the driver and the engine.

1985 Crash tests measure frontal impact.

1986 F1 circuits must have a helicopter on stand-by for medical emergencies.

1989 Somewhat like that required for the Olympic Games, drug testing is introduced. Further requirements to pit wall and track safety walls specs are introduced: pit wall must be at least 1.35 meters (about 4.4 feet) high; safety walls at track need to be at least 1 meter (3.28 feet) high.

1990 Driver rescue training is required. Steering wheels must be detachable; cars need to have larger rearview mirrors.

1991 Testing begins for roll bars, seatbelts, and survival cells.

1992 Official F1 safety car and crash tests with tighter specs are introduced.

1993 Unusual mixtures of fuel are eliminated. Certain measurements on the car are changed: reduction in rear wing height; expanded front wing to ground distance; and smaller steering wheel circumference. Protective material around driver's head is expanded from 80 square centimeters (31.5 square inches) to 400 square centimeters (157.5 square inches).

1994 The deaths of Senna and Ratzenberger in May bring a big year of change, including use of new technologies available to improve safety and computer analyses to help root out problem areas, such as twenty-seven dangerous corners on racetracks identified for required changes. Additional problem areas of the sport addressed include banning of traction control, ABS, power-assisted brakes, and automatic transmissions; required testing methods for tire barriers; and the requirement that barriers be held in place with rubber belts. Speed limits in the pit lane are now 80 kmh (48 mph) during practices and 120 kmh (74 mph) during races. Crash helmet production must meet higher spec requirements. In addition, all refueling crew must wear fireproof clothing.

1995   FIA introduces new requirements for drivers to obtain a super license for international competition. Crash tests now include lateral testing, and the specs are stricter.

1997   FIA requires accident data recorders, similar to flight data recorders for airplanes, in all race cars in F1 to improve crash analyses. Attention is paid to rear crashes now, with both required rear-impact tests and the introduction of required protective parts on cars for rear collisions. In addition, tire barriers at tracks must now be bolted, not tied.

1998   While the required width of F1 race cars shrinks from 2 to 1.8 meters (5.9 feet), the cockpits are enlarged. A new ten-second rule requires that a driver must be able to detach his or her steering wheel, get out of the car, and reattach the steering wheel him- or herself, all within ten seconds. Specs for rearview mirrors are now set at no smaller than 120 × 50 millimeters (4.7 inches by just under 2 inches).

1999   To avoid wheels flying off during crashes, wheels are now attached to the car's chassis with tethers. The construction of the cockpit is arranged so that the driver and seat may be removed at one time, together. Tighter specs are set for front crash testing. The number of required medical vehicles and so forth is increased at tracks: four medically prepared vehicles plus a car for a physician are mandatory. Asphalt replaces gravel in some runoff areas at tracks.

2000   Several spec changes include raised impact speed for crash testing from 13 to 14 meters per second (42.6 feet/second to 46 feet/second); thickness of carbon fiber cockpit wall required to be 3.5 millimeters (0.138 inches); roll bar height over driver's head increased from 50 to 70 millimeters (2 inches to 2.75 inches); and bar required to withstand 2.4 tons of lateral force.

2001   Improved safety standards for marshals are introduced. A ten-second stop-and-go penalty is imposed for failure to heed the blue-flag rule of allowing car behind to pass if a blue flag is shown three times. FIA standardizes headrest requirements. Cockpit walls at the driver's head level must rise toward the back at sixteen degrees. Lateral impact test speeds are increased from 7 to 10 meters per second.

2002   Stop-and-go (time) penalties will be applied for the following driver errors: false start; causing a crash; pushing a competitor off the track; restricting a driver trying to pass; speeding in the pit lane; and gaining track position by driving over chicanes. Rear lights are made larger: 6 × 6 centimeters. Lateral test for rear of cars has increased specs.

2003   HANS (head and neck support) device, first presented in 2001, is now required for all drivers. Several tracks make safety improvements, including runoff areas, chicanes to slow cars down, better safety walls, improved pit exit lanes with the goal of cars rejoining races at speed, and more emergency access pathways.

2004   FIA sets even stricter guidelines for driver helmet production. New racetracks at Bahrain and Shanghai give the sport a chance to design circuits with state-of-the-art safety developments in mind from the beginning. Older tracks, such as at Monte Carlo (Monaco Grand Prix), attempt to keep up in terms of safety (e.g., Monte Carlo, which is exclusively a street circuit, builds permanent team garages and pit lane).

2005   Cockpit padding thickness spec increases from 75 to 100 millimeters (2.95 to 3.9 inches). A spec of six tons' load is put on tethers holding wheels to chassis. Certain body parts on the car (front wing, other aerodynamic parts, etc.) must be coated with additional Kevlar fiber or a like material to minimize sharp carbon fiber debris on the track after accidents.

2006   Rear crash test standard is increased from 12 to 15 meters/second.

2007   Several rules are introduced regarding procedures when the safety car is deployed. LEDs in cockpit show drivers marshal's signals. Yearlong improvements to Spa bring it back to the calendar. Speed is reduced in the pit lane from 100 to 80 kmh (62 to 50 mph).

2009   Motor Sport Safety Development Fund is established by FIA to eventually train young drivers and officials in safety and offer a safety program. The process for selecting race stewards is changed, and video analysis is enhanced; FIA will publish findings after accidents online, sometimes with video.

2010   Stewards are to be assisted in their decision making about race incidents by an experienced F1 driver; each grand prix must have three permanent stewards and one local.

2011   Double-diffusers and F-ducts are banned to decrease speed of cars by decreasing downforce. More specs are introduced on roll bars; two tethers are required to keep wheels attached to uprights; regulations are imposed on where rearview mirrors may be mounted to keep them visible for drivers and not where they are most suited for aerodynamics. Further helmet development includes the addition of a Zylon strip across the top of the polycarbonate visor, thereby double-strengthening the acknowledged weakest area of the protective helmet (F1).

2015   Virtual safety car (lit "VSC" on signs around track instead of a vehicle driving out in front of the pack to slow the cars down during yellow-flag caution periods for car or debris removal, etc.) may be used instead of safety car when stewards determine it would be safer to do so.[2]

NOTES

INTRODUCTION

1. "Juan Manuel Fangio," *Independent*, July 18, 1995, http://www.independent.co.uk/news/people/obituaries-juan-manuel-fangio-1591999.html.

2. "Company History," Daimler.com, accessed May 12, 2015, https://www.daimler.com/company/tradition/company-history/1885-1886.html.

3. Ivan Rendall, *The Checkered Flag: 100 Years of Motor Racing*. Secaucus, NJ: Chartwell Books, 1993, 12–15.

4. "Rules of the Providence Horseless Carriage Race," *Scientific American* 75 (August 1, 1896): 122, accessed May 12, 2015, https://books.google.com/books?id=itkxAQAAMAAJ&pg=PA122&lpg=PA122&dq=narragansett+park+rhode+island+state+fair+1896&source=bl&ots=tbTj3LM2lS&sig=9e4Ac_vOfCkNtGFHHmu4TywIIXg&hl=en&sa=X&ei=iElSVeX4CNOwyASn1YCACw&ved=0CCMQ6AEwAQ#v=onepage&q=narragansett%20park%20rhode%20island%20state%20fair%201896&f=false.

5. Rendall, *The Checkered Flag*, 12–15; Gary Hartstein, "The Organization of Motor Sport: Origins," in *Medicine in Motor Sport*. Paris, France: FIA Institute for Motor Sport Safety and Sustainability, 2011.

6. H. L. Barber, *Story of the Automobile: Its History and Development from 1760 to 1917*. Chicago: A. J. Munson & Co., 1917, 161.

7. "Motoring History 1907–1914," Brooklands Museum, accessed May 12, 2015, http://www.brooklandsmuseum.com/index.php?/history/motoring-history-1907-1914; "History of the Milwaukee Mile," Wisconsin State Fair, accessed May 12, 2015, http://wistatefair.com/wsfp/wp-content/uploads/2013/02/Milwaukee-Mile-History.pdf; "History: The World When IMS Opened,"

Indianapolis Motor Speedway, accessed May 12, 2015, https://www.
indianapolismotorspeedway.com/history/the-world-when-ims-opened.

8. Éamon Ó. Cofaigh, "Motor Sport in France: Testing-Ground for the
World," in *The History of Motor Sport: A Case Study Analysis*, ed. David
Hassan. New York: Routledge, 2013, 5–17.

9. Cofaigh, "Motor Sport in France," 5–17.

10. Christopher Hilton, *Grand Prix Century: The First 100 Years of the
World's Most Glamorous and Dangerous Sport*. Sparkford, UK: Haynes Publishing, 2005, 13.

11. Jamie Page Deaton, "Top 10 Everyday Car Technologies That Came
from Racing," Auto.howstuffworks.com, accessed October 12, 2016, http://
auto.howstuffworks.com/under-the-hood/trends-innovations/top-10-car-tech-
from-racing11.htm.

12. Christian Sylt, "F1 Loses 25 Million Viewers Driven by Switch to Pay
TV," Forbes.com, February 1, 2015, http://www.forbes.com/sites/csylt/2015/
02/01/f1-loses-25-million-viewers-driven-by-switch-to-pay-tv/2; Amanda Kondology, "Daytona Speedweek's Viewership Up on FOX Sports 1," TV by the
Numbers, February 26, 2015, http://tvbythenumbers.zap2it.com/2015/02/26/
daytona-speedweeks-viewership-up-on-fox-sports-1/368147; "24 Hours of Le
Mans 245,000 Spectators," 24 Hours of Le Mans, June 23, 2013, http://www.
24h-lemans.com/en/news/24-hours-of-le-mans-245-000-spectators_2_2_1746_
11498.html; "2016 Le Mans 24 Hours: 263,500 Spectators!," Motorsport.com,
June 19, 2016, https://www.motorsport.com/lemans/news/2016-le-mans-24-
hours-263-500-spectators-789940.

13. John L. Matthews, *Grand Prix: The Killer Years: Extended Interviews
from the BBC Film*. Manchester, UK: Bigger Picture Projects, 2014, 43, 41.

14. Tom Wolfe, *The Right Stuff*. New York: Farrar, Straus & Giroux, 1979,
30.

15. Oliver Owen, "The Value of Stirling Still Rising at 80," *Guardian*, September 12, 2009, accessed December 20, 2016, https://www.theguardian.com/
sport/2009/sep/13/stirling-moss-interview-f1.

I. FATHERS AND SONS, SPEED AND SUPERSTITIONS

1. Derek Bell, telephone interview with the author, January 31, 2014.

2. "St. Anthony of Padua," CatholicOnline.org, accessed January 14, 2017,
http://www.catholic.org/saints/saint.php?saint_id=24.

3. Kevin Desmond, *The Man with Two Shadows: The Story of Alberto
Ascari*. New York: Proteus Book Publishing Group, 1981, 13–30.

4. Desmond, *The Man with Two Shadows*, 29.

5. Steve Small, "Alberto Ascari," in *Grand Prix Who's Who*. Malvern, UK: Icon Publishing, 2012, 24.

6. Small, "Alberto Ascari," 56.

7. Nigel Roebuck, "The Last Great Italian GP Star," *Motor Sport Magazine*, July 2012, http://www.motorsportmagazine.com/archive/page/july-2012/99.

8. Mario Andretti, e-mail to the author, March 3, 2017.

9. Roebuck, "The Last Great Italian GP Star," 102.

10. Small, "Alberto Ascari," 56.

11. "Formula 1 Grand Prix de Monaco 2016," Formula1.com, accessed May 24, 2016, https://www.formula1.com/content/fom-website/en/championship/races/2016/Monaco.html.

12. Small, "Alberto Ascari," 54.

13. Roebuck, "The Last Great Italian GP Star," 102.

14. Desmond, *The Man with Two Shadows*, 149.

15. Roebuck, "The Last Great Italian GP Star," 103; Small, "Alberto Ascari," 54.

16. Roebuck, "The Last Great Italian GP Star," 102.

17. Mario Andretti, e-mail to the author, March 3, 2017.

18. Roebuck, "The Last Great Italian GP Star," 102.

2. THE FOG OF WAR AND MOTION

1. Carl von Clausewitz, *On War*, ed. and trans. Michael Howard and Peter Paret. Princeton, NJ: Princeton University Press, 1989, 101, accessed February 1, 2017, http://slantchev.ucsd.edu/courses/ps143a/readings/Clausewitz%20-%20On%20War,%20Books%201%20and%208.pdf.

2. "Normandy American Cemetery and Memorial," American Battle Monuments Commission, accessed May 12, 2016, https://www.abmc.gov/cemeteries-memorials/europe/normandy-american-cemetery#.WJKPTVMrIqN.

3. Quentin Spurring, *Le Mans: The Official History of the World's Greatest Motor Race, 1949–59*. Dorset, UK: Evro Publishing, 2011, 215; Christopher Hilton, *Le Mans '55: The Crash That Changed the Face of Motor-Racing*. Derby, UK: Derby Books Publishing Company, 2012, 18; Richard Heap, dir., *The Deadliest Crash: The Le Mans 1955 Disaster*, DVD, Bigger Picture Films, 2010.

4. Spurring, *Le Mans*, 243.

5. Hilton, *Le Mans '55*, 22.

6. Steve Small, *Autocourse Grand Prix Who's Who*, 4th ed. Malvern, UK: Icon Publishing, 2012, 454; John Fitch, *Racing with Mercedes*. Lime Rock, CT: Fitch Wertz Publishing, 2006, 62.

7. Hilton, *Le Mans '55*, 43; Simon Taylor, "Lunch with John Fitch," *Motor Sport* magazine, November 2010, http://www.motorsportmagazine.com/archive/article/november-2010/67/lunch-john-fitch.

8. Howard Ganley, "Cowboy, Sailor, Racer, Inventor, and . . . 'Chippie,'" *Motor Sport* magazine, July 2008, http://www.motorsportmagazine.com/archive/article/july-2008/78/cowboy-sailor-racer.

9. Spurring, *Le Mans*, 215.

10. Spurring, *Le Mans*, 245.

11. Fitch, *Racing*, 66.

12. Hilton, *Le Mans '55*, 70, 84.

13. Hilton, *Le Mans '55*, 73.

14. Heap, *The Deadliest Crash*.

15. Hilton, *Le Mans '55*, 73.

16. Hilton, *Le Mans '55*, 96–97.

17. Spurring, *Le Mans*, 216; Heap, *The Deadliest Crash*; Hilton, *Le Mans '55*, 99; "Safety: Lane Width," U.S. Department of Transportation, Federal Highway Administration, accessed May 20, 2016, http://safety.fhwa.dot.gov/geometric/pubs/mitigationstrategies/chapter3/3_lanewidth.cfm.

18. Hilton, *Le Mans '55*, 101–2.

19. Fitch, *Racing*, 68.

20. Fitch, *Racing*, 69.

21. Fitch, *Racing*, 69, 61.

22. Hilton, *Le Mans '55*, 200–201.

23. Hilton, *Le Mans '55*, 204–5; Stirling Moss, public appearance, Lime Rock Park Historic Festival, Lime Rock Park, Lakeville, Connecticut, September 2012; Spurring, *Le Mans*, 249.

24. Spurring, *Le Mans*, 274.

25. "Danish Driver Allen Simonsen, 34, Killed at Le Mans," *Guardian*, June 22, 2013, https://www.theguardian.com/sport/2013/jun/22/danish-allen-simonsen-killed-le-mans.

26. "Fitch Universal Barrels® Crash Cushion System," Energy Absorption Systems, accessed February 1, 2007, http://www.energyabsorption.com/products/products_universal_barrels.asp; "Racing Safety with John Fitch," Race Safety, accessed February 1, 2017, http://www.racesafety.com/fitchbio.html.

3. SMOKE OVER THE HEARTLAND

1. Ralph Kramer, *Indianapolis Motor Speedway: 100 Years of Racing*. Iola, WI: Krause Publications, 2009, 15–16.

2. Kramer, *Indianapolis Motor Speedway*, 22; Cory Shouten, "Meet 'Crazy' Carl Fisher, Father of the Indy 500," CBSNews.com, May 27, 2016, accessed August 17, 2016, http://www.cbsnews.com/news/meet-crazy-carl-fisher-the-father-of-the-indy-500.

3. Kramer, *Indianapolis Motor Speedway*, 34; "Two Perished in Auto Race," *Evening Citizen* (Ottawa, Canada), August 20, 1909, https://news.google.com/newspapers?id=OKUuAAAAIBAJ&sjid=69gFAAAAIBAJ&pg=7237%2C2845320.

4. Kramer, *Indianapolis Motor Speedway*, 47.

5. Kramer, *Indianapolis Motor Speedway*, 19; Ralph Kramer, *Indianapolis 500: A Century of Excitement*. Iola, WI: F+W Media, 2010.

6. Kramer, *Indianapolis Motor Speedway*, 53.

7. Kramer, *Indianapolis 500*, 18.

8. "Marmon Car Wins; Death Marked Race," *New York Times*, May 31, 2011, http://query.nytimes.com/mem/archive-free/pdf?res=9B04E6D91431E233A25752C3A9639C946096D6CF.

9. Andy Hall, "ABC's First Indy 500 Broadcast in 1965," ESPN.com, May 2016, http://www.espnfrontrow.com/2016/05/tbt-abcs-first-indy-500-broadcast-in-1965.

10. "Sid Collins," Indiana Journalism Hall of Fame, Indiana University, accessed August 18, 2016, http://mediaschool.indiana.edu/ijhf/sid-collins.

11. Art Garner, *Black Noon: The Day They Stopped the Indy 500*. New York: St. Martin's Press, 2014, 52.

12. Garner, *Black Noon*, 59.

13. Garner, *Black Noon*, 61.

14. Garner, *Black Noon*, 43–51.

15. "Sid Collins' Impromptu Eulogy of Eddie Sachs Touches Racing Fans," *AutoWeek*, May 13, 2016, http://autoweek.com/article/indy-100/16-sid-collins-impromptu-eulogy-eddie-sachs-touches-racing-fans.

16. Photograph and letter, International Motor Racing Research Center, National Speed Sport News Collection.

17. Garner, *Black Noon*, 292.

18. Garner, *Black Noon*, 294.

19. "Memorial Day Traffic Toll Climbs to Record of 474," *Blade* (Toledo, Ohio), June 1, 1965, https://news.google.com/newspapers?nid=1350&dat=19650601&id=EOpOAAAAIBAJ&sjid=cgEEAAAAIBAJ&pg=3376,965348&hl=en.

4. NATURAL

1. BBC Four, *Legends of F1: Jim Clark*, Documentary film, https://www.youtube.com/watch?v=c0fMoPgsA3M&t=444s.

2. BBC Four, *Legends of F1*.

3. Jim Clark, *Jim Clark at the Wheel: The World's Greatest Motor Racing Champion Tells His Own Supercharged Success Story*. New York: Simon & Schuster, 1966, 17.

4. Clark, *Jim Clark at the Wheel*, 18.

5. Clark, *Jim Clark at the Wheel*, 18.

6. Clark, *Jim Clark at the Wheel*, 21.

7. Clark, *Jim Clark at the Wheel*, 23.

8. Clark, *Jim Clark at the Wheel*, 37.

9. Clark, *Jim Clark at the Wheel*, 38.

10. Karl Ludvigsen, "He Could Charm the Birds from the Trees," *Motor Sport* magazine, July 2010, http://www.motorsportmagazine.com/archive/article/july-2010/54/he-could-charm-birds-trees.

11. Clark, *Jim Clark at the Wheel*, 64.

12. Michael Cannell, *The Limit: Life and Death on the 1961 Grand Prix Circuit*. New York: Hachette Book Group, 2011, 261–63.

13. BBC Four, *Legends of F1*.

14. BBC Four, *Legends of F1*.

15. Derek Bell, telephone interview with the author, January 30, 2017.

16. John L. Matthews, *Grand Prix: The Killer Years: Extended Interviews from the BBC Film*. Manchester, UK: Bigger Picture Projects, 2014.

17. Danny Scott, "Me and My Motor: Derek Bell, Le Mans Legend," *Sunday Times Driving*, February 20, 2017, accessed March 1, 2017, https://www.driving.co.uk/news/interview/motor-derek-bell-le-mans-legend.

18. Graham Gauld, *Jim Clark: Racing Hero*. Köln, Germany: McKlein Publishing, 2014.

19. Matthews, *Grand Prix*, 39.

20. "In Memoriam," *Motor Sport* magazine, May 1968, http://www.motorsportmagazine.com/archive/page/may-1968/13.

21. "Jim Clark," ESPN.co.uk, http://en.espn.co.uk/teamlotus/motorsport/driver/801.html.

22. Matthews, *Grand Prix*, 41.

23. Matthews, *Grand Prix*, 40–41.

5. ACHIEVER

1. Bruce McLaren, *From the Cockpit.* Sherborne, Dorset, UK: Frederick Muller Limited, 1964, 270.

2. "Perthes Disease," Ortho Info, American Academy of Orthopedic Surgeons, accessed April 22, 2017, http://orthoinfo.aaos.org/topic.cfm?topic=a00070.

3. McLaren, *From the Cockpit*, 18.

4. "Our Story: Bruce McLaren," Wilson Home Trust, accessed April 22, 2017, http://wilsonhometrust.org.nz/our-story.

5. Eoin Young, *McLaren Memories: A Biography of Bruce McLaren.* Somerset, UK: Haynes Publishing, 2015, 24.

6. Bruce McLaren, "Autobiography," Bruce McLaren Trust, accessed April 22, 2017, http://www.bruce-mclaren.com/about-bruce-mclaren/autobiography.html.

7. McLaren, "Autobiography."

8. Young, *McLaren Memories*, 12.

9. Tyler Alexander, *A Life and Times with McLaren.* Phoenix, AZ: David Bull Publishing, 2015.

10. Johnson Wax, "Press Release: McLaren's Gone, but Team Will Carry On in Cam-Am," June 1970, International Motor Racing Research Center archives.

11. "Amanda McLaren Interview: Why She Loves F1," video posted to YouTube by Motoring Australia, January 25, 2017, accessed April 23, 2017, https://www.youtube.com/watch?v=Xpl24QA49KM&t=182s.

12. "Amanda McLaren interview."

6. ROMANTIC

1. Rick Hughey, e-mail to the author, January 18, 2017.

2. "The Tragic Tale of Francois Cevert," Racer.com, September 30, 2013, http://www.racer.com/f1/item/98165-insight-the-tragic-tale-of-francois-cevert.

3. "The Tragic Tale."

4. "Legends of F1—Francois Cevert," video posted to YouTube by F1 Legends, November 7, 2016, https://www.youtube.com/watch?v=JM62FcxLWM8.

5. Alan Henry, "Looking Back on Francois Cevert," *Motor Sport* magazine, March 1985, http://www.motorsportmagazine.com/archive/page/march-1985/62.

6. Nigel Roebuck, "Model Pupil Francois Cevert," *Motor Sport* magazine, November 2013, http://www.motorsportmagazine.com/archive/page/november-2013/55.

7. "Legends of F1—Francois Cevert."

8. "Legends of F1—Francois Cevert."

9. Steve Bieler, e-mail to the author, December 20, 2016.

10. "The Tragic Tale," 1.

11. Kevin Hughey, personal interview with the author, Watkins Glen, New York, October 6, 2013.

12. Jackie Stewart, telephone interview with the author, December 19, 2012.

13. Jackie Stewart, *Jackie Stewart: Winning Is Not Enough—the Autobiography.* London: Headline Publishing Group, 2009, 280–81.

14. "The Tragic Tale," 6.

15. Samy C. G. Beau-Marquet, telephone interview with and e-mails to the author, December 7, 2016, and March 4, 2017.

7. DRIVEN

1. Gerald Donaldson, *Gilles Villeneuve: The Life of the Legendary Racing Driver.* Toronto, Ontario: McClelland & Stewart, 1989. All quotes in this chapter are from this source unless otherwise stated.

2. Sid Watkins in Rob Widdows and Nigel Roebuck, "Gilles Villeneuve," *Motor Sport* magazine, May 2012, http://www.motorsportmagazine.com/archive/page/may-2012/56.

3. Donaldson, *Gilles Villeneuve*, 322.

4. Enzo Ferrari in Widdows and Roebuck, "Gilles Villenueve."

5. Bud Moeller, e-mail to the author, December 8, 2016.

6. Jody Scheckter in Widdows and Roebuck, "Gilles Villeneuve."

7. "View from the Stands," *On Track* magazine, June 3, 1982, 6.

8. MYSTIC

1. Christopher Hilton, *Memories of Senna: Anecdotes and Insights from Those Who Knew Him.* Sparkford, UK: Haynes Publishing, 2011, 83.

2. Asif Kapadia, dir., *Senna*, DVD, ARC Entertainment, 2011. Unless otherwise stated, quotes and much of the source material for this chapter come from archival footage shown as part of this documentary film.

3. Hilton, *Memories of Senna*, 160.

4. "Prost's Touching Tribute to Senna: Friends and Colleagues Bear a Champion to His Grave," *Independent*, May 5, 1994, http://www.independent.co.uk/sport/motor-racing-prosts-touching-tribute-to-senna-friends-and-colleagues-bear-a-champions-body-to-his-1433924.html.

5. Instituto Ayrton Senna (Ayrton Senna Institute), accessed March 1, 2017, http://www.institutoayrtonsenna.org.br.

6. Marc Giroux, e-mail to the author, December 20, 2016.

9. REBEL

1. Amy Rosewater, "Keepsakes Keep Fans Sold on Racing," *USA Today*, August 29, 2003, http://usatoday30.usatoday.com/sports/motor/nascar/2003-08-29-souvenirs_x.htm.

2. Jeff Cvitkovic, *I Am Dale Earnhardt*, DVD, Spike, 2015.

3. Cvitkovic, *I Am Dale Earnhardt*.

4. Kevin Cherry, "Cannon Mills," NCpedia.org, 2006, http://www.ncpedia.org/cannon-mills.

5. Leigh Montville, *At the Altar of Speed: The Fast Life and Tragic Death of Dale Earnhardt*. New York: Doubleday, 2001, 33.

6. Montville, *At the Altar of Speed*, 37.

7. Cvitkovic, *I Am Dale Earnhardt*.

8. Cvitkovic, *I Am Dale Earnhardt*.

9. Cvitkovic, *I Am Dale Earnhardt*.

10. "Daytona International Speedway: Through the Years," NASCAR.com, accessed April 19, 2017, http://galleries.nascar.com/gallery/61/daytona-international-speedway-through-the-years#/18.

11. Cvitkovic, *I Am Dale Earnhardt*.

12. Montville, *At the Altar of Speed*, 8.

13. "Dale Earnhardt Obituary," Legacy.com, accessed April 19, 2017, http://www.legacy.com/ns/dale-earnhardt-obituary/39595.

10. STILL HAPPENING

1. John L. Matthews, *Grand Prix: The Killer Years: Extended Interviews from the BBC Film*. Manchester, UK: Bigger Picture Projects, 2014.

2. Matthews, *Grand Prix*, 41.

3. Jules Bianchi Society, accessed February 14, 2017, http://www.julesbianchisociety.org/en.

4. "Justin Wilson," Twitter, accessed February 14, 2017, https://twitter.com/justin_wilson.

5. Andy Hallbery and Jeff Olson, *Lionheart: Remembering Dan Wheldon*. St. Petersburg, FL: Lionheart Books, 2016, 15.

6. Hallbery and Olson, *Lionheart*, 27.

7. Hallbery and Olson, *Lionheart*, 199.

8. Hallbery and Olson, *Lionheart*, 201.

11. GREAT ESCAPES

1. Brian Redman, *Daring Drivers, Deadly Tracks: A Racer's Memoir of a Dangerous Decade, 1965–1975.* Dorcet, UK: Evro Publishing, 2016, 13.

2. "Global Status Report on Road Safety," World Health Organization, http://www.who.int/violence_injury_prevention/road_safety_status/2015/Executive_summary_GSRRS2015.pdf?ua=1.

3. John L. Matthews, *Grand Prix: The Killer Years: Extended Interviews from the BBC Film.* Manchester, UK: Bigger Picture Projects, 2014.

4. Derek Bell, telephone interview with the author, January 31, 2017.

5. Sir Stirling Moss, personal interview with the author, Mayfair, London, November 23, 2015.

6. Larry Kessler, e-mail to the author, December 11, 2016.

7. Sir Jackie Stewart, telephone interview with the author, December 19, 2012.

8. Redman, *Daring Drivers.*

9. Brian Redman, telephone interview with the author, August 29, 2013.

10. "IndyCar Mario Andretti Crash—2003," video posted to YouTube by MP4/7, September 29, 2006, https://www.youtube.com/watch?v=kMeE9NAh60I; "IRL: Mario Andretti Flips at Indy," Motorsport.com, April 25, 2003, https://www.motorsport.com/indycar/news/irl-mario-andretti-flips-at-indy.

11. Mario Andretti, telephone and e-mail interviews with the author, March 3, 2017.

12. Bobby Rahal, telephone interview with the author, February 10, 2014.

13. "Franchitti Unable to Continue Racing Career," ChipGanssiRacing.com, http://www.chipganassiracing.com/News/2013/11/FRANCHITTI-UNABLE-TO-CONTINUE-RACING-CAREER.aspx.

14. Lee H. Katzin, dir., *Le Mans*, film, 1970.

CONCLUSION

1. Enda Duffy, *The Speed Handbook: Velocity, Pleasure, Modernism.* Durham, NC: Duke University Press, 2009, 4–6.

2. "Company History," Daimler.com, accessed October 11, 2016, http://www.daimler.com/dccom/0-5-1322446-1-1323352-1-0-0-1322455-0-0-135-0-0-0-0-0-0-0-0.html.

APPENDIX B

1. "History of F1 Safety," Formula1.com, accessed February 14, 2017, https://www.formula1.com/en/championship/inside-f1/safety/history-of-F1-safety.html.

2. Jonathan Noble, "FIA Announces Formula 1 Virtual Safety Car Procedure for 2015," Autosport, January 8, 2015, http://www.autosport.com/news/report.php/id/117316.

BIBLIOGRAPHY

"24 Hours of Le Mans 245,000 Spectators," 24 Hours of Le Mans, June 23, 2013, http://www.24h-lemans.com/en/news/24-hours-of-le-mans-245-000-spectators_2_2_1746_11498.html.

"2014 Japanese Grand Prix Thursday Press Conference," FIA, October 2, 2015, http://www.fia.com/news/2014-japanese-grand-prix-thursday-press-conference (accessed 14 October 2015).

"2016 Le Mans 24 Hours: 263,500 Spectators!," Motorsport.com, June 19, 2016, https://www.motorsport.com/lemans/news/2016-le-mans-24-hours-263-500-spectators-789940.

Alexander, Tyler. A Life and Times with McLaren. Phoenix, AZ: David Bull Publishing, 2015.

"Amanda McLaren Interview: Why She Loves F1," video posted to YouTube by Motoring Australia, January 17, 2017, https://www.youtube.com/watch?v=Xpl24QA49KM&t=182s (accessed April 23, 2017).

Barber, H. L. Story of the Automobile: Its History and Development from 1760 to 1917. Chicago: A. J. Munson & Co., 1917.

BBC Four. Legends of F1: Jim Clark, Documentary film. https://www.youtube.com/watch?v=c0fMoPgsA3M&t=444s.

"Bianchi's Legacy Is Better Safety," Supersport.com, September 28, 2015, http://www.supersport.com/motorsport/formula1/news/150923/Bianchis_legacy_is_better_safety.

"Birth of the Automobile," Daimler.com, http://www.daimler.com/dccom/0-5-1322446-1-1323352-1-0-0-1322455-0-0-135-0-0-0-0-0-0-0-0.html (accessed May 3, 2015).

Cannell, Michael. The Limit: Life and Death on the 1961 Grand Prix Circuit. New York: Hachette Book Group, 2011.

Cherry, Kevin. "Cannon Mills," NCpedia.org, 2006, http://www.ncpedia.org/cannon-mills.

"Chicago Times-Herald Race of 1895," Encyclopedia of Chicago, http://www.encyclopedia.chicagohistory.org/pages/2380.html (accessed May 6, 2015).

Cimarsoti, Adriano. The Complete History of Grand Prix Motor Racing. London: David Bateman, 1997.

Clark, Jim. Jim Clark at the Wheel: The World's Greatest Motor Racing Champion Tells His Own Supercharged Success Story. New York: Simon & Schuster, 1966.

Clausewitz, Carl von. On War. Edited and translated by Michael Howard and Peter Paret. Princeton, NJ: Princeton University Press, 1989. Accessed at http://slantchev.ucsd.edu/courses/ps143a/readings/Clausewitz%20-%20On%20War,%20Books%201%20and%208.pdf.

Cofaigh, Éamon Ó. "Motor Sport in France: Testing-Ground for the World." In *The History of Motor Sport*, edited by David Hassen. New York: Routledge, 2013.

"Company History," Daimler.com, http://www.daimler.com/dccom/0-5-1322446-1-1323352-1-0-0-1322455-0-0-135-0-0-0-0-0-0-0-0.html (accessed October 11, 2016).

Cvitkovic, Jeff, dir. *I Am Dale Earnhardt*. DVD. Spike, 2015.

"Dale Earnhardt Obituary," Legacy.com, http://www.legacy.com/ns/dale-earnhardt-obituary/39595 (accessed April 19, 2017).

"Danish Driver Allen Simonsen, 34, Killed at Le Mans," *Guardian*, June 22, 2013, https://www.theguardian.com/sport/2013/jun/22/danish-allen-simonsen-killed-le-mans (accessed May 13, 2016).

"Daytona International Speedway: Through the Years," NASCAR.com, http://galleries.nascar.com/gallery/61/daytona-international-speedway-through-the-years#/18 (accessed 19 April 2017).

Deaton, Jamie Page. "Top 10 Everyday Car Technologies That Came from Racing," Auto.howstuffworks.com, http://auto.howstuffworks.com/under-the-hood/trends-innovations/top-10-car-tech-from-racing11.htm (accessed October 12, 2016).

Desmond, Kevin. *The Man with Two Shadows: The Story of Alberto Ascari*. New York: Proteus Book Publishing Group, 1981.

Donaldson, Gerald. *Gilles Villeneuve: The Life of the Legendary Racing Driver*. Toronto, Ontario: McClelland & Stewart, 1989.

Duffy, Enda. *The Speed Handbook: Velocity, Pleasure, Modernism*. Durham, NC: Duke University Press, 2009.

"The First American Automobile Race," America's Library (Library of Congress), http://www.americaslibrary.gov/jb/progress/jb_progress_autorace_1.html (accessed May 6, 2015).

Fitch, John. *Racing with Mercedes*. Lime Rock, CT: Fitch Wertz Publishing, 2006.

"Fitch Universal Barrels® Crash Cushion System," Energy Absorption Systems, http://www.energyabsorption.com/products/products_universal_barrels.asp (accessed February 1, 2007).

"Formula 1 Grand Prix de Monaco 2016," Formula1.com, https://www.formula1.com/content/fom-website/en/championship/races/2016/Monaco.html (accessed May 24, 2016).

"Franchitti Unable to Continue Racing Career," ChipGanssiRacing.com, http://www.chipganassiracing.com/News/2013/11/FRANCHITTI-UNABLE-TO-CONTINUE-RACING-CAREER.aspx.

Ganley, Howard. "Cowboy, Sailor, Racer, Inventor, and . . . 'Chippie,'" *Motor Sport*, July 2008, 78.

Garner, Art. *Black Noon: The Day They Stopped the Indy 500*. New York: St. Martin's Press, 2014.

Gauld, Graham. *Jim Clark: Racing Hero*. Köln, Germany: McKlein Publishing, 2014.

Gladwell, Malcolm. *Outliers: The Story of Success*. New York: Little, Brown, and Co., 2008.

"Global Status Report on Road Safety," World Health Organization, http://www.who.int/violence_injury_prevention/road_safety_status/2015/Executive_summary_GSRRS2015.pdf?ua=1.

Hall, Andy. "ABC's First Indy 500 Broadcast in 1965," ESPN.com, May 2016, http://www.espnfrontrow.com/2016/05/tbt-abcs-first-indy-500-broadcast-in-1965.

Hallbery, Andy, and Jeff Olson. *Lionheart: Remembering Dan Wheldon*. St. Petersburg, FL: Lionheart Books, 2016.

Hartstein, Dr. Gary. "The Organization of Motor Sport: Origins," Section 01.0 in *Medicine in Motor Sport*. Paris, France: FIA Institute for Motor Sport Safety and Sustainability, 2011.

Hassan, David. *The History of Motor Sport: A Case Study Analysis*. New York: Routledge, 2013.

Heap, Richard, dir. *The Deadliest Crash: The Le Mans 1955 Disaster*. DVD. Bigger Picture Films, 2010.

Henry, Alan. "Looking Back on Francois Cevert," *Motor Sport*, March 1985, http://www.motorsportmagazine.com/archive/page/march-1985/62.

Hilton, Christopher. *Grand Prix Century: The First 100 Years of the World's Most Glamorous and Dangerous Sport*. Sparkford, UK: Haynes Publishing, 2005.

———. *Le Mans '55: The Crash That Changed the Face of Motor-Racing*. Derby, UK: Derby Books Publishing Company, 2012.

———. *Memories of Senna: Anecdotes and Insights from Those Who Knew Him*. Sparkford, UK: Haynes Publishing, 2011.

"History: The World When IMS Opened," Indianapolis Motor Speedway, https://www.indianapolismotorspeedway.com/history/the-world-when-ims-opened.

"History of F1 Safety," Formula1.com, https://www.formula1.com/en/championship/inside-f1/safety/history-of-F1-safety.html (accessed February 13, 2017).

"History of the Milwaukee Mile," WisconsinStateFair.com, http://wistatefair.com/wsfp/wp-content/uploads/2013/02/Milwaukee-Mile-History.pdf (accessed May 12, 2015).

"History of Wrestling," United World Wrestling, https://unitedworldwrestling.org/organization/history (accessed May 6, 2015).

"In Memoriam," *Motor Sport*, May 1968, http://www.motorsportmagazine.com/archive/page/may-1968/13.

"IndyCar Mario Andretti Crash—2003," video posted to YouTube by MP4/7, September 29, 2006, https://www.youtube.com/watch?v=kMeE9NAh60I.

"IRL: Mario Andretti Flips at Indy," Motorsport.com, April 25, 2003, https://www.motorsport.com/indycar/news/irl-mario-andretti-flips-at-indy.

"Jim Clark," ESPN.co.uk, http://en.espn.co.uk/teamlotus/motorsport/driver/801.html.

Johnson Wax. "Press Release: McLaren's Gone, but Team Will Carry On in Cam-Am," June 1970, International Motor Racing Research Center archives.

Jones, Robert F. "Sportsman of The Year: Leaving with Love, and the Loot," *Sports Illustrated*, December 24, 1973, http://www.si.com/vault/1973/12/24/618484/sportsman-of-the-year (accessed June 24, 2015).

"Juan Manuel Fangio," *Independent*, July 18, 1995, http://www.independent.co.uk/news/people/obituaries-juan-manuel-fangio-1591999.html (accessed March 29, 2015).

"Justin Wilson," Twitter.com, https://twitter.com/justin_wilson (accessed February 14, 2017).

Kapadia, Asif, dir. *Senna*. DVD. ARC Entertainment, 2011.

Katzin, Lee H., dir. *Le Mans*, film, National General Pictures, 1971.

Kissell, Rick. "Update: Super Bowl on NBC Ratings Hit All Time High," Variety.com, last modified February 2, 2015, http://variety.com/2015/tv/ratings/super-bowl-ratings-hit-all-time-high-with-patriots-win-on-nbc-1201421267.

Kondology, Amanda. "Daytona Speedweek's Viewership Up on FOX Sports 1," TV by the Numbers, February 26, 2015, http://tvbythenumbers.zap2it.com/2015/02/26/daytona-speedweeks-viewership-up-on-fox-sports-1/368147.

Kramer, Ralph. *Indianapolis 500: A Century of Excitement*. Iola, WI: F+W Media, 2010.

———. *Indianapolis Motor Speedway: 100 Years of Racing*. Iola, WI: Krause Publications, 2009.

"Legends of F1—Francois Cevert," video posted to YouTube by F1 Legends, November 7, 2016, https://www.youtube.com/watch?v=JM62FcxLWM8.

Ludvigsen, Karl. "He Could Charm the Birds from the Trees," *Motor Sport*, July 2010, http:/www.motorsportmagazine.com/archive/article/july-2010/54/he-could-charm-birds-trees.

"Marmon Car Wins; Death Marked Race," *New York Times*, May 31, 2011, http://query.nytimes.com/mem/archive-free/pdf?res=9B04E6D91431E233A25752C3A9639C946096D6CF.

Matthews, John L. *Grand Prix, The Killer Years: Extended Interviews from the BBC Film*. Manchester, UK: Bigger Picture Projects, 2014.

McLaren, Bruce. *From the Cockpit*. Sherborne, Dorset, UK: Frederick Muller, 1964.

"Memorial Day Traffic Toll Climbs to Record of 474," *Blade* (Toledo, OH), June 1, 1965, https://news.google.com/newspapers?nid=1350&dat=19650601&id=EOpOAAAAIBAJ&sjid=cgEEAAAAIBAJ&pg=3376,965348&hl=en.

"Milwaukee Mile Speedway and Peck Media Center," Wisconsin State Fair Park, http://wistatefair.com/wsfp/milwaukee-mile-speedway-and-peck-media-center (accessed June 15, 2015).

Montville, Leigh. *At the Altar of Speed: The Fast Life and Tragic Death of Dale Earnhardt.* New York: Doubleday, 2001.

"Motor Sport Without Danger Is Like Cooking Without Salt," ESPN.uk.com, December 10, 2009, http://en.espnf1.com/f1/motorsport/story/4802.html#KKmQsgDTfpStoW7l.99.

"Motoring History 1907–1914," Brooklands Museum, http://www.brooklandsmuseum.com/index.php?/history/motoring-history-1907-1914 (accessed May 12, 2015).

Noble, Jonathan. "FIA Announces Formula 1 Virtual Safety Car Procedure for 2015," *Autosport*, January 8, 2015, http://www.autosport.com/news/report.php/id/117316.

"Normandy American Cemetery and Memorial," American Battle Monuments Commission, https://www.abmc.gov/cemeteries-memorials/europe/normandy-american-cemetery#.VzW01YSDGkq (accessed May 12, 2016).

"Our Story," Wilson Home Trust, http://wilsonhometrust.org.nz/our-story (accessed April 17, 2017).

Paulsen. "Indy 500 TV Ratings Up Slightly, but Third-Lowest Ever," Sports Media Watch, May 28, 2014, http://www.sportsmediawatch.com/2014/05/indy-500-tv-ratings-up-slightly-but-third-lowest-ever.

"Perthes Disease," Ortho Info, American Academy of Orthopedic Surgeons, http://orthoinfo.aaos.org/topic.cfm?topic=a00070 (accessed April 22, 2017).

"Prost's Touching Tribute to Senna: Friends and Colleagues Bear a Champion to His Grave," *Independent*, May 5, 1994, http://www.independent.co.uk/sport/motor-racing-prosts-touching-tribute-to-senna-friends-and-colleagues-bear-a-champions-body-to-his-1433924.html.

"Racing Safety with John Fitch," Race Safety, http://www.racesafety.com/fitchbio.html (accessed February 1, 2017).

Redman, Brian. *Brian Redman: Daring Drivers, Deadly Tracks: A Racer's Memoir of a Dangerous Decade, 1965–1975.* Dorset, UK: Evro Publishing, 2016.

Rendall, Ivan. *The Checkered Flag: 100 Years of Motor Racing.* Secaucus, NJ: Chartwell Books, 1993.

Roebuck, Nigel. "The Last Great Italian GP Star," *Motor Sport*, July 2012, http://www.motorsportmagazine.com/archive/page/july-2012/99.

———. "Model Pupil Francois Cevert," *Motor Sport*, November 2013, http://www.motorsportmagazine.com/archive/page/november-2013/55.

Rosewater, Amy. "Keepsakes Keep Fans Sold on Racing," *USA Today*, August 29, 2003, http://usatoday30.usatoday.com/sports/motor/nascar/2003-08-29-souvenirs_x.htm.

"Rules of the Providence Horseless Carriage Race," *Scientific American*, August 1, 1896, https://books.google.com/books?id=itkxAQAAMAAJ&pg=PA122&lpg=PA122&dq=narragansett+park+rhode+island+state+fair+1896&source=bl&ots=tbTj3LM2lS&sig=9e4Ac_vOfCkNtGFHHmu4TywIIXg&hl=en&sa=X&ei=iElSVeX4CNOwyASn1YCACw&ved=0CCMQ6AEwAQ#v=onepage&q=narragansett%20park%20rhode%20island%20state%20fair%201896&f=false (accessed May 12, 2015).

"Safety: Lane Width," U.S. Department of Transportation, Federal Highway Administration, http://safety.fhwa.dot.gov/geometric/pubs/mitigationstrategies/chapter3/3_lanewidth.cfm (accessed May 20, 2016).

Scott, Danny. "Me and My Motor: Derek Bell, Le Mans Legend," *Sunday Times Driving*, February 20, 2017, https://www.driving.co.uk/news/interview/motor-derek-bell-le-mans-legend (accessed March 1, 2017).

Shouten, Cory. "Meet 'Crazy' Carl Fisher, Father of the Indy 500," CBSNews.com, May 27, 2016, http://www.cbsnews.com/news/meet-crazy-carl-fisher-the-father-of-the-indy-500 (accessed August 17, 2016).

"Sid Collins' Impromptu Eulogy of Eddie Sachs Touches Racing Fans," *AutoWeek*, May 13, 2016, http://autoweek.com/article/indy-100/16-sid-collins-impromptu-eulogy-eddie-sachs-touches-racing-fans.

"Sid Collins," Indiana Journalism Hall of Fame, Indiana University, http://mediaschool.indiana.edu/ijhf/sid-collins (accessed August 18, 2016).

Small, Steve. *Autocourse Grand Prix Who's Who*, 4th ed. Malvern, UK: Icon Publishing, 2012.

"Sprint Cup Tracks," NASCAR.com., http://www.nascar.com/en_us/sprint-cup-series/schedule/tracks.html (accessed May 6, 2015).

Spurring, Quentin. *Le Mans: The Official History of the World's Greatest Motor Race, 1949–59.* Dorset, UK: Evro Publishing, 2011.

"St. Anthony of Padua," CatholicOnline.org, http://www.catholic.org/saints/saint.php?saint_id=24 (accessed January 14, 2017).

Stewart, Jackie. *Jackie Stewart: Winning Is Not Enough—the Autobiography.* London: Headline Publishing Group, 2009.

Sylt, Christian. "F1 Loses 25 Million Viewers Driven by Switch to Pay TV," Forbes.com, February 1, 2015, http://www.forbes.com/sites/csylt/2015/02/01/f1-loses-25-million-viewers-driven-by-switch-to-pay-tv/2.

Taylor, Simon. "Lunch with John Fitch," *Motor Sport*, November 2010, http://www.motorsportmagazine.com/archive/article/november-2010/67/lunch-john-fitch.

"The Tragic Tale of Francois Cevert," Racer.com, September 30, 2013, http://www.racer.com/f1/item/98165-insight-the-tragic-tale-of-francois-cevert.

"Two Perished in Auto Race," *Evening Citizen* (Ottawa, Canada), August 20, 1909, https://news.google.com/newspapers?id=OKUuAAAAIBAJ&sjid=69gFAAAAIBAJ&pg=7237%2C2845320.

"View from the Stands," *On Track*, June 3 1982, 6.

Weaver, Paul. "F1's Refocus on Driver Safety Is Legacy of Jules Bianchi," *Guardian*, July 18, 2015, http://www.theguardian.com/sport/2015/jul/18/f1-jules-bianchi (accessed September 28, 2015).

Widdows, Rob, and Nigel Roebuck. "Gilles Villeneuve," *Motor Sport*, May 2012, http://www.motorsportmagazine.com/archive/article/may-2012/48/denis-jenkinson-motor-sport-june-1982.

Young, Eoin. *The Amazing Summer of '55: The Year of Motor Racing's Biggest Dramas, Worst Tragedies, and Greatest Victories.* Somerset, UK: Haynes Publishing, 2005.

———. *McLaren Memories: A Biography of Bruce McLaren.* Somerset, UK: Haynes Publishing, 2005.

INDEX

ABOUT THE AUTHOR

Connie Ann Kirk writes primarily in the areas of motor sport and literature, publishing frequently on the topics in print and online. She has been credentialed to cover racing trackside by Formula One, Indy-Car, NASCAR, and IMSA/WEC series as well as historic/vintage racing events such as the Goodwood Revival in England. The author of more than a dozen books, Kirk was awarded an Artist's Crossroads grant from the New York State Council on the Arts for her work on motor racing.